SHORT COURSE SERIES

WORLD TRADE PRESS®

Professional Books for International Trade

THE SHORT COURSE IN INTERNATIONAL TRADE SERIES

A Short Course in International Business Culture

A Short Course in International Business Ethics

A Short Course in International Business Plans

A Short Course in International Contracts

A Short Course in International Economics

A Short Course in International Intellectual Property Rights

A Short Course in International Joint Ventures

A Short Course in International Marketing

A Short Course in International Marketing Blunders

A Short Course in International Negotiating

A Short Course in International Payments

A Short Course in International Trade Documentation

A SHORT COURSE IN

International Joint Ventures

3rd Edition

Negotiating, Forming and Operating the International Joint Venture

Alan Gutterman, M.B.A., J.D., Ph.D

Published in arrangement with World Trade Press by

ATLANTIC
PUBLISHERS & DISTRIBUTORS (P) LTD
7/22, Ansari Road, Darya Ganj, New Delhi-110 002
Tel: 40775252, 23273880, 23275880, 23280451; Fax: +91-11-23285873
E-mail: orders@atlanticbooks.com; Web: www.atlanticbooks.com

World Trade Press
800 Lindberg Lane, Suite 190
Petaluma, California 94952 USA
Tel: +1 (707) 778-1124
Fax: +1 (707) 778-1329
USA Order Line: +1 (800) 833-8586
E-mail: sales@worldtradepress.com
www.WorldTradePress.com
www.WorldTradeREF.com (international trade and logistics)
www.BestCountryReports.com (business travel, communications and culture)
www.GiantMapArt.com (Giant maps for building lobbies, conference rooms and education)

A Short Course in International Joint Ventures
By Alan Gutterman, M.B.A., J.D., Ph.D.
Short Course Series Concept: Edward G. Hinkelman
Cover Design: Ronald A. Blodgett
Text Design: Seventeenth Street Studios, Oakland, California, USA
Desktop Publishing: Valentina Pfeil

ISBN 978-81-269-1249-0
First Indian Reprint 2009

Disclaimer
This publication is designed to provide general information concerning aspects of international trade. It is sold with the understanding that the publisher is not engaged in rendering legal or any other professional services. If legal advice or other expert assistance is required, the services of a competent professional person or organization should be sought.

This book is dedicated to my family.

Library of Congress Cataloging-in-Publication Data
Gutterman, Alan, 1955–
A short course in international joint ventures : negotiating, forming and operating the international JV / Alan Gutterman.
p. cm. — (The short course in international trade series)
1. Joint ventures. 2. International business enterprises.
I. Title: International joint ventures. II. Title. III. Series.
HD62.47 .G88 2009
658'.049--dc21

2009026825
CIP

Printed in India at Chaman Enterprises, 1603, Pataudi House,
Darya Ganj, New Delhi-110 002

TABLE OF CONTENTS

CHAPTER 1

Introduction to International Joint Ventures

IS A JV THE BEST STRATEGY?

INTERNATIONAL OPERATIONS HAVE BECOME an important part of overall business strategy in recent years, and the commencement of activities in foreign markets has become a natural milestone for any growing business regardless of its size in terms of employees, products, or revenues. Each foreign market offers unique opportunities and risks, and many firms naturally look to strategic relationships with one or more partners for assistance in entering new markets.

One of the most popular forms of strategic relationship is a "joint venture," referred to herein as a JV. A JV utilizes a separate business entity (e.g., corporation, limited liability company, or partnership) to allow two or more parties to collaborate in conducting specified business activities. By using a separate entity, parties can limit the liabilities associated with the relationship. They may also qualify for incentives and concessions under local foreign investment programs that are offered to businesses using JVs as the means for distributing products and services into the foreign market.

A JV is only one of several ways that a party might approach a given business opportunity. An understanding of the advantages and disadvantages of this type of structure in relation to your own business goals is therefore essential. For example, assume that a manufacturer desires to enter into a new foreign market. To achieve sales there, the manufacturer might use a series of contractual relationships, such as license and distribution agreements with local parties. These strategies might be an advantage because they limit the degree of integration between the parties, provide for compensation rather than a split of profits, and can usually be terminated on fairly short notice. However, if the manufacturer prefers a more dynamic relationship with the local party, it may form an equity JV in which the manufacturer contributes a license to make the products and the local party contributes the manufacturing and distribution facilities, capital, and personnel. The parties will then share the profits of the JV. Assessment of your business goals is the first step in deciding whether to use a JV, and your deliberations should include the following considerations.

General Legal Characteristics of JVs

In the broadest terms, a JV is simply a business arrangement between at least two individuals or legal entities (such as partnerships, corporations, limited liability companies, and so forth) that undertake together either (a) a single transaction or specific series of transactions for the gain of all parties or (b) a specific commercial enterprise in which the parties all share mutually in the profits and losses. This broad definition encompasses a wide variety of cooperative business relationships, all of which might be characterized as a JV. Nevertheless, certain features of a JV can be identified. In most national laws, the following characteristics are the essential elements of a JV:

1. CONTRACTUAL ARRANGEMENT JVs are established by express or implied contracts that consist of one or more agreements involving two or more individuals or organizations and that are entered into for a specific business purpose.
2. SPECIFIC LIMITED PURPOSE AND DURATION JVs are formed for a specific and definable business objective and are established for a limited duration because (a) the complementary production activities involve a limited subset of the assets of the JV participants, (b) the complementary assets have only a limited service life, and/or (c) the complementary production activities will be of only limited efficacy.
3. JOINT PROPERTY INTEREST Each JV participant contributes its own property, cash, or other assets and organizational capital for the pursuit of a common and specific business purpose. Thus, a JV is not merely a contractual relationship, but rather the contributions are made to a newly-formed business enterprise, usually a corporation, limited liability company, or partnership. As such, the participants acquire a joint property interest in the assets and subject matter of the JV.
4. COMMON FINANCIAL AND INTANGIBLE GOALS AND OBJECTIVES The JV participants share a common expectation regarding the nature and amount of the expected financial and intangible goals and objectives of the JV. The goals and objectives of a JV tend to be narrowly focused, recognizing that the assets deployed by each participant represent only a portion of the overall resource base.
5. SHARED PROFITS, LOSSES, MANAGEMENT, AND CONTROL The JV participants share in the specific and identifiable financial and intangible profits and losses, as well as in certain elements of the management and control of the JV.

Functional Types of JV Relationships

While an understanding of the general characteristics of a JV is important, the significance and usefulness of a JV can be more clearly understood by examining the most common purposes for forming JVs. A JV can be classified by its primary function. For example, a JV may be formed to conduct research and development work on a new product or technical application, to manufacture or produce various products, to market and distribute products and services in a specified geographic area, or to perform a combination of these functions. The function of the JV will be linked to the overall objectives of the parties and will dictate to a large extent the substantive terms of the JV arrangement.

RESEARCH AND DEVELOPMENT JVS

A research and development JV is particularly useful for combining the creative resources and assets of two entities to facilitate technical exchange and, hopefully, to reduce the time that might otherwise have been required to complete the development work. "R&D" JVs usually involve technology licenses from one or both parties to the new enterprise, an agreement as to scope and duration of the research plan; covenants from both parties to protect the technology developed and, in most cases, an agreement defining each party's use of that technology.

MANUFACTURING OR PRODUCTION JVS

A manufacturing and production JV is primarily dedicated to combining the resources of the parties to produce goods that would be available for use or sale by one or both of the parties. For example, a party may wish to license certain production technology and trade secrets to a new JV, while the other party would contribute facilities, equipment, and personnel to manufacture the products. The finished products could then be delivered to the licensor for sale or sold by the JV, perhaps under a distribution arrangement with the manufacturing party.

MARKETING AND DISTRIBUTION JVS

A marketing and distribution JV sells goods and services of the parties in a given geographic area. For example, if a company seeks to enter a new foreign market using the assistance of a local partner with substantial expertise in that market, a new JV might be created. The foreign party would contribute the products, as well as any trade secrets or trademarks, while the local partner would provide the capital, facilities, and human resources required to exploit fully the products in the market. In addition, the local partner may be able to provide the JV with access to various marketing channels and scarce supplies and utilities.

HYBRID JV RELATIONSHIPS

Hybrid JV relationships combine two or more of the basic product development and distribution functions described previously. A JV of this type usually serves as an integrated business enterprise, owning or controlling all of the assets and resources that might be required to develop and manufacture new products, plus marketing and distributing the products in specified markets. Each of the parties will contribute, either directly or through licensing or similar contractual arrangements, all the capital, technology, facilities, and human resources required to fulfill the objectives of the JV's original business plan.

Advantages and Disadvantages of JVs

A JV carries with it a number of advantages and disadvantages. On the one hand, it can provide a party with access to resources and skills that are unavailable to it at reasonable cost. On the other hand, use of a JV can be quite risky given the reliance that must be placed on the ability and willingness of the other party to perform its obligations during the term of the arrangement. When deciding whether a JV is the appropriate business strategy, the parties must always review the various generic advantages and disadvantages of joint venturing and consider how each might apply to the specific opportunity.

CAPITAL REQUIREMENTS

- ADVANTAGE: *FINANCIAL RESOURCES CAN BE SHARED.*

One of the most commonly cited advantages of a new JV is the opportunity to reduce the amount of capital that one party must contribute to get involved in the specific business. For example, a party may be considering a project that will require a substantial amount of investment in development work and product testing. The party may have sufficient intangible assets in the form of skilled professional labor and marketing networks, but its financial resources may be inadequate to take on this particular project alone. Such projects are good candidates for the JV structure. To undertake the project, the party may seek a JV partner to assist in sharing the financial burden and other risks of the project. A partner may even be located who is willing to provide most, if not all, of the funding in exchange for access to the other's intangible assets.

The reduction of capital requirements is usually an important factor when the parties stand on common ground with respect to their financial resources. However, this factor is likely to be more significant to a foreign party making an investment with a local partner in a developed country than in a less developed country. In either country, there will probably be costs for building a new manufacturing plant or substantially remodeling an existing one, plus expenses of assembling a trained work force and experienced management team. However, if the country is developing, as opposed to developed, the foreign party will usually assume that few local partners will be able to make a substantial financial investment, and therefore the decision to enter the market with a local partner will be based on factors other than the reduction of capital investment (e.g., relations with the local government). Accordingly, it is not surprising that partners with money are a hot commodity for projects in developed countries.

■ DISADVANTAGE: *JV PROFITS ARE SHARED.*

An obvious disadvantage of sharing capital obligations is the need to share profits generated from the actual operation of the JV. Issues can arise in this area not so much because of the cash contributed, but because of the fact that the parties will also be contributing intangible assets to the business, such as intellectual property rights and technical know-how. These assets are difficult, if not impossible, to value. The intangible contributions of one of the partners will quite possibly result in returns that are out of proportion to the profit-sharing ratio determined solely by reference to the cash made available to the JV. In fact, if one party comes to believe that the other is not carrying its weight with respect to operations, the JV is likely to end up in trouble.

REDUCTION OF BUSINESS RISKS

■ ADVANTAGE: *A JV ALLOWS FOR INVESTOR DIVERSIFICATION.*

Closely connected with capital saving is as a motive for joint venturing is the reduction in business risk. By sinking less capital into a JV and diversifying investments among industries, areas, and countries, the investor obviously gains an element of protection. In turn, diversification allows the investor to enter into a market that has significant growth potential but is a little riskier than other markets that have already proved stable and profitable.

■ ADVANTAGE: *A JV REDUCES LOCAL FRICTION.*

The entrepreneurial skills and experience of local partners facilitate adaptation to the particular dangers of a new business environment with which the foreign investor may be relatively unfamiliar. The risk of doing business in a foreign land can be further reduced if collaboration with a local partner makes the entire project less subject to the danger of adverse action by the local government.

ECONOMIES OF SCALE

■ ADVANTAGE: *A JV CAN BE USED TO REDUCE FIXED COSTS PER PRODUCT.*

One of the most touted benefits of a JV has been the opportunity for the parties to achieve beneficial economies of scale and, transactional benefits that would not have been possible with other contractual structures. For example, if sales or distribution is contracted to local representatives, a manufacturer will remain responsible for getting the goods through import and other governmental restrictions in sufficient quantity to supply the market demand, and for providing distant customer service that is adequate to retain market share. With proper planning, the parties to a JV may be able to reduce the costs associated with logistics, production, and procurement, thereby increasing profit margins or facilitating lower pricing, which will in turn create higher market share.

CONTROL OVER FUNCTIONAL ACTIVITIES

■ ADVANTAGE: *A JV ALLOWS FOR DIRECT MANAGEMENT OF BUSINESS ACTIVITIES.*

A party may choose a JV structure, rather than a network of contractual relationships, to ensure that it is in a position to directly manage the specific functional process, be it research work, manufacturing, or distribution. For example, while a party can presumably decrease its manufacturing costs through a production agreement with a local party in a country with lower labor expenses, it can instead opt for a JV as a way to retain some control over the quality of the process and the manufacturing technology used. Also, a JV may be appropriate when the party believes that it will need to provide personnel to facilitate rapid transfer of trade secrets and other information for use in the collaborative venture. While the foregoing generally makes sense, the degree of control ultimately depends on the skills of the JV's local managers and, to some extent, the policies of the local government regarding technology transfer.

SHARING TECHNOLOGY AND MANAGEMENT SKILLS

■ ADVANTAGE: *THE COMPETITIVE STRENGTHS OF TWO PARTIES CAN BE COMBINED.*

A JV generally presents a good opportunity to combine the technical and managerial strengths of both parties. A party that lacks the technology to undertake a business opportunity will welcome the chance to learn from the other party, and will often bargain for substantial amounts of technical assistance. Management expertise can be transferred during the course of the JV and then used in other areas of the party's business operations. On its side, the foreign partner may look at the JV as a way to tap into local management experience in dealing with consumers, vendors, and government officials. Knowledge exchange is another important benefit when both parties contribute roughly comparable expertise because the interaction between scientists and managers will presumably increase the rate of innovation.

- DISADVANTAGE: *SHARED TECHNOLOGIES CAN BE USED BEYOND THE JV.*

Technology and management sharing can potentially create significant problems among the parties. In particular, one party's mastery of the other's technology can lead to improvements on that technology beyond the intended services of the JV, a factor that tends to discourage companies from disclosing their technologies for fear of losing the competitive edge to their JV partner. Many commentators argue that JVs offer a structure for reducing the "free riding" of the local JV partner because both partners contribute to the costs associated with the exploitation of the technology in proportion to their expected benefits. The theory is that a JV partner will have an incentive to focus on protecting the results of the JV activities rather than trying to replicate independently the results for its own account. But studies of real world JV operations often uncover situations in which one party becomes far more interested in using the JV technology in areas unrelated to the scope of the JV without compensation to the other partner.

- DISADVANTAGE: *LOCAL MANAGEMENT OF A JV CAN BE AN UNKNOWN.*

Although the opportunity to obtain local management is sometimes regarded as a major advantage of joint venturing, the need to work with local management can sometimes be a major problem. For example, local management styles and expectations may lead to clashes with foreign partners. Potential conflicts among the management team are material and often result in early termination of the JV. Also, the advantage of having local managers who know how to deal with government officials may evaporate if a change in leadership occurs.

MARKET PENETRATION

- ADVANTAGE: *A LOCAL JV PARTNER KNOWS THE MARKET.*

A party may seek a JV with a local party in a new foreign market as a means of accelerating the pace of market penetration. The local party should be able to supply the requisite knowledge of local tastes and customs. With the incentive of equity involvement, the local partner is more likely to ensure that it puts out its best services for the JV. Of course, this advantage can quickly disappear if the local party lacks the managerial experience and skills to properly conduct the JV operations. Moreover, the rate of market penetration will also depend on the general competitive conditions within the market, including the presence of other JVs, unless the government provides some market protections.

HOST COUNTRY INCENTIVES

- ADVANTAGE: *ECONOMIC INCENTIVES ADD VALUE TO JVS.*

Many countries have created a wide range of economic incentives for using a JV structure for foreign investment (see also Chapter 11). In some cases, these incentives may be the deciding factor in a foreign party's determination of whether the rewards of the proposed venture are commensurate with the risks associated with entering an unfamiliar market. Of course, the value of the incentives depends on the ability and willingness of the local government to deliver on its promises, as well as the diplomatic skills of local managers in dealing with regulators.

Structural Components of a Typical JV

If a JV arrangement appears to be of interest within your particular business situation, you will need to do a bit more investigation before making a final decision. Specifically, you must decide on the overall structure of the JV arrangement and come to an agreement with a ready, willing, and able partner. The formation and operation of a typical JV must take into account all of the same issues that are generally encountered with any new business enterprise. Each partner will contribute various resources and skills to the new enterprise, including products, cash, personnel, facilities, raw materials, and marketing expertise. These contributions may take the form of direct investment in the JV, or may be provided under the terms of one or more ancillary agreements between the JV entity and the partners. The partners must also agree on a number of issues regarding the management and operation of the enterprise. Although the laws relating to business organizations differ from country to country, the basic structural components of the JV are described below.

FORMATION AND ORGANIZATION

The parties, referred to herein as A and B, will agree to form and organize a separate business entity (e.g., corporation, limited liability company, or partnership). The procedures for forming the entity will, of course, depend on the relevant laws in the jurisdiction where the entity is to be organized. For example, if the JV is organized in the corporate form, charter documents (e.g., articles of incorporation and bylaws in the United States) must be drafted and approved by the parties. These basic charter documents describe the capital structure of the entity as well as any specific rights granted to the shareholders with respect to voting, distributions, and liquidation of the entity. Articles are filed with the appropriate regulatory body at the time the entity is formed, while the bylaws are approved by the board of directors of the entity and ratified by the parties in their capacity as shareholders. Other entities, such as limited liability companies or limited partners, also must satisfy specified statutory filing and publication requirements. The requirements for formation and organization of the various entities are discussed in Chapter 8.

CAPITAL CONTRIBUTIONS

A and B will agree to make various contributions of cash, tangible assets, and other intangible rights to the JV. A and B are the sole owners of the JV and receive evidence of their interests in the JV in the form of shares if a corporate form is used, or partnership interests if the partnership form is used. The number of shares or partnership interests generally determines the rights of the parties with respect to voting and distribution of profits, but the parties are free to make other arrangements for special voting rights and special economic allocations. Initial capital contributions are generally made at a formation meeting, often referred to as a "closing," which is discussed in Chapter 13.

VENTURERS' AGREEMENT

In addition to the articles, bylaws, or other statutorily required documents, the parties generally enter into a venturers' agreement (e.g., shareholders' or partners' agreement), which will govern their respective rights and obligations with regard to the operation of the JV. This agreement is the key operational document for the JV and sets forth the understanding of the parties with respect to a number of matters, including initial capitalization and additional financing, management and control, the business and operational activities of the JV, transfers of ownership interests, allocations and distributions of income and other assets, and the term and termination of the JV. In addition, the agreement will include various representations and warranties by each of the parties, agreements with respect to confidentiality of information exchanged during the JV, procedures for the resolution of disputes, and a description of internal controls to monitor the progress of the JV. An annotated venturers' agreement is included in Chapter 18.

ANCILLARY AGREEMENTS

The parties may also both enter into separate contractual agreements with the JV. These agreements will cover any services that the parties will provide to the entity, as well as any agreements for either party to purchase products developed or manufactured by the JV or to use the JV's assets for activities that may, or may not, be related to the specific purpose of the JV. These various agreements might include an administrative services agreement, a supply agreement, an equipment purchase agreement, license agreements for technology or manufacturing rights, distribution agreements and agreements for the lease, acquisition, or construction of facilities. See Chapter 15 for ancillary and other operational activities of the JV.

TERMINATION PROVISIONS

Although the JV is established as a separate legal entity, the enterprise will survive for only the period that is required for each of the parties to achieve the specific goals and objectives of the relationship. When the JV terminates, the entity will either be liquidated and each party will receive its agreed allocation of the JV assets and resources, or one party will buy out the other's interest and continue to operate the business. Most of the termination provisions will be described in detail in the venturers' agreement and, in the case of a corporation, the articles of incorporation. Termination procedures are discussed in Chapter 17.

Transaction Checklist for Forming a JV

In negotiating and drafting the documentation for use in a JV arrangement, the following transaction checklist may be helpful:

1. Conduct an internal assessment to identify the goals and objectives for the proposed JV (see Chapters 1, 2, 3, and 6).
2. Identify prospective JV partners and collect preliminary information from publicly available sources (see Chapters 4 and 5).
3. Prepare and execute confidentiality agreements to govern exchange of information during the due diligence investigation and negotiations, and establish procedures to follow during the investigation (see Chapter 7).
4. Make a preliminary determination of the appropriate JV structure and commence an analysis of relevant legal (e.g., tax, corporate, securities, antitrust, environmental, employment, labor) and accounting issues (see Chapters 1, 2, and 8).

5. Prepare a timetable and list of required documents for the proposed transaction, and consider the need for a meeting of all parties to allocate responsibilities.
6. Negotiate, draft, and execute a letter of intent or commitment (see Chapter 9).
7. Draft a preliminary business plan for the JV (see Chapter 10).
8. Prepare drafts of all required agreements, including any necessary schedules or exhibits, and circulate the drafts to all parties (see Chapters 8, 9, 12, and 18).
9. Prepare and complete all required pre-transaction filings with regulatory authorities, and obtain all required consents from other third parties (e.g., lenders) (see Chapter 11).
10. Determine all required entity actions (e.g., corporate director and shareholder approvals) for the venturers to enter into the transaction (see Chapter 8).
11. Prepare all necessary documentation for transferring assets to the JV at the time of closing, including bills of sale, assignments, licenses, etc. (see Chapter 13).
12. Collect comments on all documents and prepare the final form of the agreements for execution.
13. Prepare all documents to be delivered at closing, including legal opinions, officers' certificates, etc., and arrange for copies of good standing certificates and similar documents from regulators to be available for delivery to the parties at the closing (see Chapter 13).
14. Verify that all regulatory approvals for the transaction have been obtained (see Chapter 11).
15. Complete all entity actions necessary for finalizing the transaction, including obtaining approvals from all venturers and securing formation of the new entity.
16. Ensure that all representations and warranties in the venturers' agreement are correct, and that all covenants and closing conditions have been satisfied.
17. Obtain all required signatures on the documents.
18. Prepare a closing memorandum and conduct a pre-closing review to ensure that all documents are in order and that arrangements have been made for timely delivery.
19. Close the transaction and verify that all documents have been properly dated and delivered.
20. Complete the formation of the new entity (e.g., hold the initial meeting or otherwise secure all actions by the incorporators and directors).
21. Give all required notices to the regulatory authorities and other parties regarding consummation of transaction.
22. Calendar periodic review of compliance with the covenants included in the documents, as well as dates of meetings required for the governance and operation of the entity (e.g., annual meetings of directors and shareholders).
23. Circulate copies of the documents to all parties.

Alternatives to JVs for Entering Foreign Markets

A collaboration can take any number of forms, and therefore you should consider whether an alternative strategy might be better suited than a JV to your particular situation. Some parties opt for a "contractual JV" to test their compatibility and to decide whether to form a more comprehensive relationship. Other options include direct investment, acquisition, and wholly owned subsidiaries.

CONTRACTUAL JVS

Contractual JVs do not create separate JV entities, but they resemble JVs because the parties agree to a cooperative effort in which they contribute their operations, services, and expertise for an extended time to achieve technical, manufacturing, or sales objectives. However, they retain separate ownership of their assets and resources. The following are examples of contractual JVs:

- INTELLECTUAL PROPERTY LICENSES The most basic form of strategic business relationship is a license of intellectual property (IP) rights (such as patents, trade secrets, copyrights, and trademarks). A license conveys to the licensee a right to use the IP rights without fear of liability to the IP owner for infringement or misappropriation. A license may expressly provide that it will extend to subsequent improvements or enhancements of the IP rights. Licenses are particularly advantageous in the following situations:
  - The licensee wishes to exploit its own technology, but it could potentially become liable to the licensor, whose prior technology is identical or similar.
  - The licensee desires to manufacture and distribute products developed by the other party, who agrees to a front-end payment for the right to use the IP, plus royalties based on revenues from that use.
  - The licensor seeks to offset the costs associated with development of the licensed technology. A license can provide a form of "rent" for using the technology.
  - The licensor desires to enter the marketplace quickly and to establish its credibility and technology before it is able to create its own distribution system.
  - The licensee desires to use valuable technology, free of the costs and risks associated with the initial development efforts.
- RESEARCH AND DEVELOPMENT (R&D) AGREEMENTS In an R&D agreement, the parties coordinate their efforts to make fundamental changes in, or improvements to, specific core technologies. One party usually agrees to fund the other's research in return for the rights to use the resultant technology. Parties with complimentary technical skills and assets may agree to cross-licensing and sharing of scientific and engineering personnel. An R&D agreement can be structured as a one-time "fee-for-service" arrangement, then expanded later into an arrangement for product distribution if needed.
- MANUFACTURING LICENSE Another common and important type of technology transaction involves the manufacture and purchase of technology-based goods. For example, a firm may realize greater production efficiency by granting a license to a low-cost overseas manufacturer to make its products. The licensor then agrees to repurchase the products at a fixed price, often a multiple

of the manufacturer's actual cost. This type of license must provide for technical assistance to ensure product quality.

- SALES REPRESENTATIVE ARRANGEMENTS A firm that lacks the sales network and resources to realize fully the commercial potential for its products in a particular market might contract with another party to represent it locally. The sales representative is typically entitled to a commission based on the sales volume generated from its activities. This is among the least restrictive of business relationships.
- DISTRIBUTION ARRANGEMENTS A distribution arrangement is similar in purpose to the sales representative arrangement, but more complex in its transactional structure. It involves the manufacturer selling goods to a distributor, who in turn resells the goods for its own account. This arrangement may include a license for use of the IP rights so that the distributor can market and service the products. A distribution strategy lets the manufacturer take advantage of the distributor's sales network, while the distributor can gain access to new products without incurring the costs of development.

INVESTMENT RELATIONSHIPS

An investment relationship is created when one firm directly invests equity or debt in the partner. No new entity is formed; rather one party takes a stake in the other's business. An investment is often combined with a contractual JV, as when the investor agrees to distribute products of the other company. Often, the investor will limit its initial involvement to a minority position, intending to increase involvement as the relationship evolves and matures. Investment relationships are attractive for a variety of reasons, including the following:

- A larger firm can invest in a smaller firm, allowing the smaller firm to stretch its resources more quickly.
- By investing in a another firm that has the desired capabilities, an investor seeking a window on new technologies and a good return on its investment does not need to modify its own corporate culture and internal development efforts to develop innovative technology within the timeframe necessary for market acceptance.
- A direct but non-controlling investment offers an opportunity for the investor to evaluate the utility of a long-term relationship or an acquisition.

NEGOTIATED ACQUISITIONS

A negotiated acquisition involves the purchase of an entire company or discrete assets of a company (such as a separate company division). An acquisition may, but need not, displace existing management, and the former owners may even retain an ownership interest. Many investment relationships include an option by which the investor can ultimately acquire control of the subject company, and an acquisition may become the eventual result of a contractual JV. Obviously, this strategy involves significant outlays of cash and other resources, and its success may depend on the domestic firm's ability to retain key employees and to continue to capitalize both on its local reputation and on the local contacts that it had prior to the acquisition.

FORMATION OF NEW WHOLLY-OWNED FOREIGN ENTITY

If no viable JV partner is available in a specific market, a party may decide to go it alone by forming a wholly owned subsidiary and launching its own new business. Of course, this strategy is extremely risky unless the company has substantial familiarity with the market or can recruit qualified local personnel to assist it. For this reason, foreign companies commonly recruit managers and employees from the home labor market. Despite the cost and risk, companies from developed countries have increasingly turned to this strategy as they grow disenchanted with purported incentives offered in developing markets and lack of loyal and capable support from local partners.

CHAPTER 2

Legal and Regulatory Aspects of Joint Venture Activities

THE PARTIES TO A JV will always need to consider the various laws and regulations that may be applicable to the business of the JV. The content of these laws and regulations will depend on the functional activities of the JV, as well as the countries where the JV will be operating. The most common areas of concern are the laws, rules, and regulations governing enterprises, commercial transactions, property rights, foreign investment, competition, labor, health, environment, capital markets, and securities. Understanding and complying with all these laws can be an expensive and time-consuming experience, and it is therefore important for each party to engage experienced professionals familiar with the legal requirements for each relevant country as a guide through the maze.

Enterprise Laws

While the success of any business arrangement generally turns on the compatibility of the persons and resources involved in the particular project, attention must be paid to the form of the legal entity selected for the conduct of the relationship. The characteristics of the organizational forms available for the conduct of a JV are determined by the relevant "enterprise law," sometimes referred to as "company law" or the "law of business organizations." Enterprise laws not only define the legal entities (i.e., organizational forms) or enterprises that can be used to conduct commercial activities, but also establish the rights and obligations of the enterprise, its governance process, and the rights and duties of its managers and owners. Also, enterprise laws set out the specific rules for forming, operating, and terminating business enterprises. The impact of enterprise laws on the selection of a form of business entity is discussed further in Chapter 8.

Commercial Laws

Commercial laws are those that govern market-based transactions among independent contracting parties, including between a JV and each JV participant and between the JV and any third party. Commercial laws are particularly important for developing countries, not only because of the need to formulate rules for transactions between domestic parties, but also because a reliable and predictable set of rules for commercial transactions is required to induce foreign investors to deal with local firms in licensing, distribution, production, and sales arrangements.

Ten Tips For Selecting Governing Law

In a cross-border transaction, the parties must confront the question: Which national law might govern? Although parties have some latitude in negotiating their contract terms, the governing law that they chose will determine the enforceability of their choices. It might also supplement their agreement with implied terms, to the extent that the parties fail to provide for their own rights and obligations. When selecting the governing law and projecting its impact on the interpretation of the contract, consider the following:

1. Is your choice of governing law likely to be honored by the courts that might be called on to interpret the contract? Generally, the chosen jurisdiction must bear a reasonable relationship to the subject matter of the contract, and the court's own rules must require it to abide by the decision of the parties.
2. Which terms of the agreement will be controlled by law and which can be left to negotiation between the parties? If you negotiate a point that is already fixed by law, you will be wasting your time and giving away your negotiating edge.
3. Will the agreement or provision you have in mind be valid under applicable law? If the provision is void it will be unenforceable, and you will be left either with nothing, or with a judge's guess about what the parties intended or custom dictates.
4. Which law would be more favorable to your position? Your should ask your legal advisor to explain the material differences between the relevant national laws.
5. What terms, conditions, and duties might the law imply into your agreement? If the law is inadequate, silent, or overly strict, you should insist on protective provisions within the contract itself, provided that they are enforceable.
6. Under the relevant national laws, what is the scope of your potential liability for the other party's actions during the term of the relationship? If possible, you will want to negotiate terms that limit or completely protect you against civil lawsuits and government fines or penalties, such as indemnity provisions, disclosures and mandatory proofs of authority, and required compliance certificates.
7. What enforcement and recovery remedies are available in the event of breach? Depending on its stage of development, a country may offer administrative civil and criminal, judicial civil and criminal, statutory, and conciliatory remedies.
8. To what extent will the national procedures actually be effective remedies? A law is only as good as the system created to interpret and enforce it.
9. What will your liabilities be if you do not perform the contract? Liability will depend largely on the development of a nation's laws and on the effectiveness of the enforcement mechanisms. The national laws of some countries may allow you to determine your own remedies as part of your contract provisions, or it might invalidate or set aside your choices in favor of a statutory remedy.
10. If the selected governing law is not the local law of the area where the JV will be operating, will local law override the decisions of the parties regarding governing law? In some cases, jurisdictions forbid parties from performing certain contracts within their borders even if the contract is to be governed by foreign law.

CONTRACT LAWS

Contract law is the basic legal building block for each of the essential agreements created during the course of a JV relationship. A contract is a promise, or a set of promises, that is recognized by law as imposing a duty on each party to perform the contract requirements and a liability for remedies in the event of a breach of that duty. A contract arises whenever two or more individuals or other competent parties become obligated to each other, with reciprocal rights to demand performance of the promises that each party has made. The law of contracts addresses the legal obligations that arise from the agreement of the parties.

- GENERAL V. SPECIFIC TRANSACTION LAWS In economically mature countries, such as Canada, the United States, and Western European nations, contract law is the product of lengthy periods of development and evolution, and today it focuses on broad types of commercial transactions, such as the law of sales. In contrast, the contract law in many developing countries has tended to focus on the content of specific types of contracts (e.g., supply and installation contracts, loan contracts, and agency contracts) and to set out in detail the contractual terms of transactions involving state-owned enterprises. However, as developing countries move toward market-based economies, they are now working to establish a legal framework for commercial dispute resolution and for formation and interpretation of economic contracts generally, including agreements relating to production, exchange of goods, provision of services, and development and commercialization of technology.
- UNITED NATIONS CISG When no relevant provision is made in local law, contract laws often refer to international practice for guidance. In the context of an international JV, this means the parties may look to the rules set out in the United Nations Convention for the International Sale of Goods ("CISG"). In fact, provisions in the contract laws of many developing countries are often borrowed from the CISG. Standard contracts continue to play a large part in contract negotiations between domestic and foreign parties in many developing countries, particularly because local parties still lack the experience and knowledge to assess some of the alternative provisions that might be suggested by foreign parties. This situation is changing, however, as local entrepreneurs and government specialists gradually become more familiar with JVs through increased association with foreign investors.

SALES OF GOODS TRANSACTIONS

A JV, like many other business enterprises, will continuously find itself involved in transactions involving the sale or transfer of goods. The JV might itself be engaged in the direct sale of goods to third parties. The JV participants may sell raw materials and components to the JV for the JV's use in manufacturing finished products. In addition, the JV may sell goods to the JV participants under an agreement by which the JV manufactures products that the participants then use in their own operations, or develops and manufactures products that the participants agree to distribute. In each case, the relevant law of sales will apply to the interpretation of the duties and obligations of the parties as stated in the sales agreement.

If the sales contract involves two parties in the United States, the contract will be governed by some form of the Uniform Commercial Code ("UCC"), and sales contracts between parties in other countries will be governed by the applicable law of sales in that country. If the sales contract is between parties located in different countries, the parties must choose which country's law will govern their relationship. Given the fact that many sales of goods contracts are international in nature, an ongoing effort has been made to develop a balanced set of rules that the parties can turn to in cross-border situations rather than getting into pre-performance disputes regarding which law will govern the transaction. The result of these efforts is the aforementioned CISG, which sets out rules governing the formation and administration of international sales contracts.

DEBTOR-CREDITOR LAWS

As an inducement to firms and investors to enter into commercial transactions, country laws must provide for protection of the rights of creditors who lend capital or other assets for use in a business enterprise. Legal regimes in this area cover a variety of concerns. The primary ones are discussed here.

- SECURED TRANSACTIONS Secured transaction laws provide for the registration and enforcement of security interests against property, including mortgages secured by movable and intangible property in a manner similar to mortgages on real property. Secured transaction laws permit banks and other creditors to finance a company's equipment purchases in exchange for a security interest that is held on the equipment, and that protects the lender's legal and financial rights against other creditors without the lender having to retain physical possession of the equipment. These same laws can be used to protect the JV's rights to payment for goods sold in a particular country, and such protection is particularly appropriate wherever the JV plans significant sale activities.
- REORGANIZATIONS The parties to a JV should be aware of the relevant country laws for restructuring or, if necessary, liquidating the enterprise in the event that it experiences financial or business difficulties. While bankruptcy laws have long been recognized in mature economies, developing countries have only recently begun to adopt such laws. These laws are particularly significant in countries where there is a viable but risky market because they allow an enterprise to continue operating after a period of restructuring, reformation, and rehabilitation by protecting it from the immediate claims of creditors. The foreign party in a JV should also be concerned about the effect of the local partner's bankruptcy or insolvency on the JV arrangement and whether the local partner's creditors may be able to reach any of the JV assets.
- DISSOLUTION Debtor-creditor laws can impact a JV at the time of its liquidation and dissolution. The parties should therefore take into account the relevant laws when drafting the provisions of their venturers' agreement. Each party must understand how the country's governing law will affect their expectations with respect to satisfying the JV's obligations to its creditors at the end of the JV term.

RELATED COMMERCIAL LAW ISSUES

As a further enticement to foreign investors, countries have developed a network of laws with respect to various payment and financing methods. These include laws relating to letters of credit, installment sales, wire transfers, factoring, and negotiable instruments and commercial paper. In conjunction with the laws relating to secured transactions and guarantees, laws on payment and financing can significantly reduce each party's costs related to the commercial transactions. As a result, small- and medium-sized enterprises can more easily enter into the same sorts of transactions that were previously only available to large enterprises.

Property Rights

Property rights are now commonly accepted as one of the cornerstones of a modern legal system that can support innovate economic activity. Development of private property rights, including rights of individuals and firms to own and control real and personal property, creates incentives for innovate activities and reduces the risks inherent in collaborations between parties with different backgrounds. In starting and operating a JV, the venturers will need to consider local real property laws, including procedures for transfers of title, land leases, and regulation of land usage (e.g., zoning laws). Rights related to personal property will be governed by laws on the ownership and use of equipment, raw materials, and similar items. Finally, intellectual property laws will protect the intangible fruits of creativity. All of these laws must be carefully reviewed in each country where the JV is or may be conducting business.

Investment, Financial, and Securities Laws

FOREIGN INVESTMENT REGULATIONS

Developing countries are typically dependent on inbound transfers of capital and technology from foreign countries and businesses as a means for acquiring assets and resources necessary for the development of its economic infrastructure. To ensure that foreign investment is made on terms and conditions that are perceived to be fair to the host country, many governments have implemented laws and regulations on foreign investment activities. This phenomenon is not limited to developing countries, but is also present in major industrial nations, particularly in relation to key industries.

Governments regulate inbound investment transactions in a number of different ways. Most developed countries, like the United States, treat foreign investment transactions under the same laws as any other form of business collaboration. Such transactions are analyzed for compliance with antitrust and competition laws to ascertain the effect that the relationship might have on competition in each relevant local market. A developing country is unlikely to have sophisticated laws and administrative procedures for conducting an antitrust review of a transaction, but it is likely to have foreign investment laws. These laws govern the role that foreign firms and capital may play in the domestic economy, and sometimes regulate specific forms of business collaborations (e.g., technology transfer agreements). The impact of foreign investment regulations on the structure and business activities of a JV is discussed further in Chapter 11.

CAPITAL MARKETS AND SECURITIES LAWS

Although JV operations may be financed largely from the contributions of the participants, plus capital generated from JV activities, in some situations the JV will require local market financing. In this case, the parties must concern themselves with laws and regulations relating to banking and capital-raising activities. The content of financial laws is particularly important in developing countries, because laws are being enacted to provide access to capital through a market-driven system rather than through a centralized planning mechanism. In many developing countries, banking laws and regulations address the need for the availability of credit at reasonable cost, of deposit facilities for surplus cash and temporary investment, and of facilities that permit prompt clearance and settlement of payments. Securities laws are needed to facilitate development of a market-oriented system for capital formation through the use of equity securities and debt instruments.

Antitrust and Competition Laws

JVs will usually be subject to antitrust or competition laws in the country of formation and each of the countries where the JV operates. These laws not only cover JVs, but also other types of business collaborations (e.g., mergers and licensing or distribution agreements) that might result in some combination of the business assets and resources of actual or potential competitors in a manner that reduces competition.

National practices regarding the regulation of JVs are somewhat uniform, at least in those cases where the proposed collaboration involves participants of a specified size in relation to the effected market(s). For example, in the United States, JVs may be subject to review prior to the consummation of the transaction, although recent statutory changes have led to a more liberal attitude toward JVs limited to research and development and production of the results of the joint research. The European Union also reviews JVs and other collaborative arrangements in the same manner as it deals with commercial agreements. Finally, countries that extensively regulate direct foreign investment will generally be involved in reviewing any proposed JV between a local party and a foreign investor. Competition regulation outside of the United States and the EU varies substantially, and the content of those laws is largely dependent on the general industrial policies of the country and the overall competitiveness of its domestic firms.

Labor, Immigraton, Health and Environmental Laws

JV participants must consider the labor, immigration, health and environmental laws and regulations applicable to the area where the facilities and other operations of the JV are to be conducted. Labor laws are clearly relevant when the JV intends to call on the local work force to staff its operations. In fact, in many developing countries foreign participation in a JV will be conditioned on some level of local employment. Compliance with immigration laws is often necessary when hiring domestic workers as well as when importing personnel from overseas to train, manage, set up, or otherwise work on the JV staff. Health, safety, and environmental laws, long a significant factor for JVs with operations in the United States and the EU, are now becoming more important in the developing countries. The cost of compliance with these and similar national laws and regulations must be considered in establishing the budget and economic objectives of the JV.

Consumer Protection Laws

Competition and sales of goods laws are not adequate to protect consumers from harmful product defects or from unfair competitive practices, such as publication of false or misleading information regarding goods and services. To achieve these safeguards, countries have developed legal standards for consumer protection and product quality. Consumer protection laws address the quality and accuracy of information provided to consumers regarding products and services, as well as the quality of the products themselves. For example, laws may require that products not be sold if they present "unreasonable dangers" with respect to their use. Similarly, some products can only be sold if they have been produced, stored, and transported in accordance with specified safety and hygiene standards. There are also laws regarding warranties and product performance which include the responsibilities of the manufacturer and seller with respect to damages caused by defective goods.

Dispute Resolution

The parties to a JV must carefully consider the steps to be taken in the event that disagreements arise over the course of the relationship. Arbitration and other dispute resolution procedures are often preferred as a means for settling disputes involving any economic transaction. In many Asian countries, arbitration is consistent with traditional preferences for settling disputes through "negotiation and mediation," and a number of these countries have promulgated laws and regulations that dictate the rights of parties with respect to arbitration. In addition, many countries with developed court systems have promulgated laws and rules of civil procedure that provide not only for litigation of civil cases, but also for encouraging conciliation and the honoring of arbitration clauses that might be included in foreign economic trade, transport and maritime contracts.

Dispute resolution is clearly an important issue for prospective foreign investors, and it is generally reflected in the negotiations relating to choice of law provisions and enforcement of awards and judgments. While there is still no generally accepted international agreement that requires recognition of foreign judgments, the New York Convention on the Recognition and Enforcement of Foreign Arbitral Awards of 1958 ("New York Convention") provides parties with comfort that foreign arbitral awards rendered in any jurisdiction that is a member of the New York Convention will be honored in any other jurisdiction that is also a member of that Convention.

Means of dispute resolution are discussed in greater detail in Chapter 16.

Tax Laws

Like any form of business activity, JVs generally raise a number of important tax issues. Tax laws and regulations are relevant to the contribution of assets to the JV when formed, the receipt of income by the JV while operating, the distribution of income and capital to the JV's participants, and the liquidation of the JV's assets when its term expires. The financial impact of the various taxes will depend on the form of the legal entity used to operate the JV, the tax laws applicable to the JV's operations, and the relative ownership interests of the joint venturers. In addition, a number of developing countries offer "tax holidays" as important incentives for foreign investment.

Expert advice is essential on the tax aspects of any proposed international JV. In the United States, such advice is available from tax lawyers who specialize in international transactions, as well as from accountants. In other countries, the type of professional that should be consulted depends on the tradition in that particular country. For example, in Europe, local accountants or special tax experts are usually the best source of information. On the other hand, tax attorneys are invaluable resources in Central and South America.

CHAPTER 3

Analysis of the Market

INTERNATIONAL BUSINESS RELATIONSHIPS, particularly JVs between parties from different countries, cultures, and legal systems, present unique challenges. Parties tend to focus on the business and economic terms and consequences of their relationship, but they must also respect the different values they will encounter when they approach a cross-border relationship. For the process to succeed, a careful analysis should always be made of the markets in the country or countries where the JV will be active.

Social and Political Factors

In an international JV, the cross-border nature of the transaction requires that the parties pay close attention to the social and political factors that might impact the success of the JV. The social and cultural beliefs and practices of another population are based on its history, education, and fundamental understanding about how society ought to be ordered and regulated. Political factors can extend beyond the structure of government and the rule of law to include informal methods of power and influence in the marketplace.

In many ways, the decision to enter into a new foreign market is an adventure in cultural anthropology. The foreign party needs to consider carefully all the traits and activities that make up the way of life in the subject country. This analysis requires identification and understanding of the controlling institutions and customs that regulate how people think and what goals they seek in their day-to-day lives. These cultural values will, in turn, influence the structure and operation of business enterprises. For example, consider the argument that management practices in a Japanese corporation, including the emphasis on group values and subordination of the desires of the individual, are a byproduct of the social organization in that country. Consider also how clan and extended family relationships in a small developing country can often overwhelm the nominal authority of the government, thereby reducing the degree to which foreign parties can rely on guarantees of the state with respect to the operation of a JV.

In addition, a foreign party must carefully evaluate the political environment of the subject country. Political evaluation has often been neglected, or contemptuously ignored, by managers in developed countries. The results can be disastrous, leading to misunderstandings between the parties and direct clashes between the foreign investor, regulators, and other institutions within the subject country. Relevant considerations include an estimate of the political stability and the likely direction of political development in the subject country, an appraisal of the quality of the public service, the possibilities for long-term economic growth, and the attitude of the government and people toward foreigners in general and toward the prospective venturer's nation in particular. National pride and sensitivities must be taken into account. Finally, the foreign party should remember that, particularly in smaller developing countries, an investment will often have far-reaching and unexpected effects on policy developments in the host country and on overall political relations between the countries involved.

Country Analysis

Country analysis is a holistic approach to understanding a country's past activities, particularly within its government, and its future trends during the term of the JV. Government activities are of special significance because they are chiefly responsible for establishing and maintaining the framework, including the institutions and behavioral rules, through which the country develops its economic, political, and social structure, and relates to the activities of other countries. The analysis focuses first on identifying and evaluating a country's performance and national goals and objectives. Then the analysis turns to the construction of scenarios reflecting possible trends in evolution and development of the country over the JV term. Using these scenarios, a party can make an educated guess as to the effect of future events on its interests and can attempt to build protection into the JV documentation.

ECONOMIC PERFORMANCE

One of the most important factors in selecting a new foreign market for investment is the historical and projected economic performance of the country or region. Most countries regularly publish data on economic performance. Although some indicators are more important than others for a particular JV, attention should always be paid to such factors as the balance of payments situation; the exchange rate; aggregate output, prices, and employment; savings and investment rates; productivity measures; and distribution of income broken down by demographic characteristics (area, age, ethnic group, and so on).

NATIONAL GOALS

Like businesses, countries generally have specific national goals or objectives that drive the various policies implemented by their governments. A country may have many goals, some more real than others, some more important than others. Among the most common are autonomy, productivity, and equity. Autonomy is the freedom from foreign domination, and it is generally expressed through a country's foreign investment regulations. Productivity refers to the skills and processes that can create wealth and increase the overall standard of living. The need to enhance productivity often drives incentives for foreign investment, which sometimes puts the government at odds with concerns over foreign domination of the economy. Finally, the notion of equity includes questions surrounding distribution of income and opportunity. Equity concerns can lead to substantial political uncertainty in a country, as well as to laws and regulations (e.g., required profit-sharing with employees) that impact the JV's anticipated profits.

ECONOMIC AND SOCIAL POLICIES

A country seeks to meet its goals and objectives through a series of policies. The process of policy selection involves a balancing of many public and private interests and the actual choices are subject to various constraints, including the resources available within the country, the structure of the government and other institutions, and political realities. Among the areas that must always be considered are the following:

- FOREIGN POLICY Countries tend toward one of three distinct foreign policy orientations: (1) territorial or political expansion, (2) maintenance of the "status quo;" or (3) adherence to a low profile and an inward-looking focus. The country's foreign policy focus may be relatively unimportant for short-term JVs. On the other hand, a country looking to expand is likely to devote substantial resources to defense-related activities, while a lower profile policy is more likely to free up resources for private investment and enhancement of local markets.
- FISCAL AND MONETARY POLICIES Fiscal policies relate to government spending and tax policies, while monetary policies influence the money supply, the price of money (i.e., interest rates), and the convertibility of local currency into foreign currency. Issues of concern might well include decisions of the government with regard to procurement and funding of programs in a particular geographic or industrial area, the tax rates, and foreign exchange policies. Also, if a government has substantial deficits, the entire market might well be adversely impacted.
- INCOME POLICIES A country's income policies concern the regulation of the level and distribution of income within the country. For example, countries attempting to reduce the level of inflation may adopt wage and price controls. Income maintenance programs, such as unemployment insurance and social security, are used to preserve certain minimum standards of livelihood to eligible citizens.
- FOREIGN TRADE AND INVESTMENT POLICIES Foreign trade and investment policies regulate the flow of trade and capital in and out of a country. Trade policy includes tariffs and non-tariff barriers to imports, as well as incentives for exporters who can distribute the country's products in foreign markets in exchange for valuable foreign currencies. Investment policies are particularly important to JVs because they regulate the terms of foreign participation in the local economy. Analysis of foreign trade policies has become more complex with the growth in the number of bilateral and multilateral agreements between and among various economies.
- INDUSTRIAL POLICY Industrial policy was a very popular topic during the 1980s, as developed and developing countries sought to identify strategies to promote and enhance the competitiveness of their domestic industries. At the macroeconomic level, industrial policy might have been in the form of changes to the tax system in order to promote savings and investment. But, in many cases, industrial policy consisted of a package of policies that effectively favored one industry over another. While these policies sometimes brought short-term success, they often tended to protect businesses that lacked an effective management structure, because they did not have to present themselves to the judgments of independent capital markets.
- SOCIAL POLICIES Social policies encompass some of the economic-based policies already mentioned, including income maintenance schemes and labor policies. In addition, a foreign investor must seriously consider the impact of

educational and population policies, and the government's attitude toward organized religion.

CONTEXT

The goals and policies of the government are usually established based on an understanding of the relevant constraints on the country, and its available resources during the planning period. This is often referred to as the "context" for government planning and requires consideration of the following factors: (1) the local and international political situation; (2) the country's governing ideology; (3) the institutions that support its political, economic, and social infrastructure; and (4) its geographic and demographic characteristics.

- GOVERNMENT STRUCTURE Obviously, the government is always one of the most, if not the most, important institution in a country. Foreign parties need to analyze carefully the form and structure of the government, the mechanisms for power transitions between leaders, the key power blocs, and the extent of popular support for the current regime. The identification of other sources of political influence, such as lobbyists, special interest groups, and tribal, clan and family connections is just as important.
- OTHER INSTITUTIONS Other institutions outside of the government can have a profound impact on a country's business environment. First, foreign investors need to evaluate the core business-related sectors in the local economy, including banking and finance, transportation, real estate, and construction. For example, management practices within the financial sectors can be an important indicator of the expected volatility of the domestic market. The investor should look for any mechanisms that might impact competition, including cartels, informal understandings, or interlocking directorates managed through banks. Other groups or activities that might rise to the level of an institution include farmers, agricultural workers, and organized labor. Finally, religious institutions play a key role in many countries, particularly if there is a Catholic or Moslem majority.
- IDEOLOGY The ideological context for a country is often quite difficult to define and analyze. In general, ideology speaks to the core values of the country and common understandings as to how a society should be organized, and the rights and duties of the members of the society. Decisions made regarding ideology impacts the powers that reside in the key institutions and the way in which those institutions are expected to exercise those powers. For example, if the controlling ideology emphasizes equality, then one can expect to see government policies that emphasize freedom of opportunity and access. While this may seem laudable, firms from developed countries may be chagrined to see some governments pursue equality by failing to recognize intellectual property rights out of fear that they may deprive society of access to ideas that they believe should be open to use by all, regardless of who made the original investment.

Finally, the goals and strategies of a country may well be constrained and driven by physical characteristics that cannot be changed, or changed only at substantial expense. Among the obvious features that might be expected to drive a country's economy are arable land, deepwater harbors, mineral resources, climatic conditions, and population density.

EVALUATION AND FORECASTING

The two final steps in the country analysis process are (1) evaluation of the country's performance in light of its goals and policies, and (2) development of a forecast of future performance for use in constructing an appropriate strategy for investors considering entry into the marketplace. Of course, the analyst should carefully review all the performance indicators to make a broad assessment as to how well the economy is doing. Trends should be noted, such as whether performance is getting better or worse, and comparisons might be made to comparable countries. Most importantly, performance should be evaluated relative to the stated goals announced by the government over the last few years.

■ PAST PERFORMANCE If a country's performance has been satisfactory, an attempt should be made to identify the reasons for success, and to determine if these represent specific strategic advantages that can be exploited in the future. If, on the other hand, the country's performance has been disappointing, the analyst must search for a diagnosis of the causes. For example, a country may have mismanaged its fiscal policy by following spending and taxing policies that adversely affected incentives to work and invest. In other cases, excessive growth in the money supply may have led to inflation and a high-cost, uncompetitive economy. Also, costly income maintenance and social security programs can result in the government taking too large a role in the economy.

Apart from evaluating performance, the analyst should also attempt to identify inconsistencies between the country's strategies and policies, and the context within which they are formulated and executed. For example, a strategy based on a particular rate of growth may be doomed to failure if the country lacks the requisite resources, or local firms are unable to meet the levels of productivity necessary for success. Likewise, strategies may be impossible to execute if they are not supported by key institutional groups, such as farmers or labor unions. This is a difficult area for foreign investors to evaluate because it requires an uncritical understanding of the ideology that drives local actors. Another possible problem might be that a given strategy is unrealistic in the international context, as might be the case when a country is looking to achieve growth through exports of goods that are unlikely to be accepted in other countries.

■ FUTURE PERFORMANCE If inconsistencies exist between strategy and institutions, a new strategic direction will most likely be required. Institutions often have historical roots that make them difficult to change, and any changes that are made will come quite slowly. In contrast, policies can be changed quickly, provided that consensus can be achieved within the government. However, even if policy changes are rapid, caution should be exercised in gauging the speed and efficacy of the changes and the associated political and economic costs.

Analysis of the past is designed to allow a party to make an educated assessment of the future for purposes of planning for the proposed JV. A considerable amount of time and effort has been devoted to developing methodologies for analyzing the future, and a wide variety of approaches have been used. Many businesses represent the future environment by a forecast, often by a consensus forecast reflecting a compromise between optimistic and pessimistic views. This approach works reasonably well during periods of political stability and relative smooth economic growth. On the other hand, businesses may join military planners in scenario-based planning, which calls for the evaluation of several different strategies against alternative scenarios about the future.

CHAPTER 4

Parties to the JV: The Roles

MANY CHALLENGES IN LAUNCHING AND OPERATING an international JV flow from the fact that the typical JV involves several different parties, each with its own unique set of goals and objectives. Obviously, the main parties are the joint venturers themselves. Although a JV can include more than two partners, or partners that operate primarily in the same jurisdiction, we will assume that the JV involves a foreign party (i.e., a business entity that operates outside of the country where the JV activities will be carried out) and a local party (i.e., a business entity owned and operated by parties in the country where the JV activities will be carried out).

Although success of the JV will ultimately depend on the relationship of the venturers, other parties will also play an important role. In many emerging markets, the most important of these parties is the local government, which may not only regulate the terms of the JV but may also own part of it. In addition, the tone of the JV relationship may be dictated by the advisors to the venturers, particularly their lawyers and accountants. Finally, the concerns of local managers and union leaders should always be accounted for in the planning process.

The Foreign Party

A JV offers inherent business advantages to a foreign party seeking a local business partner. International joint venturing, once limited to large corporations in developed economies, is attracting smaller businesses today as innovative technologies are making global commerce more accessible. Regardless of a foreign party's size, its key objectives usually include the following:

- IMPROVED ACCESS TO THE FOREIGN MARKET A foreign party might prefer a JV when tapping into the local party's existing market and distribution channels.
- COST REDUCTION If a local partner contributes working capital, raw materials, facilities, and other assets, the foreign party may realize significant cost savings by entering the market through the JV as opposed to starting up on its own.
- ACCESS TO LOCAL MANAGEMENT The best entry into a local market is through managers experienced in marketing to the unique needs of customers in the foreign country. A JV offers a local management structure that the foreign party would otherwise have to hire and train if it were to launch its own business.
- FAVORABLE GOVERNMENT TREATMENT The government's attitude toward foreign investment is particularly important in emerging economies. Often, a foreign party will enter into a JV only if it can receive favorable government treatment.

ACCESS TO FOREIGN MARKET

A foreign party can usually choose from several alternative strategies for entering a foreign market. When marketing and distribution are the goals, a foreign party may find that selling its products in the local market is easier in a JV form, particularly for consumer goods. Managers of foreign parties believe that involving a local partner improves sales by creating an incentive to buy and to strengthen brand loyalty. Certainly local participation is likely to be favorable if the market is small and the level of price competition between brands is not intense. However, in larger markets, the advantage is less obvious. Buyers may be uninformed about the national ownership of vendors and will usually be concerned about price and quality as opposed to whether a local party is part of the venture. As such, the use of a JV may have little advantage over setting up a wholly owned subsidiary or conducting business through a local agent.

COST REDUCTION

Almost by definition, a JV creates opportunities that significantly reduce the capital requirements to enter a market or start a functional activity. Sometimes the local party contributes cash to fund the operations, and other times contributions may be in kind, such as a right to use property and equipment that are otherwise underexploited. Cost savings do, however, come with a price in that having a partner may reduce the profit potential associated with a project.

MANAGEMENT OBJECTIVES

Capable management talent is a rare commodity, and is often the key to the success or failure of a JV. A foreign party might find that it lacks management resources for a new project in the local market, or that it cannot spare personnel plus the time and attention of the main office to set up and operate a new venture. In those cases, they will look at a JV as a means for gaining access to local managerial talent that can contribute knowledge of local conditions and experience in dealing with labor, government, and suppliers. A JV format is particularly well suited to this type of objective, given that it is difficult to attract first-class managerial talent in emerging economies without offering them true ownership positions with the firm. In many countries, local employees without an ownership position lack the status and personality to obtain favorable local treatment for the enterprise. Also, although training local managers is certainly an option, this strategy is risky, given that the early months of the JV are usually the most crucial in establishing the foundations for long-term success.

The pursuit of management objectives must be tempered by consideration of the potential problems. Assuming local talent is recruited, it must be able to cooperate with colleagues from the foreign party. Management communication problems are a key reason for JV failure, and this needs to be borne in mind from the start of negotiations. In some emerging economies, local managers customarily hire friends and relatives instead of engaging in more open recruiting programs. Such practices can lead to conflicts of interest and can make personnel changes over the term of the JV more difficult for the foreign party.

GOVERNMENT TREATMENT

Historically, foreign investors have considered the JV as a way of obtaining more favorable treatment from the local government. For many years, many countries made it legally impossible for a foreign entity to invest in specified industries except on a JV basis. In other situations, the government left open the possibility of a wholly owned subsidiary while adopting policies that clearly favored the use of a JV with respect to obtaining necessary approvals and qualifying for various incentives.

First and foremost, foreign investors look to a JV to achieve an acceptable level of friendship and cooperation from government officials. The foreign party will be seeking both assurances that the government will not take measures that might be harmful to the JV, and guarantees that incentives will be made available to the JV if local participation is sufficient. This type of relationship may, in fact, be possible if the government is highly centralized, as is often the case in smaller emerging economies, or if it consists for practical purposes of a small group of leaders and officials having long-standing relationships with local business owners. In larger economies with more decentralized government control, the utility of a JV is more dependent on the specific skills of the local party in acting as an agent to favorably influence government policies and treatment. Hopefully, a local party can exert political influence in ways the foreign party cannot, such as by initiatives through organized business groups and political parties.

Throughout the JV term, the foreign party should guard against blind reliance on favorable government treatment. Particularly in smaller economies, there is a high likelihood that government changes may occur in the future and that those changes may cause a wholesale turnover in regulatory personnel. The new regulators may well be disinterested in cooperating with parties that have aligned themselves with the former regime. The foreign party needs to make its own assessment of the political environment in the subject country, as opposed to simply accepting the intelligence offered by the prospective local partner, and it should revisit its assessment periodically to account for variations in the ruling powers.

The Local Party

The local party's objectives when offered a JV opportunity depend on the JV's purpose and the relative size and resources of the parties. For example, in a JV between two relatively equal partners, the local party may share similar goals with the foreign party, such as reduction of costs and risk. However, if the local party is smaller than the foreign one, or lacks business assets and resources needed to undertake the activity on its own, it will seek to negotiate terms to satisfy goals that may be adverse to the foreign party's interests and the JV itself.

JOB CREATION

For smaller local firms, a JV with a foreign partner may create significant new job opportunities, as well as the opportunity to refocus existing employees on new activities that might be more profitable than current operations. If the local partner will be adding new workers to perform its obligations to the JV, it will want assurances regarding available benefits and training that might be necessary to recruit and maintain the employees. Also, an inflow of new workers may have serious effects on the surrounding community, and the parties need to consider whether sufficient housing and related services are in place.

ACQUISITION OF TECHNICAL KNOW-HOW

Governments in emerging economies have often looked at JVs as an opportunity for local firms to acquire technical know-how from more advanced partners in developed countries. In fact, countries such as Japan and Korea, each of which are now powerful intellectual property producers in their own right, fueled their growth through technology transfer arrangements with partners from the United States and Europe during the 1960s and 1970s. The acquisition of technical know-how is obviously a key goal of the local participant as well as the local government. The local partner will want to be sure that it has an opportunity to become exposed to all relevant current technology in the area in which the JV will be operating. Certainly, the local partner's ability to independently exploit the foreign party's technology can, and will, be limited by law and contract. The knowledge that the local partner receives through observation, use, and training, however, will certainly upgrade its internal development capabilities.

GUARANTEED CUSTOMER OR SUPPLIER

The local partner may be attracted to a JV as a means to secure a guaranteed customer for its products, or an exclusive supplier of certain components that it needs to manufacture its products. For example, the foreign partner may be willing to provide funding to expand the local partner's manufacturing operations so that the local partner's products can be made available for distribution in the foreign partner's own markets. Likewise, a local partner might be able to substitute components that it had previously imported for parts and materials produced locally by the JV using technology provided by the foreign partner.

ACCESS TO FOREIGN PARTY'S MARKETS

A JV may be the best way to exploit sales and distribution of the local partner's products through the foreign party's own market network. The local party may decide that a straightforward distribution agreement does not provide the requisite incentives to entice the foreign party to embrace the local partner's products. A JV structure, with its shared equity structure and higher level of interpersonal dependence, is more likely to keep the foreign partner interested in its products, and inattentive to other sources.

COST REDUCTION

For smaller firms in emerging economies, cost reduction and capital raising are two key incentives for partnering with a larger foreign entity. Local capital markets may not be mature enough to provide the cash required to allow domestic firms to fund all the activities required to expand their businesses. For example, interest rates may be too high or capital providers may lack the background to understand and value an opportunity. In such situations, foreign investors may be able to provide the required cash along with invaluable management assistance.

MANAGEMENT SKILLS

Although a foreign partner often looks to a JV to tap local managerial talent, the local partner may also view the venture as a substantial learning experience that will enhance the managerial and technical competence of its employees. Not surprising, this is an area that often causes great confusion, because it raises possible conflicts among management over responsibility for the strategic direction of the JV. The local partner needs to be quite certain about the scope and amount of technical and managerial assistance that will be provided, as well as the amount of managerial know-how that it will be expected to contribute.

The Local Regulators

One reason that the JV is frequently used abroad, particularly in developing countries, is that many host countries have required that foreign investment take the form of a JV rather than a wholly owned subsidiary. This requirement has been codified in various ways around the world. Some countries have adopted absolute rules that prohibit foreign investments except in the form of a JV in which the local investors—public or private—own a majority of the equity and hold a controlling position. Other countries impose a JV requirement only in particularly important segments of the economy, such as agriculture, mining, or natural resource development. These requirements are discussed in greater detail in Chapter 11.

Host country preferences for joint ventures are driven by various objectives, each of which may become relevant during the negotiation period leading up to approval of the JV. Among the most important are the following:

- Participation by local investors will increase the likelihood that the project will be integrated into the local economy.
- A JV can enhance local management skills and facilitate the transfer of new technologies into the country.
- Local participation tends to mitigate the perceived dangers of foreign domination of important sectors of the local economy.
- A JV can improve the local partner's ability to gain access to the international marketing and manufacturing resources of the foreign partner.
- Local participation ensures that the business will be conducted in a manner that is responsive to the economic policies of the government, which presumably would be a more difficult task for a business wholly owned by the foreign investor.
- A JV can be the basis for nationalization or a negotiated purchase of the project if this strategy is deemed beneficial to the economic structure of the host country.

Of course, several of these motives are at odds with the objective of attracting maximum foreign investment. For example, a foreign party will be understandably reluctant to invest resources in a foreign JV if there is substantial risk that it will lose control over any technology it transfers to the JV. Also, local government pressure on foreign investors to divest themselves of part of their equity by inviting in specific local interests may cause the foreign party to take its capital elsewhere. The impact of the government's motives will vary depending on the specific project. If the foreign party might fund the entire venture on its own but for the national laws that require local involvement, the project is more likely to be cancelled if government conditions are too strict. On the other hand, a foreign party that needs some local capital to initiate the project may be more willing to accede to local policy objectives.

Six Tips to Engaging Foreign Counsel

Once you have identified foreign counsel, you must consider the scope of the relationship and the mutual expectations of the parties regarding the type of work that is to be done, billing practices, deadlines, and other matters. The following tips are useful:

1. Be specific about the issues and questions that the foreign lawyer is expected to address. Prepare a detailed summary of the relevant facts, and transmit copies of all documents that the foreign lawyer may need to review.
2. Be sure all the important terms and concepts are clearly defined from the outset, particularly because commercial and legal words and phrases have different meanings in different countries.
3. Obtain an estimate of fees from the foreign law firm, including the names of the attorneys who will be involved in the matters and their billing rates, and be clear on how and when payments are to be made.
4. Impress on foreign counsel the need to meet deadlines. Also, require progress reports, ask for an oral report of legal analysis before authorizing a written opinion, and request an assurance that the partner in charge will remain personally responsible for supervising the matter.
5. Probe carefully into whether the firm has any real or apparent conflict of interest, particularly if you have any suspicion that it has previously represented a competitor. In many jurisdictions outside of the United States, Canada, and Europe, conflict of interest rules are less than strict.
6. In most cases, have your foreign lawyer communicate with your domestic counsel rather than with you directly. In this way, your domestic counsel can monitor the advice, ensure that all issues are being addressed, and integrate the advice on foreign law with its own research to develop an answer that is most useful to you.

Professional Advisors

Each principal in the JV negotiations is usually supported by professional advisors, including attorneys, accountants, and consultants with special expertise in the particular market or industry. The challenge for the principals is to extract the best advice and counsel from these professionals without losing sight of the fact that the JV is first and foremost a relationship between the managers of the JV partners and their respective business organizations.

INSIDE OR REGULAR OUTSIDE COUNSEL

In nearly all cases, the participants will turn first to their domestic legal counsel, who may be either employed directly by the party (i.e., "inside counsel") or part of an independent law firm that the party retains regularly (i.e., "outside counsel"). Counsel should be a trusted and experienced member of the party's management team and should already have a good sense of the possible goals and motives for the particular JV. The primary role of counsel is to manage the process of negotiating and documenting the terms of the JV, including formalities of establishing the entity and ensuring that all statutory and regulatory hurdles have been satisfied. By its very terms, an international JV is a cross-border transaction heavily influenced by the laws of the jurisdiction where the JV will primarily operate, and therefore the value and effectiveness of counsel will depend on its ability to identify competent foreign counsel to assist in the representation.

FOREIGN COUNSEL

During negotiations, a JV party will often retain foreign legal counsel who is licensed to practise law in the other party's country to advise on the laws and legal customs of that other country. Foreign counsel is most commonly employed by the foreign party to the JV—the party that is outside the country where the JV is created. Assistance from foreign counsel can be invaluable on matters relating to local law and procedures related to the formation and operation of a JV, and foreign counsel can also be the primary contact with local officials and regulatory bodies. Although less common, a local party who has sufficient resources might retain counsel who is familiar with the laws of the other party's country and who can provide insight into the meaning of unfamiliar contractual terms and legal tactics. Foreign counsel can be particular helpful in:

- Advising on issues of local law and practice in the other party's country.
- Dealing with foreign government officials, courts, and regulators.
- Advising on government policies and developments relating to legislation, regulations, and case law in the local market for the JV.
- Advising on local customs, culture, and business practices in the other party's country.
- Advising on the legality of contracts under the local law of the JV's country.
- Assisting in negotiations with other local residents and firms of the JV's country.
- Resolving any issues arising from language differences between the parties.

A party's regular counsel should be able to provide assistance in engaging competent counsel in the other party's country. Directories such as Martindale-Hubbell's *International Law Directory* list law firms on a country and city basis. Listings typically describe the practice areas of the firms and may include the names of representative clients. Foreign counsel may also be located through a multinational client, an international accounting firm, or a bank with foreign branch offices or affiliates. Many firms offer information about their services on the Internet and can be contacted electronically. Finally, a list of local firms may be obtained from the embassy's commercial office for the country of interest.

SELECTION FACTORS

In reviewing potential candidates for foreign counsel, the JV party should look for someone with experience in drafting and negotiating JV documents, preferably with other clients from the same countries as the JV participants. The foreign party is best advised to consider counsel who has experience in dealing with the local government and who can provide assistance in negotiations with local regulators, and advice on the competencies of the local partner in relation to government discussions. Foreign counsel should be able to represent you in court in the event a problem arises in the future. Finally, the ability to communicate with foreign counsel is essential and it is therefore necessary to find counsel who speaks your own language and grasps your business policies and intentions. In particular, seek out foreign counsel that has had experience with your country's legal system, either as a practicing attorney, an intern with a law firm, or perhaps through training at a law school in your country.

OTHER ADVISORS

Other professional advisors that may be involved in a JV transaction include the following:

- Accounting and tax professionals, who will advise on the financial reporting and tax obligations attributable to the JV. These issues can be quite complex, and it generally makes sense to engage professionals with substantial experience in the country where the JV will conduct its activities. The foreign party needs to bear in mind that accounting and record keeping practices in the host country may vary substantially from those used by the foreign party in other parts of its business.
- Business or marketing consultants, who will assist in selecting the appropriate market and in evaluating potential JV candidates. Careful consideration should be given to defining the scope of this engagement. The engaging party should be sure to obtain guarantees from the consultant that it will comply with all applicable laws and regulations, including laws restricting the use of gifts to obtain favorable treatment from government officials and others.

Other Business Partners

The activities of the JV may require involvement by one or more other business owners who will contract with the JV to provide goods or services. For example, a manufacturing JV may depend on various local suppliers for parts or raw materials. If so, the JV partners must consider whether they will be able to enter into a long-term arrangement with an outside party that has no ownership interest in the JV itself. If the JV appears to depend too heavily on other businesses, the parties need to consider whether the JV might develop its own capabilities for producing the specified goods or service. Alternatively, a business owner may be offered an ownership interest in the JV to assure availability of the goods or services, and to align the interests of all of the parties toward the success of the JV.

CHAPTER 5

Parties to the JV: The Selection

BEFORE ENTERING INTO A JV, the parties should engage in preliminary activities that can be of tremendous importance in properly structuring the deal and ensuring that their objectives will be incorporated into the JV documentation. Although the importance of each step depends on the transaction, consideration should always be given to the means by which reliable JV partners may be located and evaluated, and to the initial exchange of information between the parties to determine whether a basis for a relationship actually exists. An essential part of this process is the signing of a Confidentiality Agreement (see Chapter 7).

Locating Potential JV Partners

Much time and effort is generally spent in locating appropriate candidates for a JV. On the other hand, an existing relationship can be built with a current supplier, distributor, or customer. Information about potential candidates can be solicited from experts in the area of interest, such as trade associations, chambers of commerce, investment and commercial bankers, lawyers, accountants, and independent consultants. Firms with complimentary strengths and needs can be identified by reviewing information in published reports, such as the periodic reports that may be filed with the United States Securities and Exchange Commission (SEC) and with similar regulatory agencies in other countries. Government organizations in many countries (e.g., Ministry of Commerce, Ministry of Trade and Industry) often serve as catalysts for foreign investment and JV transactions.

Due Diligence Investigation

The preliminary exchange of information between potential JV partners is generally referred to as a due diligence investigation. It involves a review of each party's business and affairs as a condition to consummation of the deal, and it is typically conducted by first obtaining publicly available information and next exchanging information made available by the potential parties.

REVIEW OF PUBLIC INFORMATION

A preliminary investigation of information that is publicly available should reveal whether the potential JV partner is in good legal standing, has a good reputation among traders and consumers, has government or extended family connections, or has a long, stable, and profitable history. The public records that are available depend on the country's regulatory laws and the organizational type of the potential partner's entity. These records might include trade name and business registrations, trademark and patent registrations, credit reports, press releases, and tax, financial, and securities registrations. The usual practice is to employ an investigator, accountant, or law firm

Due Diligence Documentary Checklist

The items on this due diligence checklist are designed to provide the requesting party with a better idea of the proposed partner's general business activities, organizational structure, and skills and experience in the specific functional areas that are most relevant to the particular JV.

Certified copy of the charter documents of the prospective partner (e.g., articles of incorporation).

Copies of any studies, reports, or business plans prepared by, or on behalf of, the prospective partner with respect to the proposed activities of the JV.

All consents, filings, and correspondence with or to local regulatory agencies relating to the partner's proposed activities on behalf of the JV.

Description of the partner's business activities within the geographic scope of the JV, and in other areas where the partner will be conducting activities similar to those to be performed for the JV.

List of the partner's major shareholders or other equity owners, and a description of any agreements among the owners with respect to management of the partner's business.

A list of key executives and managers of the partner, and biographical information for each listed person.

A list of key personnel in the functional areas relevant to the partner's activities for the JV.

Financial information regarding the partner, including consolidated balance sheets and income statements for at least three years prior to the date of the proposed formation of the JV.

A list of the partner's key customers, suppliers, and financial partners.

All material contracts, including deeds, leases, JVs, material supply, purchase, services, development, merchandise, equipment, license, marketing, and distribution contracts to which the partner is a party.

Lists of all patents, trademarks, and copyrights held by or licensed to the partner.

A list of pending, threatened, and historical litigation to which the partner is or has been subject, to the extent it is related to the activities of the partner for the JV.

within the country where the potential partner claims to exist. Such a local expert will be familiar with local official registers, banking and financial resources, industry networks, and the like. The investigation can be performed reasonably quickly at minimal cost, and it will indicate whether a company is worth approaching.

EXCHANGE OF PRIVATE INFORMATION

Assuming that preliminary due diligence suggests the potential partner might be a worthy venturer, the next step is to approach the company and to determine its interest in a JV. The parties should then sign a Confidentiality Agreement (see Chapter 7) and proceed with a more thorough due diligence check in which they voluntarily exchange relevant data about their own separate organizations.

The type of information exchanged depends on the circumstances and the amount of preparation each party has made in advance. One party may have already conducted a substantial study of the proposed JV project, and may have developed some form of preliminary business plan to demonstrate the economic feasibility and attractiveness of the proposed JV. If so, the plan should identify the assets and resources that each party is expected to contribute to the JV, and these elements should be carefully analyzed during the due diligence investigation.

GOALS OF THE INVESTIGATION

Much time and effort goes into a due diligence investigation, and therefore it is important to remember the purpose for the investigation. All concerns should be resolved with an eye toward accomplishing the following objectives:

- Collect enough information about the other party to make a reasoned and informed decision about whether or not to proceed with the transaction.
- Identify and, if possible, quantify the potential risks and liabilities associated with the proposed JV, with the intent of crafting a contract that resolves these concerns.
- Confirm the accuracy and completeness of the other party's representations and warranties that will be included in the documentation for the transaction.
- Identify all the legal and regulatory hurdles that must be overcome to form and launch the JV, including governmental approvals and authorizations, and consents from other third parties.

UNIQUE PROBLEMS IN CROSS-BORDER DUE DILIGENCE

Any cross-border transaction raises special due diligence challenges. Each party must be sensitive to, and become informed about, the cultural, geographic, and legal environment in which the other party operates. Consideration must be given to the problems associated with closing the particular transaction and participating in a long-term business relationship in a foreign jurisdiction located many miles and time zones away.

Even what may seem to be the simplest things can be difficult in a foreign country. For example, weeks or months can pass before "public" documents are received because recrudescing and indexing procedures may be poor, or even nonexistent, in some countries. One party may need simply to rely on the accuracy of the other party's representations and warranties to proceed with the transaction in a timely fashion. Be cautious, however, of taking short cuts merely to keep to a time schedule. Keep in mind that remedies for breach of a representation only kick in after the deal has been completed and cash and assets have been transferred to the JV. This means that a party may be left with having to litigate in a foreign jurisdiction because it was unable to perform the type of due diligence investigation that would have uncovered the problem at the preformation stage.

- **CULTURAL DIFFERENCES** Successful due diligence for a new international JV requires attention to other unique factors, many of which follow from differences in language and custom. The first thing you need to do is to learn how the concept of due diligence is understood in the relevant country. If you already have experience with transactions in that particular country, then this can serve as your guide. If not, you will want to consult books or articles about the business culture and the general customs associated with doing business in the specific country.

  Countries that follow the common law tradition tend to adopt or accept due diligence practices that are similar to those in the United States and Europe. Thus, one can expect that a fairly comprehensive investigation will be an accepted part of the pre-closing preparations and negotiations. But, in many countries in Asia and Latin America, due diligence may be viewed as a sign of mistrust or bad faith, and any attempt to conduct a full-blown review may destroy the relationship before it begins. To some extent, these differences reflect the fact that European and United States parties and attorneys tend to attach great importance to the documents associated with the transaction, while business people in other societies view the deal in terms of the relationship that exists between the parties.

- **REGULATORY COMPLIANCE** When requesting information from a foreign party, consideration must be given to the need to comply with foreign country regulations relating to the export of sensitive information. In all but the smallest transactions, both parties will execute confidentiality agreements that include undertakings by both parties to maintain the secrecy of information received from the other party. Government restrictions, however, may prevent the foreign party from disclosing financial or technical information without first obtaining the approval of the appropriate administrative authorities. The need to comply with these regulations should be factored into the timetable for completing the due diligence review and the transaction as a whole.

- **RELIANCE ON FOREIGN COUNSEL** Foreign counsel can often provide useful assistance in determining the acceptable scope of the due diligence transaction and in assisting the foreign party to understand the questions that are being asked. In addition, legal opinions from local counsel may be used to supplement the representations and warranties of the foreign party. Don't forget that the opinion will only be as good as the review made by the local counsel. Lawyers in many countries are not familiar with the rigorous back-up investigation undertaken by lawyers in the United States and Europe as a condition of rendering an opinion. Also, lawyers in many countries are not accustomed to delivering opinions, and the foreign party may have a good deal of difficulty in explaining the elements usually included in a legal opinion.

  Another thing to remember is that, although due diligence is usually conducted by attorneys in the United States, practices differ in other jurisdictions. In Japan and other parts of Asia, for example, lawyers are rarely used for due diligence investigations. Instead, the foreign party will be dealing with business people and accountants in the host country. In many cases, these persons have some form of legal training, but you should be prepared to describe fully the type of information that you are seeking. Language skills may be particularly important at this juncture, and you may need to rely heavily on local counsel to translate your requests and the means for compliance.

PROCEDURES FOR DUE DILIGENCE INVESTIGATION

There is no standard set of procedures for conducting a due diligence investigation in the context of a proposed JV. The amount of effort will depend on the countries where the parties are operating, each particular company, the style of the company conducting the investigation and, to some extent, the size and importance of the proposed transaction in relation to the other activities of the investigating party.

In most cases, the participants should sign a Confidentiality Agreement (see Chapter 7) and agree on a formal investigation plan for the due diligence investigation. Each of the elements of the plan should be discussed during preliminary negotiations, so that the results can be available well in advance of the projected closing date. This will allow the participants to utilize the information to achieve the proper structure for the relationship and to establish communication about their questions and concerns over the resources that will be used in the actual JV. Also, a written investigation plan can expedite the transaction by setting deadlines for collecting the information.

ADDITIONAL DUE DILIGENCE PROCEDURES

Document review should be supplemented with interviews of key officials of the proposed partner, the partner's accountants, suppliers, and customers, and other persons who might have useful information relating to the partner. Also, special procedures should be followed in connection with functions and assets that are particularly important to the JV. For example, if one partner is to contribute patents or other intellectual property rights to the JV, the other partner will want to do a thorough technology review that covers the creation, ownership, and protection of those rights. Finally, the foreign partner should do its own analysis of the business, legal, and political environment in the host country, and in each country where the JV will be operating.

MANAGEMENT AND THE DUE DILIGENCE INVESTIGATION

Prospective JV partners can derive a number of significant sideline benefits from a due diligence investigation. For example, each party will have the opportunity to observe how the managers of the other party handle detailed inquiries into significant aspects of its prospective business plan. In many cases, parties can learn a good deal about the judgment and competence of the other party's managers and analyze how they have organized and managed their existing operations. If the managers have clearly mismanaged or neglected important areas, this may raise concerns about whether they have the basic competence to carry out their part of the tasks for the JV.

Evaluating Potential JV Partners

Once the due diligence investigation is completed, a careful evaluation of the information gleaned is needed to decide whether a long-term JV relationship is feasible. Few subjects have been more extensively analyzed then the selection of potential JV partners. Clearly, a JV presents special problems because, by its very nature, it requires partial integration of the skills, attitudes, bias, and experiences of each party's organization and the many persons within them. Accordingly, the

Building a Cultural Profile

When preparing to negotiate the terms of a new JV, take the time to build a cultural profile of your potential business partner. This important step will allow the negotiators to anticipate and understand cultural differences that might impact the negotiations and the actual operations of the JV. At a minimum, a cultural profile will improve your understanding of the other partner's behavior. Profile questions should include:

1. Is behavior in the business culture influenced by a particular religious philosophy?
2. How important is nonverbal communication, such as body language and facial expressions, in the other party's culture?
3. What is the role of humor in business negotiations?
4. Does the culture appreciate independent thinking and achievement, or is the status of the group more important?
5. What is the basis for authority in the culture (e.g., meritocracy, age, education)?
6. Are the social rules different for men and women, and are there any potential racial concerns?
7. Do businesspeople prefer detailed and precise communications or will general expressions of intent be sufficient?
8. How does the concept of time drive the decisions of businesspeople in the other culture? Will they stick to a schedule or use time simply as a rough framework?
9. What local manners and customs need to be recognized in the negotiation process (e.g., greetings, socialization, gifts)?

evaluation should focus not only on functional characteristics, but also on the likelihood of compatibility between the partners. A number of factors to consider are listed below. In addition, a party might refer to the discussion in Chapter 6 of some of the situations that create trouble for a JV.

- COMPATIBILITY Each potential JV partner should be compatible in a number of areas, such as the level of commitment to the JV, the size and structure of the organization, and the underlying national and corporate cultures. Under the best of circumstances, the parties will have had some sort of prior relationship. If concerns about compatibility exist due to lack of information, some other form of business arrangement might be considered as a way to begin building trust.
- FUNCTIONAL SKILLS AND RESOURCES The functional skills and resources of the potential partner should compliment those needed for the JV. For example, if a JV is primarily formed to take advantage of the local partner's ability to access the market rapidly, the distribution skills of the prospective partner should be of greater importance than its ability to assist in developing new products.

- MANAGERIAL RESOURCES The potential partner should have the managerial resources required to provide all necessary assistance to the JV, particularly in the areas where the partner is to have primary functional responsibility. This is often a difficult hurdle for JVs in emerging markets where the pool of qualified managers may not be as deep as in other countries. The foreign partner may want to consider whether to provide training to local managers and whether the JV will be able to retain the trainees after the know-how has been transferred.
- FACILITIES AND SUPPORT A partner may provide facilities and administrative support for part of the JV's activities. This contribution can reduce the overall capital investment associated with the JV. Careful review of the available facilities and support must be made, however, to ensure that they are reliable, efficient, and capable of meeting the needs of the JV.
- GOVERNMENTAL AND REGULATORY ACUMEN In some situations, the skill and experience of a prospective JV partner in dealing with the government can be extremely important. Familiarity with government procedures and policies can be strategic when the venture involves products that are subject to government testing and approval. In a number of foreign countries, the government also exercises actual or *de facto* authority over local distribution, and the local JV partner's experience and expertise could be essential to the JV's success.
- FINANCIAL RESOURCES The potential partner must have sufficient financial resources to support the JV and its functional activities for the JV. Failure to supply adequate capital is a major pitfall in any business.
- REPUTATION A JV is perhaps the most visible form of business relationship. If possible, an effort should be made to find a partner with a solid reputation in the market, as well as in the functional skills and resources that the partner is being asked to provide to the JV. Although a JV is a separate entity and will build its own reputation, the JV parties bring to the table their own respective reputations as the foundation on which the JV will build.

A Few Final Questions

Much study is required before proceeding with even the most preliminary stages of a JV relationship. Managers on both sides of the potential transaction need to systematically review the potential trouble spots and, if possible, map out strategies that can be used in negotiations to minimize possible risks. The final essential step is for key personnel of both parties to consider a few fundamental questions before proceeding to full-scale negotiations:

- Is the potential partner a direct or potential competitor and, if so, in what markets?
- How important does the JV appear to be to the potential partner's own long-term strategic and technical objectives?
- What is the potential partner's track record with respect to other collaborative relationships?
- What measures can reasonably be taken, both from a legal and business perspective, to protect the value of the contributions made to the JV?

CHAPTER 6

Factors Affecting Success or Failure

NUMEROUS STUDIES HAVE BEEN MADE regarding why international JVs get into trouble. Each JV is, of course, unique, and it is therefore difficult to draw sweeping generalizations from these studies. Nevertheless, it is useful to understand some of the more common problems that tend to arise. In each case, the parties need to consider appropriate changes in JV operations and/or the overall business strategy of the JV. Recognition of early warning signs is important because failure to deal with a specific problem may doom later attempts to reach a solution through one of the formal dispute resolution procedures described in Chapter 16.

Poor Pre-Formation Planning

Many problems that might arise during the operation of a JV are in fact created by pre-formation planning that is inadequate and, perhaps, too hasty. For example, a distribution relationship might fail if a product was inappropriate for the target market, or the parties failed to assess correctly the competitive factors in the market. Before you leap into a JV, consider the following:

- Pay careful attention to country and market analysis, due diligence investigation, and entity selection and formation. This is time well spent, even if the timeline for becoming operational must be extended a bit.
- Take assertive steps to guard against communication failures, which may occur due to language, cultural, or geographic constraints.
- Reach a consensus on the fundamental objectives of the JV. Often, discussions during formation and negotiation unduly emphasize methods and procedures, without clarifying or expanding on the overall objective. As a result, the JV is less able to adjust if another method is needed to accomplish its prime objective.

Unexpectedly Poor Financial Performance

Nothing can strain a relationship between two parties more than unexpectedly poor financial performance by the JV, whether in poor sales, cost overruns, or otherwise. Poor financial performance can result from such factors as inadequate preformation planning, failure to approach the market with sufficient management flexibility and efficiency, and unanticipated changes in the country's situation. Although business risks cannot be completely eliminated, factors that might adversely influence the JV's financial performance can be identified and monitored. These factors should be reviewed before finalizing formation of the JV and periodically during its operation so that adjustments can be made if problems are found.

Management Problems

One of the biggest challenges for parties to an international JV is the effective coordination of managers drawn from diverse countries, cultures, and educational backgrounds. Managerial styles reflect the expectations of workers and their tolerance for confrontation, factors that also differ among countries. The fact that many JVs fall apart over misunderstandings about leadership strategies is not surprising. Successful management requires compromise, respect and understanding of the differences, and integration of the strengths of both styles to overcome the weaker points.

EXAMPLE: A number of JVs between US and Japanese partners reached a crisis point when US managers, who prefer strong direction from upper management, clashed with Japanese executives, who prefer to rely on consensus built from within the organization. Adding to the strain was the fact that Japanese management philosophy tends toward a less formal organizational structure. A byproduct of this was that Japanese managers relied more on verbal communications without keeping the extensive written memoranda and informational reports that US executives tended to expect.

INAPPROPRIATE MANAGEMENT STRUCTURE

Contrasts in management style can be magnified if the management structure selected is inappropriate for the JV's activities. Many parties, particularly those with little or no experience with JVs, insist on a shared management system to protect themselves from what they perceive as an attempt by the other party to extract an unfair advantage from the relationship. As a result, daily operational decisions that are best made quickly must instead be approved by a committee, making rapid movement by the JV more difficult, and increasing the possibility that the parties will become embroiled in disputes over matters that are immaterial to the JV's success. For this reason, the parties should consider letting one assume control over daily operations while reserving joint approvals for major issues.

A cumbersome management structure can increase the costs associated with operating the JV, particularly if the partners work in different languages and decisions must be frequently reviewed by home office personnel in disparate locations. Delegation of daily decisions to on-site personnel is therefore not only time and labor efficient, but can save significant costs, as well.

EXAMPLE: Early JVs between United States and Japanese companies struggled under high costs for translating company documents and sending constant communications from the JV in Japan to the US headquarters. Time differences placed significant strains on personnel, particularly in the US, where managers had to be available during business hours for Japan. Many of these problems could have been avoided if the US companies had delegated more authority to on-site personnel in Japan.

Strategy Problems

For many JVs, the problem is not the execution of the JV's business strategy, but rather the strategy itself. During formation, the parties should try to anticipate strategy changes and allow for flexibility within the JV's operations so as to avoid at least some of the following strategy pitfalls:

- **FAILURE TO ANTICIPATE PROBLEMS** A JV's initial strategy may be faulty if the parties did not lay their plans with careful analysis. For example, a distribution JV may fail if the parties did not expect to adapt their product for sale in the local market.
- **FAILURE TO ADAPT TO CHANGING MARKET CONDITIONS** A business strategy should always reflect market conditions, which means that it must be revised periodically as those conditions change. For example, if a distribution JV is paying substantial costs for importing goods produced in another country with higher labor costs, the parties might revise their strategy and decide to expand the activities of the JV to include manufacturing operations as a way of reducing costs.
- **FAILURE TO GRAB NEW OPPORTUNITIES** A business should be encouraged not limited by strategy decisions. Strategy decisions that impose, for example, unreasonable limitations on product lines or targeted customers, tend to work against the JV.
- **FAILURE TO FOLLOW A PARTNER'S ALTERED POSITION** Strategy changes are sometimes a function of revised objectives within one of the JV participants. The other party might resist such changes, and at the least they should be open to negotiation. Consider a situation where one party decides that the JV is no longer merely a manufacturing opportunity, but also has potential for marketing the product in the host country and elsewhere. That party might shift the mix of the personnel that it assigns to the JV to include marketing experts and general managers with experience in operating a multifunctional marketing and manufacturing subunit.

Improper Choice of JV Format

In some cases, the JV format is inappropriate for the particular product or service that is being exploited in the collaboration. As a general rule, a JV works fairly well for a standardized product, such as chemicals, drugs, plastics, and automobiles. On the other hand, construction of a dam or a steel mill does not lend itself to establishment of a separate enterprise, but rather is best accomplished through a network of contractual relationships covering various activities, each of which is coordinated through a single owner-manager.

Inappropriate Performance Milestones

Even if JV participants appear to agree on the fundamental objectives of the relationship, confusion often occurs if assets are transferred to the JV over time, particularly if one party transfers technology or other intangible property. A fairly common phenomenon is that the other JV partner fails to recognize the value of acquiring knowledge and process experience, which can be used in a diverse set of product and market areas. In such cases, performance should not be measured by revenues or market share, but instead by performance milestones that measure how well the local operation has been able to absorb and exploit the relevant know-how and other intangibles. Properly used, these milestones may uncover problems arising from the unwillingness or inability of one party to actually transfer its technology and other intangible rights through the JV.

Personnel Problems

As with any business, personnel problems can significantly harm the viability of a JV, resulting in poor performance and ultimately in high personnel turnover. The range of possible problems is quite broad, and may stem from poor training, low benefits, difficult work conditions, and difficulties with managers. To the extent possible, JV parties should try to anticipate these problems during the formation stage. In particular, they should address these basic personnel concerns:

- *What will the personnel policies be in view of the contrasting management styles of the parties?* Personnel problems may actually be a byproduct of some of the differences in management styles. For example, while Japanese workers may value job security and the intangible comforts of sharing in management decisions, US employees may not be satisfied with those perks if they have to sacrifice performance-based incentives, which are more commonly used in the US.
- *What mechanisms will be used for performance reviews?* Countries tend to use different systems for performance reviews, which may create uncertainty and stress for workers who may not receive the guidance and feedback they expect.
- *How will directors, officers, and managers of the JV be selected?* Nepotism can be a cause for controversy. Substantial conflict can arise if a foreign party imposes professional criteria for selection of executives and key managers of the JV, while the local owners want to give influential posts to their relatives.
- *What will be the timeline for phasing out foreign staff in favor of national management, and what is the compliance period under national laws?* Disagreements can arise when local partners, or the local government, hasten the replacement of foreign staff by nationals more rapidly than the foreign partner feels is warranted by the training and experience of the local employees.

Conflicting Objectives

As a JV grows, the possibility increases that one or both of the parties will begin to have business objectives that conflict with the ongoing operation of the JV. Periodic review of the JV's performance and the business objectives of each of the JV participants should be conducted to ensure that both parties remain committed to the JV. Common scenarios to watch out for include the following:

- One party becomes interested in developing business relationships outside the JV.
- The JV is considering selling its products into markets where one of the JV parties is already active, either on its own or through another agent or distributor.
- One party may develop, and wish to independently exploit, new products that may compete with or replace the products made by the JV.
- One participant may simply lose interest in the project, perhaps because of a revised focus of the company independent of the JV's success or failure.

Divergent Values

Perhaps the most challenging problem for an international JV is that the parties typically have divergent values which impact how they interpret the objectives of the relationship. For example, in JVs between parties from developed countries, there is a certain community not only of tradition but also of scientific, technical, and legal standards, and there is also more experience with responsible business and investment practices and legal supervision. In contrast, these standards typically have not yet been established in the business environment of less developed countries where power and wealth remain concentrated in a small group of companies and individuals, and where workers and consumers are not well protected. On the other hand, companies in the developed world tend to lack appreciation for building an enterprise over a long time to achieve continuous profitability. Instead, they seek to make a quick profit, even if long-term viability of the relationship is compromised.

Perceived Differences in Contributions by Parties

After a JV has been operating for awhile, a foreign party may express discontent with the level of contribution and commitment from the local party. The lack of commitment may be real, as when a local party has realized all the benefits from the initial transfer of technology and is eager to strike out on its own. Alternatively, it might simply be a byproduct of unrealistic initial expectations caused by the foreign party's inability or failure to make a due diligence investigation. In other cases, one partner might accuse the other of a lack of commitment, such as when a foreign party is unwilling to commit senior managers to the JV and is slow to contribute cutting edge technology.

Financial Difficulties for One Party

One JV partner may, for reasons unrelated to the JV activities, experience financial difficulties that impact the projected growth and stability of the JV. For example, if a party has made a long-term commitment to provide additional funding to the JV, and that source of funding become uncertain, the parties would need to consider whether alternative sources might be available. In many cases, financial difficulties of one partner will trigger the other party's right to terminate the JV or to buyout the interest of the distressed party.

Local Business and Regulatory Conditions

In some situations, adverse local business and regulatory conditions may doom the JV relationship. Even if the parties do their best to analyze the local economy and to identify any anticipated trends that might impact sales by the JV and local cost factors, the JV may fall victim to an unforeseen recession based on local factors that are beyond the control of the participants. The risk is exacerbated in developing countries because local policy makers may lack the regulatory tools and experience to manage problems in the economy effectively.

National tax laws and foreign exchange considerations can be regulatory sources of conflict. For example, the foreign party may want the JV to retain surplus and not to remit dividends in order to be free of home country taxes at a given time. However, this goal may directly conflict with the needs of the local partner to take cash out of the JV to fund other activities. Conversely, a foreign party may want to avoid accumulation of profits because of concerns about depreciation of the local currency, while the local party may rightly argue that it doesn't make sense to fund the JV's working capital requirements from bank borrowings that carry a heavy interest burden. In either case, having to deal with a partner significantly reduces the degree of flexibility that a party might otherwise have to exploit profit opportunities from tax and currency situations. It is worth considering, however, that undue focus on tax and foreign exchange strategies may be counterproductive and distract attention from the operation of the core business.

Legal and regulatory changes can also impact the risk-adjusted financial return on investment from the JV. For example, changes in local labor or environmental laws, although impacting all businesses in the country, may significantly alter the cost structure for the JV and erase any pricing advantage that the parties may have anticipated from operating in the particular country. Again, the parties need to analyze carefully the political environment when they are planning the JV.

Political Factors

Political factors always play a substantial role in an international JV, particularly when the parties come from countries with different social, cultural, and economic backgrounds. If the local political situation is unstable, the foreign party can expect substantial scrutiny from regulators. Moreover, if the local partner should fall out of favor with the government, as is likely to happen if new regimes take over on a regular basis, the chances for success for the JV are significantly impaired. It is worth noting, however, that unstable political conditions probably would have threatened the foreign party's investment regardless of the form of its operation, and it remains important for foreign investors to conduct a thorough country analysis before deciding to enter a new market under any strategy.

Local political factors are especially important when one of the parties is the local government, a government agency, or a local company that is controlled by the government. If there are changes in political leadership or public policies regarding foreign investment, the government may begin to push for changes in the original agreement between the parties. These changes could potentially have significant impact on the JV, such as a demand that the JV increase the number of local employees or grant preferences to local suppliers. While this may improve the local economy, it may at the same time adversely impact the overall return on investment for the foreign party. Of course, the government may contemplate more drastic measures, including expropriation.

CHAPTER 7

Confidentiality Agreements

ONCE A POTENTIAL JV PARTNER HAS BEEN SELECTED, the next step is to establish a process for exchanging the technical and business information necessary for the parties to determine if there is actually a basis for a relationship. The exchange of information allows each party to evaluate its prospective partner and to find out their potential compatibility, respective functional strengths and weaknesses, and respective management structures and ideologies, with a view to deciding whether these various factors are or can be made complementary.

No information regarding the proposed JV or the current operations of either of the parties should be exchanged before the parties enter into an appropriate agreement to preserve the confidentiality of sensitive technical or business information and to restrict the disclosure of the information. These confidentiality and nondisclosure agreements can take a variety of forms, ranging from simple one page letters to long and elaborate documents, which themselves require a good deal of negotiation. The effort spent on preparing a confidentiality and nondisclosure agreement will depend on the scope of information to be disclosed and its importance to each of the parties, as well as relevant common and statutory law protections for trade secrets and confidential information.

In all cases, the agreement should be executed before the initial exchange of information between the parties. In most cases, disclosures made during the negotiation of the terms of a potential business relationship will be protected by the agreement, as will information discovered by any party during the pre-contract, due diligence investigation period. If the parties reach agreement on the terms of a formal JV, the JV agreement will either incorporate the terms of the pre-existing confidentiality agreement or will include new provisions covering the information disclosed prior to formation of the JV as well as during its operation.

Sample Contract: Nondisclosure Agreement

This Agreement is made as of [*date*], between [*name of first party*] [*a/an*] [*specify* e.g., individual residing in (*country*) *or* corporation *or other type of entity* organized and existing under the laws of (*state and/or country*)] (hereinafter the "First Party") and [*name of second party*] [*a/an*] [*specify* e.g., individual residing in (*country*) *or* corporation *or other type of entity* organized and existing under the laws of (*state and/ or country*)] (hereinafter the "Second Party"). The First and Second Parties are each referred to herein as a "Party" or the "Parties" whenever a term or condition applies to either or both of them, respectively. A Party that is disclosing "Confidential Information" (as defined subsequently) is referred to herein as a "Disclosing Party", and a Party receiving such Confidential Information is referred to herein as a "Receiving Party."

COMMENT: The parties to the agreement should be clearly identified. If disclosures are to be made by or to a subsidiary or affiliate of one party, the identification should be extended to include that additional entity. It is also important to give an effective date for the agreement, although this may be placed to where the parties sign at the end. Keep in mind that, in a cross-border transaction, this agreement may be signed by the parties on different dates, which could cause some confusion unless a single effective date is clearly chosen.

WHEREAS the Parties have each previously furnished to one another certain Confidential Information (as hereinafter defined) to assist them in determining whether to enter into negotiations with respect to [*specify purpose*, e.g., forming a joint venture for the manufacture of certain products] (the "Business Purpose");

WHEREAS the Parties contemplate furnishing to one another certain additional Confidential Information prior to the consummation of a definitive agreement between them with respect to the Business Purpose; and

WHEREAS each Party wishes to furnish to the other such Confidential Information without conveying any interest or right therein to the other Party and without making any Confidential Information public or common knowledge;

NOW, THEREFORE, in consideration of the mutual covenants and conditions herein contained, and in contemplation of an association between them, the Parties hereto agree as follows:

COMMENT: The recitals provide an indication of the intent of the parties in forming this agreement. In general, the recitals should cover the following matters:

- A description of the parties' purpose for disclosing confidential information.
- Relevant past actions of the parties regarding the subject matter of the contract.
- Relevant future actions contemplated by the parties with regard to the subject matter of the contract.
- The primary intent of the parties with regard to how the disclosure of the information will affect the parties' respective rights in that information.
- The description of the purpose for the disclosures is often referred to as the "Business Purpose." The description sets limits the scope of the disclosures, as well as the permitted uses of the information by the receiving party.

1. DEFINITION OF CONFIDENTIAL INFORMATION. "Confidential Information" shall mean all information, regardless of whether communicated orally, in writing, through personal observation or otherwise, that relates to the Business Purpose specifically, all products and services generally, and all business affairs of the Disclosing Party to the extent that such information is of a proprietary or confidential nature. Such Confidential Information shall include, by way of illustration and not limitation, information concerning the following: (i) research and development activities; (ii) manufacturing and processing techniques and know-how; (iii) software, firmware, and computer programs and elements of design relating thereto (including, for example, programming techniques, algorithms, inference structures, and the construction of knowledge bases); (iv) designs, drawings and formulae; (v) costs, profits, and markets; (vi) financial and other business matters with respect to the Disclosing Party that the Disclosing Party has not made publicly available; (vii) customer business matters, including ordered and sold products of the Disclosing Party, prices, and delivery schedules; and (viii) any matters that a third party has disclosed to the Disclosing Party and that the Disclosing Party has agreed, or is otherwise obligated, to treat as confidential or proprietary.

COMMENT: A basic element of a confidentiality agreement is a provision defining the information, commonly referred to as "Confidential Information" or

"Proprietary Information," to be treated in confidence by the receiving party. The definition should be broad enough to cover information that would otherwise qualify for trade secret protection, plus any other information in which there is a proprietary interest and a legitimate business reason for guarding it against unauthorized use or disclosure. While the information will either be disclosed to the receiving party in writing or communicated orally, the agreement should be drafted so as to include information that the receiving party might learn through observation or examination of the facilities or procedures of the disclosing party.

Several different drafting approaches can be used for this provision. One common method is to describe types of information and the general business areas to which the information pertains, as illustrated here. Other techniques highlight a list of information protected as trade secrets, with a separate list of other proprietary information that might not otherwise qualify as a trade secret. The advantage of such a separation is that the party can retain specific labeling of materials protected by trade secrets, which may be important for showing the exercise of diligent efforts against public disclosure in a lawsuit for misappropriation of a trade secret. The parties may also limit the definition to specific items, provided there is in fact such a limit.

2. EXCLUSIONS. Neither Party, however, shall have any liability to the other Party under this Agreement with respect to the disclosure and/or use of any Confidential Information that it can establish:

a. Has become generally known or available to the public without breach of this Agreement by the Receiving Party;

b. Was known by the Receiving Party before receiving such information from the Disclosing Party;

c. Has become known by or available to Receiving Party from a source other than the Disclosing Party subsequent to disclosure of the information by the Disclosing Party, and without any breach of any obligation of confidentiality owed by the Receiving Party to the Disclosing Party;

d. Has been disclosed to persons regularly employed by the Receiving Party who have previously agreed in writing not to disclose such information or to use such information for any purpose other than to assist it to determine whether to pursue the Business Purpose;

e. Has been independently developed by the Receiving Party without use of or reference to the Confidential Information by persons who had no access to the Confidential Information;

f. Has been provided to the Receiving Party with a written statement that it is provided without restriction on disclosure; or

g. Has been approved for release or use by written authorization of the Disclosing Party.

COMMENT: It is common to provide for a number of exclusions to the receiving party's overriding obligation to maintain the confidentiality of information received during the due diligence investigation and the subsequent term of the JV. However, it is important to note that this clause does not authorize the receiving party to simply run out and start disclosing excluded information to whomever. Rather, the clause limits the receiving party's liability provided the receiving party can prove application of an exclusion. In other words, if the receiving party discloses or uses any of the excluded information, the receiving party must demonstrate to the disclosing party, and possibly to a court of law or other dispute resolution forum, that an exclusion applies.

It is further important to note that these exclusions tend to cover information that, for whatever reason, would no longer meet the legal standard for protection as a trade secret, that is the standard applied by statute or court rulings. In other words, the receiving party will not be liable if this information is found to have already been disclosed in some other way, whether because it is common public knowledge, it has been previously released to the public by the disclosing party, or it has been independently developed or acquired by the receiving party (in which case the receiving party might have claimed it as a trade secret, too). Accordingly, this clause may be modified to account for variations in national laws and court decisions that protect trade secrets.

The burden of proof for exclusions should be placed on the receiving party, but this general term may need to be altered to ensure that this burden is not overwhelming, depending on the application of national laws. For example, the receiving party could be required merely to present documentation to support its entitlement to the exclusion. Alternatively, the receiving party may be placed under an extraordinary burden of proof, which would require that it prove that it is entitled to an exclusion by clear and convincing evidence (beyond doubt), rather than by a preponderance of the evidence (beyond a reasonable doubt).

3. OBLIGATIONS OF RECEIVING PARTY. The Receiving Party acknowledges that irreparable injury and damage will result from disclosure of any Confidential Information to third parties, or utilization of such Information for purposes other than those connected with the Business Purpose. The Receiving Party agrees:

a. To hold the Confidential Information in strict confidence;

b. Not to disclose such Confidential Information to any third party except as specifically authorized herein or as specifically authorized by the Disclosing Party in writing;

c. To use all reasonable precautions, consistent with the Receiving Party's treatment of its own proprietary and confidential information of a similar nature, to prevent the unauthorized disclosure of the Confidential Information, including, without limitation, protection from theft, unauthorized duplication and discovery of contents, and restrictions on access by unauthorized persons;

d. Not to make or use any copies of any of the Confidential Information, or of any synopses, abstracts, summaries, or photographs thereof supplied by the Disclosing Party or compiled by the Receiving Party, except as are necessary for the Receiving Party's internal communications and examinations in connection with the Business Purpose; and

e. Not to use any Confidential Information for any purpose other than the Business Purpose.

COMMENT: The obligations of the receiving party with regard to protection of the confidential information should be described in the agreement. In general, the agreement will provide for an overriding obligation on the receiving party to protect the confidentiality of covered information, and will also restrict the party's ability to make copies of the information or engage in unauthorized uses or disclosures. In some situations, specific obligations should be included as part of the agreement, including language relating to:

- Execution of written confidentiality agreements with third parties to the extent a party to this agreement is authorized by it to make a disclosure;
- Maintenance of a log regarding uses and location of the confidential information;
- Segregation of documents and other tangible embodiments of the confidential information;
- Use of legends and other markings to indicate that the information is to be maintained in confidence; and
- Initiation of legal proceedings to protect the confidentiality of the information.

4. REQUIRED DISCLOSURES. The Receiving Party may disclose the Confidential Information if and to the extent that such disclosure is required by applicable law, provided that the Receiving Party uses reasonable efforts to limit the disclosure by means of a protective order or a request for confidential treatment and offers the Disclosing Party a reasonable opportunity to review the disclosure before it is made and to interpose its own objection to the disclosure.

COMMENT: The receiving party may be compelled by law to disclose the information to a court or regulatory body. Such disclosures should not be treated as exceptions to the definition of confidential information, because the information should still be considered confidential for other purposes.

The disclosing party should have an opportunity to participate in the steps taken to limit disclosure of its trade secrets. For example, the agreement should put the receiving party under an obligation to give notice to the disclosing party of any subpoenas or other requests for production of records and documents that may relate to the trade secrets, including any information submissions or filings required by government agencies. Notification gives the disclosing party the opportunity to make a motion for a protective order, which might be granted on a showing that the owner's interest in secrecy outweighs the need for disclosure in the particular dispute for which a subpoena is sought.

5. RETURN OF CONFIDENTIAL INFORMATION. At the request of the Disclosing Party, the Receiving Party shall return all written material, photographs, and all other documentation made available or supplied by the Disclosing Party to the Receiving Party, all copies and reproductions thereof, and all notes, abstracts, reports, commentaries, or other materials prepared by the Receiving Party with respect to such documentation, copies, and reproductions.

COMMENT: The agreement should always provide that, at termination of the relationship or on any earlier demand by the disclosing party, the receiving party must return or destroy of all documents and other tangible items (e.g., notes, abstracts, tapes, etc.) containing the trade secrets or confidential information. Return of the documents is part of the disclosing party's larger program of diligently protecting the information by ensuring that the unnecessary circulation of the information is minimized.

6. RETENTION OF LEGAL RIGHTS. The Disclosing Party retains all rights and remedies afforded to it under the patent, trademark, and other laws of all applicable jurisdictions,

including without limitation any laws designed to protect proprietary or confidential information.

COMMENT: Athough a written confidentiality agreement can serve to bolster protection that would otherwise be available to the owner of the information under intellectual property or other laws, it is also important that the agreement indicate that is not intended to limit the available protections. For example, information exchanged under the agreement may continue to be protected under trade secret, copyright, trademark, and patent laws after expiration of the agreement, and the agreement should make it clear that none of those rights are intended to be limited by, or abandoned on expiration of, the agreement.

7. INJUNCTIVE RELIEF. Each Party acknowledges that the unauthorized use or disclosure of the Confidential Information of the other Party would cause irreparable harm to the other Party. Accordingly, each Party agrees that the other Party will have the right to obtain an immediate injunction against any breach or threatened breach of this Agreement, as well as the right to pursue any and all other rights and remedies available at law or in equity for such a breach.

COMMENT: Each party should specifically acknowledge that breach of the agreement will lead to irreparable harm to the disclosing party, and that the disclosing party will have to obtain immediate injunctive relief. Even though irreparable harm will often be presumed in trade secret cases, the acknowledgments of the receiving party can be important in any subsequent litigation, although they are not binding on a court. This clause may need to be modified to accommodate variations in remedies afforded by national laws.

8. TERM OF AGREEMENT. This Agreement applies to all Confidential Information that is disclosed by either Party to the other Party during the period that begins on the date set forth at the front of this Agreement and ends [*number*, e.g., six] months thereafter. The obligations of this Agreement will remain in effect for [*number*, e.g., five] years after the date of the last disclosure of Confidential Information hereunder, at which time this Agreement will terminate.

COMMENT: The agreement should define the time during which any disclosures made by the disclosing party will be covered by the protective obligations in the agreement, as well as the duration of the obligations themselves. The periods selected will usually depend on the difficulties that the disclosing party expects to have in monitoring the confidentiality agreement. A party making substantial disclosures will generally attempt to have the obligations continue for the useful life of its trade secrets. However, the receiving party will want the obligations to extend for some determinate period of time (e.g., two years after execution of the agreement or two years following termination of the JV). If appropriate, different time periods may be set for different classes of information.

9. ENTIRE AGREEMENT. This Agreement sets forth the entire agreement and understanding of the Parties and merges all prior discussions between them as to Confidential Information. Neither Party may be bound by any definition, condition, representation, or waiver other than as expressly stated in this Agreement or as subsequently set forth in writing signed by the Parties hereto. This Agreement shall survive the termination of any business relationship between the Parties and shall supplement any subsequent agreement between the Parties with respect to the subject

matter hereof to the extent that the terms contained herein are not inconsistent with any such subsequent agreement.

COMMENT: The agreement should include a merger clause that makes it clear that the agreement between the parties regarding protection of the confidential information is to be confined to the terms in the agreement. Amendments to the agreement must be set forth in writing and agreed to by both parties.

10. GOVERNING LAW. This Agreement shall be governed by the laws of as applied to contracts entered into and to be performed entirely within [*location*].

COMMENT: The agreement should identify the law that is intended to govern the nondisclosure obligations. The choice is important because the laws of countries (and states or other subdivisions) often vary with respect to the definition of trade secrets and the scope of protection afforded to other proprietary information.

11. SUCCESSORS AND ASSIGNS. This Agreement shall be binding on and inure to the benefit of the Parties hereto and their respective heirs, administrators, executors, successors, and assigns.

COMMENT: The agreement should clearly declare that its provisions will continue to apply to any successor or assigns of the parties, such as a business entity that acquires a party following the beginning of the underlying business relationship.

IN WITNESS WHEREOF, the Parties execute this Agreement in recognition and understanding of the obligations and conditions imposed.

FIRST PARTY

Date: [*date*]

By [*signature*]

[*typed name and title*]

SECOND PARTY

Date: [*date*]

By [*signature*]

[*typed name and title*]

CHAPTER 8

Selecting a Legal Entity for the JV

ALTHOUGH THE SUCCESS OF ANY JV generally turns on the compatibility of the persons and resources involved in the particular project, attention must be paid to the form of the legal entity selected to conduct the relationship. The characteristics of the organizational forms available for operating a JV are a function of relevant company law, sometimes referred to as "enterprise law" or the "law of business organizations." Company laws not only define the legal entities or enterprises that can be used to conduct commercial activities, but also establish the rights and obligations of each enterprise, its governance process, and the rights and duties of its managers and owners. Also, company laws set out the specific rules for forming, operating, and terminating business enterprises.

The law of business enterprises in a particular jurisdiction is heavily influenced by the particular legal traditions that prevail there. Investors will find certain similarities in business enterprise law among countries sharing the common law heritage, such as the United States, England, Australia, and English-speaking Africa. However, notable divergencies exist even among these countries, such as the fact that company laws in many English-speaking African countries are based on historic, rather than current, English law. Other countries, particularly in Europe, base their legal systems on civil law traditions that include concepts, principles, rules and procedures that vary substantially from common law countries. In spite of these basic differences, both common and civil law jurisdictions typically offer a choice between partnership-type entities, which impose unlimited liability on some or all participants, and corporate-type entities, which offer limited liability to the participants in exchange for more elaborate statutory regulation of the business operation.

Which Entity: Compare the Major Distinguishing Factors

The process of selecting the proper form of business entity generally requires a comparison of the entities in relation to a variety of distinguishing factors. Among the factors that you should consider are the following:

- FORMATION FORMALITIES The formalities and procedures involved in forming and organizing the business entity.
- FINANCING FACILITY The manner in which the business entity facilitates the fulfillment of the financing and credit requirements of the underlying business, either through the issuance of ownership interests, or by credit arrangements based on the assets of the business and its owners.
- MANAGEMENT AND CONTROL The rights of the owners to participate in managing and controlling the activities of the enterprise, as well as the ability of the owners to enter into contracts and other arrangements with outside parties.

Strategies for Selecting the Business Form

While there is no established strategy or process for selecting the proper business form, it may be useful to consider the following questions in the order presented here:

1. ARE THERE ANY NON-TAX FACTORS THAT WOULD REQUIRE UTILIZING THE CORPORATE FORM?

For example, the need or desire for limited liability may dictate the use of a corporation, as may the restrictions imposed by law on the use of partnerships or other non-corporate forms to conduct certain business activities. Also, it is generally easier to attract outside investment capital and bank credit to a business organized in the corporate form.

2. WILL THE BUSINESS GENERATE LOSSES DURING THE EARLY YEARS OF OPERATION?

If so, the parties may want to elect to use an entity that allows for losses to pass through to the owners to offset income from other activities. On the other hand, if this is not important, the parties may use a corporate form and allow losses to accumulate to offset anticipated income in later years. Projections for income and loss should be prepared to evaluate possible scenarios.

3. WHAT ARE THE EXPECTATIONS OF THE PARTIES REGARDING PARTICIPATION IN MANAGEMENT?

Parties who must be actively involved in managing the business must be general partners, members of a limited liability company, or shareholders. The choice depends on the need for limitations on liability from the entity itself, rather than from insurance. The degree of involvement in the business may also impact the deductibility of losses for partners under "passive activity" tax rules.

4. ARE THERE ANY SPECIAL TAX PLANNING CONSIDERATIONS THAT MUST BE TAKEN INTO ACCOUNT?

For example, if the parties want to allocate the tax benefits associated with a particular asset or activity to one of the partners in a manner that is disproportionate to the relative capital contributions, they may need to select an entity (i.e., a partnership-type entity) that permits special allocations.

5. ARE THERE ANY SPECIAL NON-TAX CONSIDERATIONS THAT MUST BE CONSIDERED WHEN NO CLEAR CHOICE HAS EMERGED FROM THE BALANCE OF THE REFERENCED FACTORS?

If the preferred entity from a non-tax perspective is different than the choice for tax purposes, reference must often be made to some of the minor non-tax factors, such as administrative convenience and complexity, and the specific requirements of local regulators.

- PROFIT AND LOSS ALLOCATION The allocation of profits and losses from the activities of the business among the owners.
- PERSONAL LIABILITY The extent to which the owners will be directly liable for the debts and obligations of the business.
- RESTRICTIONS ON TRANSFERS The ability of the owners to transfer their ownership interests in the enterprise without causing a disruption or termination of the business.
- CONTINUED EXISTENCE The effect of the withdrawal of one of the business owners on the continued existence of the business.
- TAX TREATMENT The tax consequences associated with forming, operating, making distributions from and terminating the business entity, as well as the tax consequences of transferring an ownership interest in the business.

Partnerships

Partnerships are probably among the oldest forms of cooperative relationship, and have long been recognized in the common and civil laws of many jurisdictions. The most basic definition of a partnership is an association of two or more persons to carry on as co-owners of a business for profit. Distinctions can be drawn between general partnerships, with unlimited liability for each of the participants, and limited partnerships, with limited liability for at least some of the participants.

Although national requirements differ, in most countries the formation of a general partnership does not require the completion of any statutory formalities. It simply requires the agreement of the parties, which can be inferred from their conduct as well as from any oral or written contract. In contrast, limited partnerships are a creation of statute and only come into existence after compliance with strict statutory formalities including, in most jurisdictions, execution and filing of specified charter documents with the appropriate government authorities. Partnerships are almost never utilized as vehicles for JVs in manufacturing enterprises, but certain types of partnerships are often employed in extractive enterprises—primarily for tax considerations.

GENERAL PARTNERSHIPS

A general partnership consists of two or more partners, referred to as general partners, each of whom is usually active in the conduct of the business. For most activities, each general partner has the authority to manage and control the business of the partnership and to bind the partnership in relationships with third parties with respect to matters that fall within the apparent scope and authority of the partner. While this mutual agency relationship among the general partners can be limited in the partnership agreement, such agreements do not, as a rule, affect the rights of third parties against the partnership and its partners. General partners are subject to potentially unlimited personal liability for the debts and obligations of the general partnership, and stand in a fiduciary relationship to one another. Because of the fiduciary relationships and mutual agency powers associated with this form of entity, general partnerships usually place strict restrictions on the transfer of interests and admission of new partners, and the dissociation of a partner typically dissolves the partnership.

Which Entity: Compare the Major Distinguishing Factors

The process of selecting the proper form of business entity generally requires a comparison of the entities in relation to a variety of distinguishing factors. Among the factors that you should consider are the following:

FORMATION FORMALITIES

The formalities and procedures involved in forming and organizing the business entity.

FINANCING FACILITY

The manner in which the business entity facilitates the fulfillment of the financing and credit requirements of the underlying business, either through the issuance of ownership interests or by credit arrangements based on the assets of the business and its owners.

MANAGEMENT AND CONTROL

The rights of the owners to participate in managing and controlling the activities of the enterprise, as well as the ability of the owners to enter into contracts and other arrangements with outside parties.

PROFIT AND LOSS ALLOCATION

The allocation of profits and losses from the activities of the business among the owners.

PERSONAL LIABILITY

The extent to which the owners will be directly liable for the debts and obligations of the business.

RESTRICTIONS ON TRANSFERS

The ability of the owners to transfer their ownership interests in the enterprise without causing a disruption or termination of the business.

CONTINUED EXISTENCE

The effect of the withdrawal of the business owner on the continued existence of the business.

TAX TREATMENT

The tax consequences associated with forming, operating, making distributions from and terminating the business entity, as well as the tax consequences of transferring an ownership interest in the business.

LIMITED PARTNERSHIPS

A limited partnership has one or more general partners and one or more non-general partners, referred to as limited partners. A general partner of a limited partnership has the same rights of control and exposure to liabilities as do general partners in a general partnership. On the other hand, limited partners are passive (inactive) investors who contribute cash and other assets to the partnership for the general partners to use in operating the business. Limited partners have few rights to exercise any control over daily business of the partnership, although they may have some right to be heard on major policy decisions. In turn, the liability of the limited partners for debts and obligations of the partnership is restricted to their investment in the business. The interest of a limited partner is, subject to any contrary agreement, freely transferable, and the death or withdrawal of any limited partner generally has no effect on the operation of the business.

PARTNERSHIP AGREEMENTS

While the relationship among partners will be governed by statute and case law in many countries, partners are usually permitted to vary the partnership relationship by express agreement, and it is generally advisable to define the rights and duties of the partners between themselves, as distinguished from their relationship with third parties, in a written instrument known as "articles of partnership" or "partnership agreement." Unlike corporate-type entities, which are often subject to laws granting stockholders certain fixed rights including voting rights and preemptive rights to purchase stock, partnerships have greater flexibility. Through the use of written agreements, which are essentially private contracts, partnerships can be structured in almost any way agreed to by the partners with only a minimal amount of interference by law.

In the JV context, the partnership agreement should cover all the essential matters for the operation of the JV, including its name, purpose, and location; its duration; the contributions of each partner, such as real and personal property, cash, and services; the sharing of profits and losses among the partners; management and voting powers; procedures for settling disputes as an alternative to dissolution; transfer restrictions; accounting and banking arrangements; and the authority of the partners with respect to matters such as signing checks, making loans, recruiting and discharging employees, and fixing their salaries.

EXAMPLES OF PARTNERSHIP ENTITIES

The national law of a country will determine the availability, scope, limitations, and regulatory treatment of partnership entities. Examples of partnership-type entities around the world include the following:

- UNITED STATES Each of the states in the United States have their own rules regarding partnership-type entities; however, many of the state laws are based on model rules developed by academics and practitioners. In the general partnership area, reference is made to the Uniform Partnership Act or Revised Uniform Partnership Act, which are comprehensive codifications of prior statutory and common law with respect to the organization, operation, and dissolution of general partnerships, and provide default rules for the operation and management of a partnership in the absence of a contract among the partners. Limited partnerships in the United States are creations of statute and not a part of the common law. Each state also has its own statutes, but as a general rule, the state limited partnership statues are based on some version of the Revised Uniform Limited Partnership Act, and therefore the basic requirements and conditions tend to be similar across the nation.

- GERMANY Under German law, *Kommanditgesellschaft* and *Offene Handelsgesellschaft* are the limited and general partnership entities, respectively. There is also the *Stillegesellschaft*, or so-called "silent partnership," which is more like a creditor-debtor relationship than a partnership. In the case of the *Kommanditgesellschaft auf Aktien*, which is a special form of limited partnership, the capital of the partnership is divided into transferable shares.
- NETHERLANDS. In the Netherlands, a *Vennootschap Onder Firma* (VOF) is a general partnership, and a *Commanditaire Vennootschap* (CV) is a limited partnership. The VOF is the ordinary form of commercial partnership, with all partners being jointly and severally liable for the debts of the partnership. A VOF is not considered to be a separate legal entity. Limited partners in a CV are only liable for amounts up to their capital contributions.
- MEXICO The *Sociedad en Nombre Colectivo* (SNC) is a separate legal entity in which each partner is jointly and severally liable for all entity obligations. The *Sociedad en Comandita Simple* (SCS) and *Sociedad en Comandita por Acciones* (SCA) are limited liability partnerships that differ in the way the partners' interests are represented. The equity interests in the SCA are reflected in shares that in the hands of the limited partners are freely transferable, but the transfer of a general partner's shares requires an affirmative vote of the limited partners.
- FRANCE A *Societe en Nom Collectif* (SNC) is similar to a common law general partnership, but the partners, of which there must be at least two, can be limited liability companies. The *Societe en Commandite Simple* (SCS) and the *Societe en Commandite par Actions* (SCA) are similar to the Mexican limited liability partnerships, with the SCA being essentially a limited partnership with shares.
- JAPAN The *Gomel Kaisha* is similar to a general partnership in that it has joint and several liability for its members and limitations on transferability, but it is considered to be a separate legal entity for all purposes and is subject to corporate income taxation. The *Goshi Kaisha*, the limited commercial partnership company, is similar to the *Gomei Kaisha* except that there are limited partners as well as partners subject to unlimited liability. A *Kumiai* is a "Civil Code Association," which is considered to be a separate commercial entity that can carry on business even though it is not recognized as a company under the Japanese Commercial Code. A *Kumiai* is essentially a contractual relationship amongst the members with respect to a common undertaking, and may be administered by one or more managers or through a majority vote of its members. A *Kumiai* is a pass-through entity under the Japanese tax laws, meaning it is not considered an entity apart from its members.

Corporations and Public Companies

The business form most often selected for a productive enterprise organized as a JV is one of the corporate types, whether a civil law corporation, English public company, or American general business corporation. Examples of such entities include the following: (a) *Aktiengesellschaft* or A.G. (Germany), literally a "stock company;" (b) *Societe Anonyme* (France, Switzerland, Belgium), *Societa Anonima* (Italy) or *Sociedad Anonima* (Spain, Mexico, Latin America) or S.A., literally "anonymous company;" (c) *Naamlooze Vennootschaap* or N.V. (Netherlands, Netherlands Antilles), literally "anonymous (nameless) company;" (d) *Kabushiki Kaisha* or K.K. (Japan) a public company; and (e) British PLC, an entity traded publicly, typically on the London Stock Exchange. Many of these entities are referred to as "public companies" in civil law countries, but the share interests are not necessarily publicly traded. Rather, the term "public" refers to the fact that these entities are required by law to publish annual accounts and retain public auditors.

The flexibility of the corporation or public company and its adaptability to effective centralized management, notwithstanding dispersed ownership, usually make it the most advantageous form of organization for large-scale JVs. From a practical view, these types of entities enjoy greater prestige in the public eye than other business forms. When the equity participation of the local interests is to be widely held by the public, the corporation or public company will be the only practical alternative because it is usually the only company form in which the shares are readily transferable.

ATTRIBUTES

A corporation is an artificial body, invisible, intangible, and existing only in contemplation of law. Like a limited partnership, a corporation is a creature of statute, with an identity or personality separate and distinct from that of its owners. It must, by necessity, act through its agents. The essential attributes of a corporation are as follows: the capacity of perpetual succession; the power to sue or be sued in the corporate name; the power to acquire or transfer property and do other acts in the corporate name; the power to purchase and hold real estate; the authority to have a common seal; the power to make bylaws for internal government; and the power to act generally in its own name.

Formation, organization, operation, and dissolution of corporations is governed by statutory provisions contained in the companies law of the jurisdiction—that is, state or country—where the corporation is incorporated, although a number of state and national constitutions also contain provisions that apply to business associations, including corporations. The specific corporation laws of each jurisdiction differ widely with respect to a variety of matters, including the election, removal, and composition of the board of directors; voting rights of shareholders; capitalization and the issuance of new shares; distributions to shareholders; indemnification; mergers and sales of assets; and dissolution and liquidation. However, in most cases, the law of corporations will be more specific than comparable statutes that apply to the partnership forms of organization, and it will be often supported by well-developed case law. In addition, participants in an enterprise conducted in the corporate form must adhere to the rules and provisions that are contained in the articles of incorporation and bylaws of the corporation, resolutions approved by the shareholders and board of directors of the corporation, shareholder agreements, loan agreements, indentures, employment agreements, voting trusts and agreements, proxies, and share certificate legends.

Although a JV may be equally owned and jointly managed by the parties, it is not uncommon for negotiations to create a minority interest (e.g., one party owns less than 50 percent of the economic and voting interests in the JV). If so, the minority owner should take note that corporate law has probably done a better job than any other form of business entity in spelling out minority rights with respect to management and control, preemptive rights, and general fiduciary obligations of majority owners. However, because corporate law in this area is so fully developed, the minority owner may have difficulty implementing protective provisions (e.g., cumulative voting) that are not part of the local regime, even if they are widely-accepted outside the jurisdiction. If, in fact, there are too many problems in implementing innovative provisions, the minority owner may need to balance some of the advantages of the corporation form (i.e., limited liability, innovative capitalization, and transferability of interests) against the flexibility offered by one of the partnership-type entities.

CORPORATE FINANCE

Shares or stock are the units into which the proprietary interests of the corporation are divided. As a general rule, the holders of shares may participate in corporate management through voting rights, in corporate surplus profits through declared dividends, and in the assets of the corporation distributed on dissolution and after the payment of corporate debts. In most cases, a corporation can issue various types of stock to allocate control or vary the nature of the various shareholders' potential risks and return on investment. Corporate securities can take a number of forms, including common and preferred stock, options, warrants, convertible securities and debt securities, which are often subordinated to the rights of outside creditors and may themselves be convertible into one or more different forms of equity securities of the corporation.

The most frequently used classes of stock are "common" and "preferred." Common stock ordinarily allows the holder to share in any growth in the value of the business, and generally includes full voting rights. Preferred stock ordinarily represents a more predictable return on investment, generally as periodic dividends and a fixed redemption date and price. Preferred stock usually carries limited or no voting rights. In addition, a corporation can obtain credit by issuing debt securities, which further enhances the flexibility of its capital structure.

Corporate profits are retained at the entity level until distributed in the form of dividends to the shareholders. As a general rule, dividends will be payable to the shareholders in proportion to their share ownership. However, various classes of shares may be created with dividend preferences and other rights with respect to distributions. Profits may also be used to fund the redemption of outstanding capital stock of the corporation.

CORPORATE MANAGEMENT

The laws of the jurisdiction where the corporation is organized generally provide detailed rules relating to management of the entity. Legal responsibility for the management of the corporation is typically vested in the board of directors, who are elected by the owners (shareholders) of the corporation. In turn, the board of directors usually delegates responsibility for the day-to-day operation of the business of the corporation to its various officers and agents. The officers commonly include a president, treasurer, and secretary, and may also include a vice-president and other officers. The directors are limited in number and have the job of making policy decisions and long-range plans for the corporation. Thus, even though there may be a large number of shareholders, the management of the corporation is centralized in a limited number of officers and directors.

The management structure for the corporation varies depending on the jurisdiction. For example, many laws permit a two-tiered management system with a board of directors being the body responsible for daily operations, and another supervisory board exercising powers to elect and remove the management board, to approve financial accounts, and to determine the overall direction of corporate activity. In general, shareholders are free, within the broad parameters of the relevant corporate statutes, to enter into various contractual agreements relating to management of the business, voting rights, transferability of shares, compensation, and other matters relating to the operation of the business.

Certain aspects of a country's corporate law may be focused on the accomplishment of specific social and economic objectives. For example, workers may have special rights to participate in corporate management, either through required election to the board of directors or in some advisory capacity. Some countries impose qualifications for service as directors and officers, including requirements that only nationals can be managers or hold board positions, or a portion of the seats on the board. In many cases, these requirements are not inconsistent with the joint decision-making anticipated by the parties at the outset of the JV. However, they can make future changes more difficult for a foreign party that is looking to assume more control over the operation of the business.

THE PROCESS OF INCORPORATION

Incorporation generally requires the preparation and submission of documents that include statutorially required information (e.g., corporate purpose, names of initial shareholders or incorporators, amount of authorized capital, etc.). These are known by a variety of names, including "Articles of Incorporation," "Corporate Charter," "Memorandum of Association," or "Statute." In some jurisdictions, the required information is fairly basic; in others, it may be extensive and even include background data on the promoters of the corporation and initial shareholders. Some jurisdictions require incorporations to follow model articles or bylaws, and problems may arise with governmental agencies when the JV partners wish to deviate significantly from the models. In addition to filing appropriate documents, the incorporators may be required to make some form of publicity, such as a legal announcement in a newspaper.

TAXATION OF CORPORATIONS

As a general rule, corporations are treated as a separate taxable entities. Accordingly, income, deductions, capital gains, depreciation and credits arising from the business of the corporation are accounted for at the corporate level and the corporation bears the burden of taxes owed and retains the benefit of any losses that may be offset against income generated in subsequent periods. If the corporation distributes net earnings after taxes to its shareholders in the form of dividends, the amount of such distributions must be included in that shareholders' individual taxable income. Accordingly, distributions from a corporation are said to be subject to "double taxation."

Limited Liability Companies

For a JV of modest size in which the equity participations are to be closely held, the limited liability company (e.g., *societe a responsabilite limitee, sociedad de responsabilidad limitada,* or *Gesellschaft mit beschrankte Haftung*) is often the preferred vehicle in jurisdictions where it is available. This type of company combines certain features of the corporation with features more characteristic of the partnership. Like the corporation, the limited liability company affords limited liability and continuity of existence. Unlike the corporation, whose capital is divided into readily transferable shares, the limited liability company's capital is divided into members' quotas, which usually can be transferred to a non-member only with the consent of a fixed percentage of the other members, or after the other members have declined to exercise a first option to purchase. The limited liability company is usually subject to less regulation and fewer filing requirements than a corporation, and may also bear a lower tax burden. In the United States, owners of a limited liability company can effectively choose whether the entity and its activities will be taxed as a partnership or as a corporation.

FORMATION AND MANAGEMENT

Formation procedures for a limited liability company will obviously vary depending on where the entity is organized. Most jurisdictions tend to require limited liability companies to file documents similar in form to those required of corporations (e.g., articles of organization). Limited liability statutes usually provide default rules for operation and management, but the parties will typically adopt an operating agreement or regulations to govern their relationship. The owners of a limited liability company, referred to as "members" in the United States, can usually choose to reserve all management powers to themselves, as in a partnership, or to delegate management powers to appointed managers and decentralize management, as in a corporate form. Regardless of the management structure, as a general matter, neither the owners or managers are personally liable for business debts or liabilities that arise from management activities.

In some jurisdictions, a serious disadvantage to a limited liability company as opposed to a corporate entity is the relative lack of flexibility in the capital structure. Some limited liability company statutes restrict the ability of the owners to create separate classes of ownership interests with different voting and economic rights, and some civil law systems prohibit limited liability companies from selling bonds and debentures to finance operations.

EXAMPLES OF LIMITED LIABILITY COMPANIES

A number of countries recognize some form of legal entity that permits the owners to enjoy limited liability. Among these private limited liability or stock companies are the following:

- UNITED STATES A limited liability company is a relatively recent creation of statute in the United States. It offers the benefits of pass-through taxation, as in a partnership, and limited liability for each of the owners associated with the corporate form. Today, limited liability company acts have been adopted in every state; however, work continues on a unifying prototype limited liability company statute. As is the case with limited partnerships and corporations, formation of a limited liability company requires filing of articles of organization with the appropriate government office in the state of organization.

- GERMANY The formation of a German *Gesellschaft mit beschrankte Haftung* (GmbH.) permits the equity holders to limit their liability to the amount of their capital contributions. Equity interests are not represented by stock certificates or other security instruments and may be transferred by notarial deed. Interests may be freely transferred or made subject to transfer restrictions. The law requires the entity to have a managing director, but provision can be made to authorize the director to act only pursuant to instructions given by the equity holders.
- FRANCE, SWITZERLAND, BELGIUM A *Societe à Responsabilité Limitee* (SARL) can have up to a maximum of 50 shareholders and as few as one. While the laws relating to the formation and operation of a SARL are typically less flexible than those that relate to the GmbH, a SARL does offer many of the same sorts of advantages as the German entity.
- MEXICO, LATIN AMERICA, SPAIN The *Sociedad de Responsibilidad Limitada* (S. de R.L.) has characteristics of both a partnership and a corporation. There must be at least two members, and the liability of each member is limited to the amount contributed to the S. de R.L. Equity interests are not negotiable and may not be transferred without the approval of the other members. An S. de R.L. may be managed by one or more managers chosen by the members, or by all of the members in the capacity of managers.
- NETHERLANDS The *Besloten Vennootschaap met beperkte Aansprakeljkheid* (B.V.) is the most common form of entity in the Netherlands and can be compared with the GmbH, the SARL, or the S. de R.L.
- JAPAN *Yugen Kaisha* (Y.K.) are authorized under the Limited Company Law of Japan, which incorporates many of the provisions of the Commercial Code applicable to the Japanese public company, the K.K. The Y.K. has limited liability for investors, centralized management, and perpetual life, although it is possible to limit the life of the entity in its articles. The shares of the Y.K. are freely transferable among members; however, transfer to a non-member must be approved by a majority vote of a quorum of members holding at least one-half of all voting rights.
- UNITED KINGDOM A Limited Company (Ltd.) is a company with limited liability, but it is not a pass-through entity for purposes of local tax laws.

Choice of Entity Factors

Entity selection is part art and part science. No selection procedures are absolute, and it is difficult to generalize a system of selection. Rather, it makes sense to sit down with legal, tax, and accounting advisors who are familiar with the laws of both the host country and the other partner's home domicile, to compare the various forms and to develop scenarios that might be anticipated from selecting one form of entity versus another for operation of the JV. The selection process should take into account the impact of the following issues:

1. How is the business going to be capitalized and financed? What, if any, tax considerations will arise in the course of developing the capital structure of the JV?

2. How are the partners going to be compensated for their activities in connection with the JV? What, if any, tax considerations arise in the course of developing the compensation structure of the JV?
3. What additional tax factors might affect the formation and operation of the JV, including elements of taxable income, and the expense and ease of converting to another form of business organization?
4. On what terms, if any, may interests in the enterprise be transferred between the partners, or to third parties?
5. How will the day-to-day operations of the JV be managed? What relationship will exist between operational control of the JV and the ownership of equity interests in the JV?
6. How will risks and liabilities be allocated among the partners with respect to the operations of the JV?
7. What fiduciary or contractual obligations will exist among the partners as to the operation of the JV?
8. What is the understanding of the partners with regard to the duration of the JV, the effect of the withdrawal of one or more of the participants, and the dissolution or termination of the JV?
9. What costs and formalities are associated with formation and maintenance of the particular form of business organization, including any regulatory, reporting, or record-keeping requirements?
10. What, if any, legal requirements exist with respect to the form in which the business must be conducted?
11. What, if any, legal requirements exist regarding the type of business that the JV might conduct?
12. What provisions are to be made for resolution of disputes and deadlocks relating to control and management of the JV?
13. What additional legal issues need to be addressed in connection with the formation of the enterprise, including issues with respect to securities law, labor law, trade secrets and intellectual property, real estate law, and compliance with various licensing and regulatory requirements?

CHAPTER 9

Negotiating the Joint Venture Terms

AFTER THE PARTICIPANTS HAVE IDENTIFIED all relevant legal and business considerations regarding the possibility and desirability of a JV arrangement, they must focus on the formation of the venture and negotiation of the key economic and legal terms of the relationship. There is no standard negotiation method. In some cases, the parties may exchange informal written proposals before final face-to-face meetings are conducted. In other situations, the parties may gather together to work out the terms in one lengthy session. Although the parties can actually draft all of the substantive documents relating to the JV during the negotiation process, it is more likely that the negotiators will limit their discussions to the important terms and concepts and leave the detailed drafting to the respective counsel of the parties.

Key Terms of the Joint Venture

Negotiations should start with establishing the primary concepts and features of the JV arrangement, leaving specifics for a later stage, because the details tend to be numerous and even overwhelming. Parties who have come to the point of negotiating a deal should have sufficient trust in each other to concentrate on the essential, major points of their JV arrangement on the assumption that the details will be worked out and won't be breaking points. For the parties to proceed with a JV, they need to reach agreement on each of the following key terms and issues:

- OBJECTIVES AND ACTIVITIES The first issues for discussion are the business and financial objectives of the JV and the activities that need to be conducted to achieve the objectives. For example, the objective of the JV might be to market and distribute a particular product in the local party's home country. If so, the JV activities will certainly include distribution, and may also require the manufacture of a sufficient volume of products to meet the needs of the market.
- CONTRIBUTIONS Each party will be expected to make certain contributions to the JV. One or both parties may provide cash to fund JV operations. In addition, the parties will likely deliver other tangible and intangible assets, including equipment, raw materials, labor, intellectual property rights, and technology.
- MANAGEMENT AND CONTROL As with any other new business, consideration needs to be given to the day-to-day management of the JV, and the procedures to be followed in connection with major decisions regarding the business and strategy of the JV. Initial directors and officers of the JV should be identified. Dispute resolution mechanisms should also be established before the JV is formed and organized.

- ALLOCATION OF PROFITS AND DISTRIBUTIONS The parties need to reach agreement on the allocation of profits and losses from JV operations, and the timing for distributions of profits and capital by the JV. The respective interests of the parties in the profits and losses may be tied to the value of their initial contributions, or the parties may agree on special allocations. The interests of the parties in profits and losses need not be the same as their voting interests.
- TERM AND TERMINATION The term, or duration, of the JV should be determined along with any events that might trigger a premature termination of the relationship. Early termination may require liquidation and dissolution of the entity, or the purchase of the ownership interest of one of the partners. Procedures for transfers of ownership interests should be carefully considered, as should the possibility of allowing one of the partners to force the other either to purchase the first partner's interest or to sell its interest to the first partner.

Other issues, such as responsibility for operational activities of the JV (e.g., administration, research, manufacturing, distribution, and sales), should be addressed as the parties develop the JV's business plan. As suggested in Chapter 10, the parties should make every effort to complete the business plan before moving forward with the formalities of launching the JV.

Letter of Intent or Memorandum of Understanding

The results of the negotiations are usually memorialized in a written document, typically referred to as a "letter of intent" or "memorandum of understanding." There is no legal or other requirement to prepare such a letter or memorandum, and it is common practice to make expressly clear in the document itself that the letter or memorandum is not intended to be binding. However, it serves to memorialize the fundamental understandings and intentions of the parties. It also can be used to obtain any necessary legal or regulatory authority necessary for further negotiation of the JV, and it clearly is the first step toward a definitive set of JV agreements and documents. Finally, such a document is generally taken as an assurance that both of the parties are serious and, in fact, the letter or memorandum will often include a covenant that neither party will attempt to locate an alternative JV partner for some period of time while they attempt to complete their own negotiations.

No standard form is followed when drafting the letter of intent or memorandum of understanding, but it should be detailed enough to provide a skeleton of the proposed JV. In some cases, the letter or memorandum is extremely detailed, and it may be as strenuously negotiated as the actual JV documents. In such instances, subsequent efforts to finalize the documents may be reduced, but the parties should be mindful that the overall time and expense of the negotiations will generally be about the same. If timing is important, the letter of intent may establish a deadline for completing the formation of the JV.

If possible, the letter of intent or memorandum of understanding should deal, at least in some basic fashion, with each of the key business issues identified previously in this chapter. In addition, the letter should address the steps that need to be completed for the JV to be formed. For example, provisions might be included regarding the exchange and protection of confidential information, and the obligations of the parties to refrain from negotiating with others regarding

Ten Tips for Completing Contract Negotiations

Once negotiations have begun, you have already spent time, labor, and money on the transaction. It is important to put your best foot forward in an honest attempt to complete the negotiations. At best, this task is difficult when the transaction is with another party who is from your own community. In a cross-border transaction, you will also face variations in culture, social traditions, political views, educational opportunities, and living standards. Your commitment to the task at hand is essential to your successful completion of contract negotiations. Remember these ten tips:

1. KEEP AN OPEN MIND You may not understand why the other party has acted in a certain way. Don't automatically assume that the other party is at fault.
2. AVOID THREATS Do not bow to the temptation to threaten dire consequences and penalties, or the termination of the negotiations. This is not the way to resolve honest differences and build a long-term relationship.
3. ADAPT TO THE CULTURE Attempt to incorporate local business culture into your negotiating style, and always respect the customs of the other party.
4. BUILD TRUST SLOWLY Time may seem to be of the essence when forging a business relationship, but remember that a JV is meant to be long term. Take as slow a pace as is appropriate, and allow new ideas to germinate. Allow the other party to consider your views and to make a reasoned response.
5. TAKE A STEP AT A TIME Be patient. Small steps are better than none, and don't expect to resolve all the issues at the very first meeting.
6. SET THE TOUGH ISSUES ASIDE WHILE YOU BUILD TRUST Do not let negotiations break down over a single point. Talk it over, and then if necessary, shelve it and move on to topics that can be easily resolved. Building a backlog of successes may give you confidence and insight to tackle the tough questions.
7. ACCOMMODATE THE OTHER PARTY Be prepared to compromise on various issues, provided you believe that the contract will benefit you over the long term. If you give in on a point, be certain that you will not regret it. You don't want to be saying ". . . if I only had held my ground on that point."
8. BE FIRM WITH GENTILITY State your position firmly and professionally, but when the point is won be sure to offer the other party a way to save face without embarrassment or obligation to you. Use a little humor, too, to show that your attitude is not one of contempt or superiority for the other party.
9. STAY ON AN EVEN KEEL Keep emotion away from the bargaining table. Theatrics generally raise a red flag and undermine any trust that you may have started to build. Make your point without temper tantrums or overt agitation.
10. PRIME YOUR CASE Plan and prepare before each meeting. Ensure that you have a real and positive vision of the results that you want to reach from the session. At the beginning of the meeting, make sure the other party knows the general points that you would like to discuss.

the proposed activities of the JV. The parties may also impose deadlines for completion of further negotiations.

Negotiation Considerations

The negotiation of a letter of intent or memorandum of understanding is a crucial time for the JV and its participants because it is the first opportunity to see whether the parties can work together to solve the problems that must be surmounted for the JV to be successful. A number of potential problems may arise during the negotiations, and the parties should be mindful of some of these from the start so as not to allow them to break the deal before it is begun. Although a resolution may not be readily apparent at the time negotiations begin, tolerance and awareness of the difficulties may pave the way for reaching an accommodation as the negotiations progress.

One of the biggest potential problems in negotiating a JV stems from the fact that the partners often have divergent long-term objectives. For example, one party may be interested in cash returns, while the other is concerned about obtaining market share. Differences of opinion may come up as a result of different management philosophies and ethics, marketing strategies, approaches to human resources, pricing considerations, and expectations regarding earnings reinvestment. Formation of a JV can also raise uncertainties for managers who are faced with the loss of exclusive control over one or more functional areas, and who are thrust into a new and complex management structure that may be materially different from the one with which they are already familiar.

While one cannot predict successful negotiations with absolute certainty, a number of rules should be kept in mind to ensure that the preliminary negotiations leading to creation of a JV uncover and deal with the real concerns of the parties, even if it means that a mutual decision is made not to proceed with the JV.

- STAY FOCUSED ON MAJOR OBJECTIVES AND CONCERNS Although relationship building is an important phase of the negotiation process, the parties should not be afraid to isolate the most important objectives and areas of concern, and put them on the table for discussion at an early stage of the negotiations. After the objectives have been stated, make sure that they remain the primary focus of the negotiations. Parties should avoid getting lost in details and contractual language, and should be flexible enough to consider alternative methods for achieving their objectives and overcoming concerns. Nothing brings negotiations to a halt faster than one partner's proposal of final plans or offers that, at least in the eyes of the other partner, must either be accepted or rejected without much discussion.

- MAKE SURE THE RIGHT PEOPLE ARE NEGOTIATING Participants in the negotiations should include all persons who will have substantive responsibilities in executing the relationship, as well as representatives of senior management with authority to make commitments on behalf of each party. Each party should have at least one person who will champion the relationship within his or her organization when problems arise and quick decisions are required. It is also wise to pay careful attention to the rank and status of the negotiators for the other side.

- **AVOID ADVERSARIAL NEGOTIATIONS** Every effort should be made to keep the negotiations from becoming adversarial. The parties must understand that the negotiations serve as the foundation for a long-term relationship, which will not end when the contracts are signed. If at all possible, the parties must not become wary of each other's motives and intentions as a result of problems during the negotiation stages. Certainly the parties will not be in agreement on every point. However, whenever a party reaches a difficult point in the negotiations, they should try and reiterate shared positions and mutual strengths so as not to discourage either party from working to reach an acceptable accommodation.
- **ACKNOWLEDGE CHANGING CIRCUMSTANCES** A JV is a long-term commitment, and the parties must realize that their objectives are likely to shift over time in response to changing conditions in the marketplace, new technological developments, changes in personnel and management styles, and revised company policies. The possibility of shifting objectives should be recognized by the parties at the negotiation stage, and provision should be made for periodic review of the scope and goals of the JV.
- **BE PATIENT, POLITE AND RESPECTFUL** Good negotiating requires patience, courtesy, and respect. The JV will hopefully last a long time, and the parties should always allow more time than they think will be necessary for negotiations. Business people in many countries are interested in long-term relationships, and etiquette and custom are extremely important and cannot be rushed or ignored. Parties should work hard to overcome their fear of conducting negotiations away from home, perhaps at the site selected by the other party. Treat this as an opportunity to observe the management and social culture of the other party, as well as the characteristics of the market itself. Increased knowledge of the actual opportunity can be extremely important in structuring the transaction, and will permit the foreign party to define the contribution that it can make to the market.
- **PAY SOME ATTENTION TO DIVORCE PLANNING** Planning for termination of the relationship should begin at the time the relationship begins so that the parties do not become anxious as to what might happen in the future. The parties should establish the procedures for "divorce," including trigger mechanisms, put and call rights, and most importantly, a clearly defined formula for valuing the interests of each of the parties.
- **GIVE PROPER INSTRUCTIONS TO THE NEGOTIATING AGENTS** Although responsibility for the big picture lies with the managers and representatives of the participants, the details are often left to agents of the parties, including their respective counsel. Each party must give proper instructions to its negotiating agents and must educate them regarding the fundamental points underlying the agreement of the parties. Without proper guidance, the deal can quickly stall as the agents quarrel over minor points and delay the launch of the JV. A timetable for completing the documentation should be established, and the parties should insist on regular updates regarding the status of the work.

Sample Contract: Memorandum of Understanding for Joint Venture

The purpose of this Memorandum of Understanding is to set forth certain nonbinding understandings and binding agreements between [*name*] ("Venturer A") and [*name*] ("Venturer B") with respect to our recent discussions regarding the formation and operation of a new joint venture company (the "Company") for the purposes further described below. Venturer A and Venturer B are sometimes referred to herein collectively as the "Venturers."

COMMENT: This introductory sentence is crucial to distinguishing between a nonbinding and binding document. In this case, the parties are following the common practice of emphasizing that the description of the proposed terms of the transaction in the next section be construed simply as preliminary understandings, subject to negotiation and execution of a definitive agreement. If, however, the parties intend for these terms to be binding even if no further documentation is ever signed, they should make that clear in the introductory sentence. In most situations, both parties will prefer to defer final agreement until further documents have been drafted. In fact, the need to satisfy additional conditions (e.g., regulatory approvals and/or financing) may make it impossible for the parties to reach agreement at the time the memorandum is executed.

TERMS OF TRANSACTION

The following numbered paragraphs reflect our understanding of the matters described but are not legally binding and do not impose an enforceable obligation on either of us to negotiate or conclude an agreement regarding the Company on such terms. This is not a complete statement of all terms and conditions of the proposed transaction but provides a basis for further negotiations.

COMMENT: This form of memorandum is divided into two parts. The first part, referred to as "Terms of Transaction," covers the understanding of the parties regarding the economic and business terms of the proposed relationship, including the purpose of the JV, the contributions and ownership interests of the parties, and the management structure. The second part, entitled Certain Covenants and Restrictions, includes agreements between the parties that relate to the negotiation stage itself and therefore are usually intended to be binding even if the parties do not ultimately complete the transaction.

1. FORMATION. Venturer A and Venturer B shall form and organize the Company for the purposes set forth in this Memorandum. The name of the Company shall be [*name*] and the Company shall be a [*description of type of entity*] organized under the laws of [*name of state and/or country*].

COMMENT: This section sets out the general undertaking of the parties to form and organize a new company to conduct the JV. The exact language depends on the type of entity selected and the country where the new entity is to be organized. Refer to Chapter 9 for a full discussion of these issues.

2. PURPOSES. The purpose of the Company shall be to [*specify*, e.g., engage in the manufacture, production, and commercial sale of (*description of*

products) within (_description of territory_) and to do all things necessary, appropriate, or advisable in furtherance thereof as may be approved by the Managing Board (as defined below).

COMMENT: No JV should be consummated without a clear understanding between the participants regarding the general business purpose of the relationship. Although the ability of the participants to develop a concise and clear statement of the proposed business purpose is no guarantee of the overall success of the JV, it does ensure that the basic parameters of the future business activities have been discussed. Each statement of purpose has several common elements: a description of the functional activities (e.g., development, production, manufacturing, and/or distribution) that will be undertaken directly or indirectly by the JV; a definition of the products that are to be commercialized by the JV; and, finally, an identification of the geographic territory where the JV will conduct its activities.

3. TERM. The Company shall terminate on the date that is [_period of time_] after its formation (the "Term") unless sooner terminated as otherwise provided in Section 12 herein.

COMMENT: Almost by definition, a JV is an enterprise created for a specific purpose and for a finite period. The parties must reach some agreement as to the term of the JV. The term will depend on the amount of time that the parties anticipate will be needed to achieve the business objectives of the relationship. For example, it may be that the parties believe that it will take at least five years to recover the amount of their initial investment in the venture and at least three or four additional years for the total return on investment to meet or exceed their required investment needs. In that case, the JV might extend for 10 to 12 years, thereby allowing some time to wind up the affairs of the enterprise.

In considering the duration of the JV, the parties should also discuss the utility of providing for various performance milestones during the early years of the venture. Failure to achieve these milestones may be an indication that the ultimate business objective may not be attainable, or that the original forecasts of the parties were in error. In such cases, it may be appropriate to provide for an early termination of the JV, including distribution of the remaining assets to the parties.

4. INTERESTS AND CAPITAL ACCOUNTS. The interests of the respective Venturers in the assets, liabilities, profits and, losses of the Company shall be as follows:

Venturer A..............................[_number_] %

Venturer B..............................[_number_] %

A separate capital account shall be maintained for each Venturer. The initial capital accounts of the Venturers shall be the amounts of their initial capital contributions as set forth in Section 5 below. All items of income, gain, loss, or deduction shall be allocated between the Venturers in accordance with their respective interests set forth above and shall increase (in the case of income or gain) or decrease (in the case of a loss or deduction) each Venturer's capital account. Distributions to a Venturer shall reduce its capital account.

COMMENT: Compensation to the parties in a JV can take a number of tangible and intangible forms. Although many JVs are pursued for purposes of ensuring access to new technologies, improved production methods, new distribution channels, and innovative management skills, it is the promise of exceptional cash returns on invested capital that often serves as the overriding consideration in analyzing any specific business opportunity. Accordingly, this section lays out the interests of the parties in the gains and losses of the JV.

The actual language for this term depends on the type of entity selected for operating the JV and on the specific agreement of the parties. For example, the language in this form is suitable for partnership-type entities in which the parties own percentage interests in the business assets and revenues. If, on the other hand, the selected entity is a corporation, the proportionate economic interests of the parties would be expressed in the number of shares issued to each party. Special allocations are possible regardless of the form of entity, and the parties may provide for a preferential return to one partner before the agreed sharing formula is triggered.

Certainly, the proportion ownership interests of the parties is one of the most complicated issues, both from a psychological as well as a practical point of view. Obviously, national legislation will have a lot to do with whether the foreign party will be forced to accept a minority interest in the JV. In other cases, the percentage interest that a party is willing to accept may depend on the activities of the JV. For example, some firms in industries that are particularly suitable to joint venturing, such as chemical products, draw a distinction between specialty products (a patented drug) and a general production line (plastics). For specialties, they will insist on majority control, but for general products they are prepared to accept a minority interest. Also, a minority interest may be acceptable so long as there are other mechanisms in place that allow the party to retain control over key assets, such as know-how and technology that is being made available to the JV.

5. **CONTRIBUTIONS.**

a. At the time of formation of the Company, Venturer A shall contribute to the Company, as its capital contribution, [*amount*], and shall receive therefor the ownership interest in the Company described in Section 4.

b. At the time of formation of the Venture, Venturer B shall contribute to the Company, as its capital contribution, [*description of assets*], and shall receive therefore the ownership interest in the Company described in Section 4. The Venturers have agreed that the initial capital contribution of Venturer B will have a fair market value of [*amount*].

c. The Managing Board (as defined below) may call for additional capital contributions to the Company, provided that the timing and amount of such a call is reasonable in view of the current and reasonably foreseeable future needs of the Company. The amount that each Venturer must contribute shall be in the same proportion as each Venturer's percentage interest in the Venture as provided in Section 4. However, no Venturer shall be required to make contributions pursuant to this Section 5(c) that in the aggregate shall exceed [*amount*].

COMMENT: The first step in establishing any JV is determining the contributions that each party will be making to the enterprise. In this area, consideration should be given not only to the amount of cash that each of the parties will be expected to contribute to fund the various activities of the JV, but also to the content and valuation of any "in-kind" contributions. It is also essential to consider the relative rights that are to be associated with the stock instruments to be issued to the parties in connection with their capital contributions, the obligations of the parties to contribute additional capital to the JV or to guarantee any borrowings by the JV from commercial lending institutions, and finally, the nature of other contributions to the JV by the parties other than in the form of capital.

6. MANAGING BOARD. Except as reserved to the Venturers as described in Section 9 below, the business and affairs of the Venture shall be managed under the direction of a Managing Board. The Managing Board shall at all times consist of four members, two of whom shall be appointed by Venturer A and two of whom shall be appointed by Venturer B. Unless otherwise agreed to in writing by the Venturers, the Managing Board shall have responsibility for the following actions, all of which shall require the unanimous approval of the members of the Managing Board:

a. **Approval of the Company's Annual Budget and Strategic Plan as described in Section 8 below;**

b. **Approval of any contract, agreement and commitment with a value in excess of [*amount*] or a term longer than [*period of time*];**

c. **Approval of all contracts that are proposed to be entered into between the Company and any Venturer or affiliate of a Venturer;**

d. **Approval of all distributions to the Venturers;**

e. **Approval of the conveyance, sale, transfer, assignment, pledge, encumbrance, or disposal of, or the granting of a security interest in, any assets of the Company; or**

f. **Approval of the transfer of any assets of the Company, or any interest therein, other than in the ordinary course of business, the fair market value of which may reasonably be expected to exceed [*amount*].**

COMMENT: This generic language regarding the composition and duties of the managing board is suitable for use with any type of business entity, including non-corporate forms. As discussed in greater detail in Chapter 14, the parties need to carefully consider the management structure and strike an appropriate balance between having all decisions made at the senior management level of each partner, and delegating authority to a group of managers who will be dealing with the operation of the JV on a daily basis. Each of the listed issues are important, however, it is worth considering how available cash will be handled. For example, the activities of the JV will presumably generate income to the enterprise, and any sale of assets that might be owned by the JV will also provide cash that would be available for distribution to the partners or for reinvestment in the activities of the business. External financing opportunities for the JV may be limited, and therefore it is important for the parties to consider carefully the policies that are to be followed with respect to distributions of operating income and the internal application of funds. As such, it is important to maintain an ongoing capital budgeting process that ensures that the enterprise will not distribute funds that should be used for expansion and related purposes.

7. OFFICERS. The Managing Board shall unanimously agree on and appoint a chief executive officer (the "Chief Executive Officer"), who will manage the day-to-day affairs of the Company, carry out the directions of the Managing

Board, and effectuate the business plan as set forth in the Company's Annual Budget and Strategic Plan as described in Section 8 herein. Unless otherwise agreed to by the Venturers, the initial Chief Executive Officer will be [*name*]. In the event of [*name*]'s death, retirement, resignation, termination, or inability to serve, a successor Chief Executive Officer shall be appointed by the Managing Board. The Managing Board shall unanimously agree on and appoint a treasurer, a secretary, and a vice president with such duties and responsibilities as may be established by the Managing Board.

COMMENT: The Managing Board will delegate significant responsibilities to the officers of the JV, particularly the president or chief executive officer. If at all possible, agreement should be reached on the identify of the chief executive officer before the JV is formed or, at a minimum, a process should be put in place for selection of the managers. If the JV has other human resources needs, such as establishing an employee equity incentive plan or other benefits arrangements, this might also be covered in the memorandum.

8. ANNUAL BUDGET AND STRATEGIC PLAN. The Chief Executive Officer shall prepare and submit to the Managing Board as soon as practicable after formation of the Company for the fiscal year ending [*year*] and at least [*number*] days prior to the commencement of each subsequent fiscal year, an annual budget and a strategic plan (the "Annual Budget and Strategic Plan"), which describes the business plan for the Company for such fiscal year. Each Annual Budget and Strategic Plan approved by the Managing Board shall remain operative until amended by the Managing Board or a successor Annual Budget and Strategic Plan is approved by the Managing Board.

COMMENT: Careful budgeting and strategic planning is essential to the success of a JV, particularly when one of the parties is situated far from the headquarters location of the JV. This provision reinforces the importance of strategic planning by requiring the chief executive officer to prepare an annual budget and strategic plan on a regular basis during the term of the JV. The plan would be subject to review and approval by the Managing Board. While this provision anticipates that the strategic plan will be completed after formation of the JV, an effort should be made to pull together a relatively complete draft before the parties decide to proceed. Refer to Chapter 10 for a full discussion of strategic planning for the JV.

9. ACTIONS REQUIRING CONSENT OF VENTURERS. Notwithstanding anything herein to the contrary, the following actions shall require the consent and approval of both of the Venturers:

a. **Amendments to the Company's charter documents and/or any other agreement setting forth the rights of the Venturers with respect to the operation of the Company;**

b. **Any sale of all or substantially all of the assets of the Company;**

c. **Any change in the size of the Managing Board;**

d. **Any issuance of securities representing an ownership interest in the Company other than as provided for in Section 5(c) above;**

e. **Any merger or consolidation of the Company with any other entity, or**

f. **The dissolution or liquidation of the Company, as well as the continuation or reestablishment of the Company following dissolution.**

COMMENT: Although the parties will generally be equally represented on the Managing Board, certain decisions regarding the JV usually require participation and consideration by senior managers of both parties who might not otherwise be involved in the operation of the JV at the Managing Board level. This provision might be eliminated if senior managers of the parties also serve on the Managing Board, because presumably they would be in a position to speak for the owner firms themselves.

10. REPORTS. The Company will deliver to each Venturer: (i) an unaudited balance sheet, statement of operations and statement of cash flows for each month within [*number*] days following the end of such month; (ii) an unaudited balance sheet, statement of operations, and statement of cash flows for each quarter within [*number*] days following the end of such quarter; and (iii) an audited balance sheet, statement of operations, and statement of cash flows for each fiscal year within [*number*] days following the end of such year.

COMMENT: Timely information about the operations of the JV is essential to good decisionmaking, and this provision sets out the general requirements regarding preparation of financial reports. Of course, the parties may expand the list to include other items, such as sales reports, notices of important contracts and litigation, and communications from regulators.

11. RESTRICTIONS ON TRANSFER OF INTERESTS. In the event that any Venturer (the "Selling Venturer") desires to sell, transfer, or dispose of any of its interest in the Company, it shall offer to sell such interest first to the other Venturer (the "Nonselling Venturer") and second, to the Company, at a price and on terms equal to: (i) in the event a third party offers to purchase such shares, the price and terms at which the prospective purchaser intends to purchase such shares, provided the Selling Venturer first delivers to each Nonselling Venturer a written copy of the offer that includes the name of the third party, the number of shares the third party intends to purchase, the price it intends to pay, and the payment terms; (ii) in the event the Selling Venturer desires to transfer the shares for no consideration, the fair market value thereof as determined in good faith by the Board of Directors with consultation of the Company's independent accounting firm; or (iii) in any event, on such other price and terms as the Venturers may agree.

COMMENT: Procedures regulating proposed transfers of ownership interest in the JV should always be included in the documents. This standard provision creates a right of first offer in favor of the non-selling party in the event the other party wants to transfer its ownership interest. Key issues in actual drafting include the method for determining the price at which the interest will be offered, the manner of payment, and the amount of time available to the non-selling party to decide whether to exercise its rights. Other procedures that might be used in connection with changes in ownership are more fully described in Chapter 16.

12. TERMINATION. The agreements between the Venturers with respect to the Company may be terminated by a Venturer (the "Terminating Venturer") by giving written notice of termination to the other Venturer in the event that the other Venturer (hereinafter the "Defaulting Venturer"):

a. **Commits a material breach of any agreement between the Venturers with respect to the Company and fails to remedy such breach within ninety (90) days from the date of notice of breach;**

b. Becomes insolvent or becomes a party voluntarily or involuntarily to bankruptcy, composition for the benefit of creditors, or reorganization proceedings; or

c. Becomes dissolved and liquidated or discontinues its business.

In the event that the agreements are terminated as provided herein, the Terminating Venturer shall be have the following rights, which are exercisable by means of written notice to the Defaulting Venturer delivered no later than [*number*] days following delivery of the notice of termination: (i) to dissolve the Company or (ii) to purchase the Defaulting Venturer's interest in the Company at a purchase price determined by [*description*].

COMMENT: As mentioned above, the parties need to give some consideration to divorce planning even before the JV is formed. Specifically, the parties need to identify events or actions that may trigger a right in one or both of the parties to terminate the JV. The list above is by no means exclusive and it is common to provide for termination on failure of the JV to meet certain goals with respect to performance. In this case, the parties have chosen to include an option in favor of the non-defaulting partner either to liquidate the JV, thereby ending the underlying business, or to continue the business as the sole owner by purchasing the defaulting partner's interest on terms agreed on in advance.

13. **CONDITIONS TO FORMATION FOR VENTURER A.** Notwithstanding anything herein to the contrary, Venturer A shall be under no obligation to enter into any definitive agreements regarding formation of the Company unless:

a. The parties are able to agree on a preliminary draft of an acceptable Annual Budget and Strategic Plan for the initial year of the Company ending [*date*] within [*number*] days of the date of this Memorandum of Understanding;

b. Venturer B delivers, within [*number*] days of the date of this Memorandum of Understanding, a letter from [*name of regulatory agency*] indicating that it has completed its initial review of the materials presented to it regarding the Company and that it does not intend to take any action that would result in delay or disapproval of the Company; and

c. A preliminary commitment, in form and content reasonably satisfactory to Venturer A, is received from [*name of vendor*] with respect to [*description of products or services to be provided to Company*] no later than [*date*].

COMMENT: Even though by its nature the memorandum is nonbinding and subject to further negotiations, the parties may elect to explicitly describe key conditions to completing the JV. The parties are free to list almost any condition; however, it is best to limit the matters to those that are actually material to the decision of a party to proceed. In this case, one party is seeking assurance regarding the content of the strategic plan, regulatory attitudes toward the JV, and the availability of products and services from an identified outside vendor. Of course, conditions may be included for both parties.

CERTAIN COVENANTS AND RESTRICTIONS

By signing this Memorandum of Understanding, we agree that the following lettered paragraphs will constitute a legally binding and enforceable agreement between us. In consideration of the significant expenses that we both will incur

in pursuing an agreement with respect to the formation of the Company and the mutual undertakings described, we agree as follows:

COMMENT: Regardless of whether the parties intend to be bound to the economic and business terms described previously, the memorandum should cover a variety of other topics to which the parties intend to be bound. These topics relate to the activities of the parties during the negotiation stage, the parties' mutual understanding as to exchange and protection of trade secrets and other confidential information, as well as any agreement regarding discussions with other parties.

The language in the main form is for use when the parties do not wish to be bound by the statement of economic and business terms included previously. To distinguish between the nonbinding and binding terms, the drafter has used numbered and lettered paragraphs and has stated that the following lettered paragraphs are, indeed, intended to be binding. Slightly different language should be used when the entire letter is intended to be binding.

A. GOOD FAITH NEGOTIATIONS. We shall negotiate in good faith and make our best efforts to arrive at an agreement with respect to the formation of the Company at the earliest practicable time.

COMMENT: This language actually is a statement of the obligations that would usually be imposed on the parties as a matter of law. Courts will typically imply a duty on both parties to negotiate with each other in good faith to iron out any open points in the memorandum. In fact, failure to bring up a material term or condition at the memorandum stage may be deemed to be a breach of the duty to negotiate in good faith, and expose a party to a claim for damages. Some commentators have advised against including a covenant regarding good faith negotiations in the binding provisions, for fear that a court might construe a binding element to the nonbinding provisions in the first part of the memorandum. These commentators suggest that the parties simply rely on a liquidated damages provision for protection in the event that a party acts in bad faith after the memorandum has been executed and negotiations on the definitive agreement are to proceed. Unfortunately, liquidated damage provisions are not valid in all jurisdictions.

Covenants regarding good faith negotiations might be supplemented by language that obligates the parties to cooperate in obtaining necessary consents and approvals to complete the transaction. For example, if information must be filed with regulatory authorities, the parties will need to work together to collect all the necessary information and organize it into the form required by the regulators. This can be a very time-consuming process, yet it must be completed quickly to ensure that the review does not drag on beyond the date the parties have set for combining the businesses.

B. EXCLUSIVE DEALING. While we are negotiating the agreements with respect to the formation of the Company, neither of us shall enter into discussions nor consummate an agreement, whether directly or indirectly through an owner, employee, or agent, with any other party with respect to any transaction relating to the proposed purpose of the Company set forth above.

COMMENT: One of the main reasons for negotiating a memorandum of understanding is to secure some commitment from the other party that it will devote all its efforts to consummating the deal at hand as opposed to entering into discussions with other parties. This section makes it clear that neither party is to begin talks with other parties regarding a similar relationship until the term of the memorandum has expired. In some cases, one or both of the parties may be restricted from entering into a JV with another party for an agreed period after negotiations break down. In the alternative, a party may be given a right to match any competing offer from another firm.

C. ACCESS TO INFORMATION. Immediately after the execution of this Memorandum of Understanding, and for so long as this Memorandum of Understanding has not been terminated as set forth in Section F below, each of us shall permit the other party and its accountants, counsel, and other representatives and agents to have reasonable access to our properties and the books, records, contracts, and other documents and information concerning our businesses, finances, and assets, solely for the purpose of evaluating the proposed joint venture relationship. Each party shall also have reasonable access during standard business hours and on reasonable notice to legal, financial, accounting, and other representatives of the other party who have knowledge of the businesses, finances, and assets of the other party. Each party agrees to hold all confidential information about the other party learned by it during the course of its activities under this Section C, in the manner provided for in that certain confidentiality agreement by and between the parties dated as of [*date*].

COMMENT: A good deal of due diligence should be completed before the parties execute the memorandum. However, it is customary for the parties to agree on procedures that allow them to have access to business and financial information regarding each other. The degree of access depends on the circumstances, such as the size of the deal and the assets involved. Certain restrictions might be included, such as limiting the access to a specified time period, and requiring advance notice before contacts are made with employees or customers. Note that in this case the form refers to a separate confidentiality agreement that should govern information exchanged during the due diligence process. If such an agreement is not in place, it can be set out in this document, or executed contemporaneously with the memorandum. Refer to Chapter 7 for a sample confidentiality agreement.

D. EXPENSES. We each shall be solely responsible for expenses that we incur in connection with the negotiations for the formation of the Company.

COMMENT: Negotiating and documenting a JV can be quite expensive, and the parties need to consider carefully the allocation of legal fees, accounting expenses, and other costs. The language in this paragraph takes the popular approach by simply requiring each party to bear its own expenses of the deal. In some cases, a portion of the expenses might be paid out of the initial contributions to the JV; however, this only makes sense if restrictions on the amount of reimbursement are agreed upon in advance. Other possible expenses that need to be taken into account include finders' fees that may be due on formation of the JV.

E. PUBLIC DISCLOSURES. We shall consult with each other and must agree as to the timing, content, and form before issuing any press release or other

public disclosure related to this Memorandum of Understanding or the formation of the Company. However, this does not prohibit either of us from making a public disclosure regarding this Memorandum of Understanding and the formation of the Company if, in the opinion of its legal counsel, such disclosure is required by law.

COMMENT: One or both of the parties may wish to avoid extensive disclosure of the pending negotiations until they have had an opportunity to iron out all the terms and enter into a definitive agreement. This paragraph is intended to ensure that the parties consult with each other before announcing publicly that they are in negotiation. For example, the local party may not want the foreign party to announce that it is in discussions regarding a possible JV until the local party has had an opportunity to speak with its employees and customers, and to address any concerns that they might have regarding the impact of the proposed transaction. Note that the restrictions are not intended to prevent a party from making any announcement or disclosure that might be required by law or regulation, such as securities or antitrust laws. For example, in the United States, a party may be under a duty to disclose arising under Section 10(b) and Rule 10b-5 of the Securities Exchange Act of 1934, as well as the periodic reporting requirements included in that Act. Moreover, disclosures may be necessary to comply with the pre-merger notification requirements of the United States Hart-Scott-Rodino Antitrust Improvements Act of 1976.

F. TERMINATION. We each have the right to terminate this Memorandum of Understanding if no agreement to form the Company is reached by [*date*]. Following termination, neither party shall have any obligations under this Memorandum of Understanding, other than under Paragraphs C and D above.

COMMENT: Termination provisions in the memorandum are generally designed to force the parties to complete the transaction by a certain date in the future. Without a deadline, one or both of the parties may be prevented from pursuing other opportunities. Moreover, uncertainty about the deal may undermine the ongoing operations of their respective businesses. In setting the termination date, the parties should carefully consider all the steps that need to be completed for the closing to occur and, if possible, should allow some additional time for unanticipated delays. Depending on the circumstances, other termination provisions might be added. For example, the obligations of the parties might terminate if one of the stated conditions set out elsewhere in the memorandum is not satisfied by a certain date (e.g., regulatory approvals). Following termination, almost all of the obligations will terminate but for the restrictions on disclosure of confidential information and the agreement of the parties to bear their own expenses.

G. BINDING EFFORT. This Memorandum of Understanding is intended to be a confirmation of interest between the parties in pursuing negotiations for a definitive agreement based on the terms hereof and, except for the lettered paragraphs hereof, shall not constitute a binding agreement between the parties hereto. Neither party intends, by setting forth in this Memorandum of Understanding the provisions of a possible transaction, to create for itself or any other person, any legally binding obligation of liability. No subsequent oral agreement or conduct of the parties, including partial performance, shall be deemed to impose such obligation or liability. No agreement shall be binding

unless and until each party has reviewed and approved (in its sole discretion) a definitive written agreement incorporating all the terms, conditions, and obligations of the parties, has had such agreement reviewed by legal counsel, and has duly executed and delivered such agreement. The legal rights and obligations of each party shall be only those that are set forth in the definitive written agreement.

COMMENT: This section is one of the most important provisions in the memorandum because it states the position of the parties with respect to the binding effect of the statement of economic and business terms in the letter. The language in the form is for use when the memorandum is nonbinding and makes it clear that the parties do not intend to create legally binding obligations with respect to the terms of the transaction. As in other parts of the memorandum, the requirement of a definitive written agreement has been included. The reference to oral agreements is to protect against the possibility that a party can assert that a binding relationship was created in conversations that were not recorded in the memorandum, or by other conduct or dealings between the parties. Of course, if the letter is to be binding, this section would reiterate that the memorandum is intended to be a legally binding agreement.

IN WITNESS WHEREOF, the Venturers have entered into this Memorandum of Understanding as of [*date*].

[*Venturer A*]

By [*name of representative*]

[*typed name and title*]

[*Venturer B*]

By [*name of representative*]

[*typed name and title*]

CHAPTER 10

Developing a Business Plan for the JV

AS PART OF THEIR NEGOTIATIONS on the basic terms and conditions of the JV, the partners will certainly consider the overall purposes and objectives of the relationship. However, before they proceed with formation of the JV, the parties should spend time preparing an initial business plan for the JV.

The business plan should set forth in reasonable detail the field of activity, line of products and services, and territorial scope for the JV. In addition, the plan should cover the goals and objectives of the JV with respect to research and development, production, distribution, licensing, and such other matters as the parties may determine are relevant. Remember that, although a JV is a combination of the assets and strengths of the parties, it is also a separate business that must be planned and managed just like any other independent enterprise.

Creating a Meaningful Plan

The development of a business plan is essential to the successful operation of any business. All of the other formational documents—confidentiality agreements, memorandums of understanding, venturers' agreement, and so forth—deal with the overall concept of the business and the ownership and operational rights of the JV participants. The business plan starts with the concept of the business and builds the process and procedures by which the concept will be realized. This task should therefore be taken seriously, with the goal of creating a meaningful plan. Keep in mind the following points:

- FOCUS ON YOUR COMMITMENT TO THE JV, NOT ON MINOR PREFERENCES In the context of a JV, the development of a business plan is no easy task, and the issues cannot be resolved in isolation. The difficulties are multiplied by the inherent conflicts of interest that tend to arise between the participants because of their shared ownership rights in the assets and resources of the JV. Each party is likely to have its own preferences for allocation of business assets and resources. Conflicts related to ownership rights can, of course, simply be avoided if the parties enter into a different arrangement that does not involve equity sharing—such as manufacturing or distribution license agreements. They could then operate their own separate businesses and dictate the manner in which their own assets and resources will be utilized.

  Nevertheless, the parties selected the JV form because they believed that a collaborative effort was necessary to achieve the desired result. Accordingly, each party should first identify their separate concerns and preferences, review each other's list, and consider which items can be incorporated into the plan without further discussion. Once they have refined the issues, the parties can discuss the remaining concerns and come to a resolution. In their discussions, both parties should stay focused on their initial commitment to the venture, which may mean that they will have to accommodate each other to make the business work.

- DEVELOP A REALISTIC PLAN, NOT A FORCED ONE By the time the parties consider a business plan, they have already initially committed to work together in a joint endeavor and have probably spent some time and labor in working out a memorandum of understanding, reviewing due diligence information, and learning about each other's operational styles, strengths, and weaknesses. Given all this effort, the parties will probably be reluctant to stop the formation process merely because they cannot decide on the details of a business plan. It is for this very reason, however, that a business plan should be created. While developing a business plan, the parties may come to find that in fact their initial concept is not viable. A business plan can point out the gaps and weaknesses, as well as the strengths, involved in sharing resources and common goals. If the parties cannot come up with a realistic plan for the operation of the JV, perhaps they need to reassess their objectives and even their relationship.
- MAKE CREATION OF A BUSINESS PLAN A PRIORITY IN THE FORMATION PROCESS If at all possible, the business plan should be completed prior to formation of the JV. In developing a business plan the JV participants will start to see their concept come alive and should be able to identify the primary barriers that must be overcome to ensure success. All major problems with the implementation and operation of the venture should be resolved before a separate entity is created for the JV. Otherwise, the parties could incur even more expense in dissolving a separate venture that never became fully operational.

  A major concern frequently voiced by parties during the formation stage is that they do not have time to create a full-blown business plan. Often, a business plan is hastily conceived, if at all, because the parties are focused on quick action to get their products and services into the market. This argument misses the point: the business plan developed during the formation process should be an *initial* plan. It is not essential for it to contain every minute operational detail. Rather, a business plan extends the initial concept of the JV by creating specific business policies, identifying assets and resources available and needed, and carving out the overall anticipated financial model.

  A common practice in developing a business plan is for discussions to continue in earnest during the first few months after the initial capital contributions are made to the JV. If this strategy is selected, the parties should consider the possibility that they may have to dissolve the JV if they are unable to reach agreement on a business plan. Given this concern, the parties should agree to a specific period of time by which they must finalize their business plan, to avoid committing resources to a never-ending project, and to reasonable dissolution provisions, including allocation of expenses and contributed capital.
- BE DETERMINED TO USE THE PLAN FROM BEGINNING TO END Planning doesn't stop with the initial plan. It is essential to revise the initial plan to account for comments from the management that is responsible for implementing the plan, for discoveries made as market research progresses, and for changes made to the JV policies and structures as the formation process is completed. Moreover, procedures for updating the plan, usually on a semiannual or annual basis, should be established so that the plan continues to be viable in the face of changing

political, regulatory, social, cultural, and market conditions, as well as transformations that can be expected to occur within each of the separate entities of the JV participants as time passes.

- REALIZE THE SIGNIFICANCE AND POTENTIAL VALUE OF THE PLAN In general, there are no set requirements for the form and content of the business plan. Members of the drafting group, which should include each person who will be actively involved in the actual management of the JV, should be prepared to produce a realistic and viable business plan that can be presented for review and approval within each of the parent organizations. In addition, some or all of the plan may be used in presentations to investors and bankers when seeking loans or financing, to regulatory agencies when seeking approval of the JV's activities, and to tax, financial, and legal advisors when requesting advice specifically relevant to the JV's situation. The business plan can therefore become the key to the future success of the JV.

Field of Activity

The JV will engage in one or more functional activities, often referred to collectively as the "field of activity." In its broadest sense, the field of activity may include the development of new technologies or products, the manufacture and production of products, and the distribution of products into the relevant marketplace. If the scope of a JV's activities is to be more limited, the JV may simply distribute products that have been independently developed and manufactured by one of the participants. The JV need not actually undertake the specific function itself, but it may choose to contract the activity, such as manufacturing or distribution, to one of the participants or even to a third party.

- IDENTIFY THE CONTRIBUTIONS The first step in determining the field of activity for the JV is to identify the respective contributions of each participant. If a JV is formed based on synergistic functional strengths and capabilities of its participants, the potential exists for a broad scope of business activities, because presumably the functional skills of each party can be adapted to meet the needs of new customers and markets. However, a JV that is formed for a very limited purpose, such as exploiting distribution channels in a specified market, will necessarily have a narrower focus, at least in the beginning. It is conceivable, of course, that the relationship may be expanded over time to include new products and services that are suitable for the market and compatible with the distribution capabilities of the local participant.

- IDENTIFY FUNCTIONAL CAPABILITIES After evaluating the strengths of each JV participant, the next step is to identify the functional capabilities needed in the JV to achieve its desired objective. For example, the JV may require a distribution network, manufacturing facilities, raw material suppliers, personnel training, and quality control programs. The field of activity can extend beyond the development, production, and distribution functions to include activities that might be essential to commercial exploitation of the JV's products and services. For example, in a technology JV, it may be necessary to secure government approvals for production and sale of products. A JV may need to secure funding from public agencies that provide specified cost advantages or licenses and permits necessary for the conduct of its business activities. All such prerequisites should be identified, and for those that are material to the success of the JV, the participants must give each other assurances that they will be able to perform and complete the necessary tasks.

- MATCH CONTRIBUTIONS TO CAPABILITIES The JV can undertake one or more functional activity only if the participants are willing to provide the expertise for completion of the function, or to contract it to a third party. In addition, the JV parties must be able and willing to contribute the capital necessary for the enterprise to develop the capability. Accordingly, decisions regarding overall financing will depend, in large part, on the expected functional requirements of the JV during the term of the relationship.

As a general rule, the participants will tend to limit the field of activity of the JV to the areas that correspond to existing strengths of at least one of the participants. However, if the direction of the JV is more uncertain, such as when the participants intend to develop new technologies and products, the parties may prefer to allow for flexibility and to reserve judgment on the ultimate field of activity. Just as it makes little sense for the JV to undertake activities for which neither participant has any skills, it is also unreasonable to base the JV's success on competence in a function that is unfamiliar to the participants. For example, while the JV might be formed to exploit the local participant's distribution skills within a specified territory, profitability may depend on low-cost manufacturing capabilities. Therefore, the key issue is whether expansion of the venture's field of activity to include manufacturing by the local participant is reasonable, which decision hinges on the specific resources and skills of that participant.

Products and Markets

An integral part of establishing the field of activity for the JV is the definition of the specific products and services to be produced or distributed by the JV. In turn, selection of the appropriate products and services requires a keen understanding of the potential uses of, and markets for, the basic strategic skills of the JV and its participants. Although some flexibility should be allowed for later expansion of products and markets, it is important to establish some parameters in the beginning. The greatest degree of uncertainty exists when the JV is engaged in development activities that have uncertain future commercial utility or value. Even if a product or service can be identified, the JV participants must decide on a specific potential customer base.

- PROTECT PRODUCT RIGHTS DEVELOPED BY THE JV If a JV is being formed to exploit a product but the precise content and use of that product has not yet been determined, the JV participants will need to engage in frequent dialogue regarding the direction of the product development effort. Care should be taken to set up an efficient communication system. Often, the resultant technology may be utilized in ways that fall outside the original expectation of the participants, creating fertile grounds for conflict. The issue becomes whether the new opportunity must be exploited through the JV.

EXAMPLE: Assume that a JV is formed to develop new products for a specified market utilizing technology that is contributed by one of the participants. In the initial business plan, the JV parties have defined the products and markets to be served by the JV. The respective capital contributions of each participant is calculated based on certain assumptions about the ultimate size and profitability of the specified markets. A new product or market is developed through the efforts of the JV. Should the JV's activities be limited in scope to those anticipated by the plan, should the JV expand its focus to include this new field, or should one of the JV participants be allowed to use the same technology to pursue other commercial applications?

At the formation of the JV, it is essential to anticipate and, if possible, eliminate conflicts over product development and use. The parties may consider various options when negotiating the documents of formation and ownership. One possibility is to provide for a "right of first refusal" in favor of the existing JV to expand its business activities to include the new commercial application. Whether a first refusal right will be a viable alternative depends on the circumstances of the particular JV, including such factors as the relationship of the parties, the nontechnology participant's willingness to contribute additional capital, and the suitability of the combined skills of the participants for the new and different market challenges that may be presented by the expansion.

The participants may conclude that the current JV is unable in practical terms to pursue the new opportunity. In that case, the participant who desires to exploit the opportunity could do so by means of a separate business to license or purchase the rights from the JV or the other party. However, such an arrangement is often difficult to negotiate, particularly if the exploitation is likely to create additional competition for the JV or to lessen one party's commitment of resources to the JV.

In any event, each participant is well advised to examine closely the other party's apparent strategies, objectives, and motives outside of the JV. Particular care should be taken in investigating the other party's intentions when the JV's target is a market or industry in which progress and competitiveness is driven by access to new and improved forms of technology. A technology provider might prefer to use the initial JV to fund the development of the technology, to allow exploitation rights limited to very narrowly defined product and geographic areas, and to retain the rights to all expanded commercialization. This position leaves very little incentive to the nontechnology participant to increase the profitability of the JV, but it would potentially preclude unauthorized exploitation. To assess the stance of the other party on these issues, it is important to find the answers to questions such as these:

1. How does the specific JV fit into the overall strategy of the other party?
2. Does the other party have alternative uses for the resources devoted to the original JV, and could those alternatives preclude a future expansion of a JV relationship?
3. What is the other party's strategy for entering a geographic or product market?
4. Is the other party capable of using the technology to compete with one or more existing products of the JV?
5. Is the party capable of forming other JV relationships with third parties active in the same geographic market where the JV was originally formed?

- **DETERMINE RIGHTS IN ENHANCED TECHNOLOGIES** Whether a JV is developing technologies or is selling developed products or services, the parties must consider the effect of future enhancements and improvements to the initial technology products on the JV. The parties should clearly address their rights with regard to improvements or new products that might replace, supplement, or compliment the original products during the JV term. Similar questions should be asked for product development. Keep in mind that the importance of this issue depends on the demographic characteristics of the specific market. For example, expending the time and effort necessary to transfer enhanced technology to the JV may make little sense if the customer base lacks the skills or technical capabilities for using the improvements.

- CONSIDER THE CUSTOMER BASE Finally, the customer base for the JV's products must be considered. Although the JV may be able to produce a generic form of a specific product or service, successful commercialization of that capability depends on identification of a distinguishable customer base and adaptation of the product or service to suit the particular needs or requirements in that market. This process of selecting the target customer base will influence each of the functions undertaken by the JV, as well as the costs, risks, and rewards associated with its business activities. In addition, the identity of the target customer base also dictates the selection criteria for the JV participant that is expected to engage in local distribution activities.

Territory

Territorial issues revolve around the original rationale for the particular JV. On the one hand, a JV established for the specific purpose of distributing already existing products and services in a new geographic market will, by definition, be limited in its scope of activities to that market, and presumably the local participant will have been selected based on its acumen and experience in the relevant territory. Similarly, a JV created for purposes of only manufacturing products, within a particular country or region where there are significant production cost advantages would be limited to that territory.

On the other hand, a JV that brings together technology and capital may make a number of different decisions regarding the territorial scope of its activities. The JV participants may anticipate regional or worldwide exploitation of the products created through the development effort. The participants must then decide on the appropriate means for apportioning this global territory, perhaps by reserving part of it to the JV, contracting it back to the JV participants, or permitting the JV to contract with third parties in places where neither of the JV participants has any competitive advantage.

Consideration of the territorial boundaries of the JV's activities hinges on a comprehensive evaluation of the marketplace, as well as competitive factors and distribution channel strategies. The local partner should be able to take the lead in developing this information, which should be incorporated into the JV's business plan and updated regularly as the JV matures.

- MARKET SIZE An effort should be made to estimate the current and potential size of the market in the territory where the JV will be located, as well as the potential markets for export operations. Market size will depend on a number of factors, such as purchasing power and demographic trends, consumer tastes, and the logistics involved in moving the products to sale points within the territory.

- COMPETITION Competitive factors must be considered, including domestic firms and imports. Competitive or substitute products should be assessed in terms of the quantity of products available, the quality and uses of the various products, and the value offered to the consumer. Competition is a growing concern for international JVs in light of the globalization of business and the increase in the number of firms looking to capitalize on opportunities in previously ignored markets.
- DISTRIBUTION CHANNELS The nature of the proposed distribution channels should be investigated, including use of wholesalers, retailers, sales representatives, exporters, and forwarders. The importance of this factor varies depending on whether the local partner is responsible for distributing the JV's products and services.
- OBTAINING MARKET INFORMATION As with any business plan, the planning effort for the JV will only be as good as the reliability of the information collected on market characteristics. Sources for market information include government statistics and special reports, local chambers of commerce, banks, trade and industry associations, and private market research agencies. Information provided by the local partner can be extremely useful. However, the foreign partner should always do its own independent investigation and analysis.

Operational Activities

The business plan description of the overall strategic objectives and scope of the JV should be supplemented by an expanded discussion of the specific key operational activities of the JV, including research and development, manufacturing and supply, and marketing and distribution.

RESEARCH AND DEVELOPMENT

In the JV context, research and development can take several different forms. For example, research can be conducted within the JV itself by researchers hired specifically to work for the JV and by researchers on loan to the JV from one or more of the partners. In other cases, the JV may enter into a research contract with one or more of the JV participants or with a third party (e.g., a university or a not-for-profit research center) to conduct the specified research work. When a separate research contract with a JV partner is used, the JV often funds the research and the researching partner enjoys the benefits of the research work through the JV, either by sharing in revenues from sales of products developed or by licensing from the JV the right to exploit the technology outside the JV's field of activity. The business plan should cover the following features:

- RESEARCH BUDGET The scope of the research program will be driven, in large part, by decisions made by the parties with respect to the products and services to be provided by the JV. Beyond that, the business plan should specifically address funding of the research program. Preparing an accurate estimate of the anticipated expenses associated with the proposed research work is one of the most difficult tasks facing the parties, because it is difficult to predict the cost of research work, particularly when the project may extend over a long period of time. However, every effort should be made to prepare at least a preliminary research budget for the initial stage of the project. While some plans actually include a budget for the entire project, it makes better sense in multi-year projects to review the budget on an annual basis.

The research budget either can be fairly general, leaving the details to the discretion of the researching party, or can be set out in great detail with a number of different line items. Whatever the method, the parties must consider how the costs associated with the following items should be allocated: wages, contract labor, fringe benefits, facilities and equipment related expenses, supplies, development and prototype materials, freight and transportation, training and education, travel expenses, data processing costs, license fees, insurance, professional services, depreciation and amortization of capital acquisitions, sales and use taxes, and periodic lease payments under capital or financing leases. In addition, the budget may include an allocation for indirect costs, such as overhead incurred by the researcher in performing under the contract.

- STAFFING The parties need to consider how the research project will be staffed. In a number of cases, the researching party will be obligated to contribute a minimum amount of time, often expressed as "person-years," that personnel of the researching party will devote to the research project, as well as a percentage of that time which is to come from internal resources. For example, the researching party may agree to devote at least 20 person-years each year to conducting the research work, at least 75% of which will be from internal resources rather than from outside consultants. The plan might also refer to a list of specific persons who are to work on the project, including their respective time commitments.

MANUFACTURING AND SUPPLY

Manufacturing and supply arrangements are always an important part of the JV's functional portfolio. In some cases, the JV itself is formed to provide manufacturing support or raw materials for the partners. If, however, the operations of the JV focus on sales and distribution, the JV may still need to concern itself with obtaining manufacturing resources, either from one of the partners or from a third party.

- RAW MATERIALS The availability of raw materials is obviously a significant consideration. In some situations, the local partner may be able to provide the necessary materials. If so, the parties still need to consider all of the essential elements of any supply arrangement, including pricing, quality, continuity, and delivery. If the local partner cannot fulfill the supply function, attention turns to other domestic suppliers, or the possibility of using imported materials. If an outside source is selected, the parties need to consider their location, productive capacity, and level of service.
- LOCAL SERVICE AND SUPPORT FACILITIES Local service and support facilities are an important factor in the manufacturing process. Consideration needs to be given to the size, location and quality of local machine shops, tool and die shops, pattern shops, plant maintenance services and related functions. Even if the JV or one of the partners takes on primary responsibility for the overall manufacturing process, it may still be necessary to subcontract a portion of the process to local firms. Accordingly, the size and quality of such firms should also be ascertained.

- COMMUNICATIONS AND TRANSPORT FACILITIES Communications and transport facilities are important to both the manufacture and distribution of the JV's products. Among the issues to consider are the availability and quality of telephone and telegraph capabilities near the JV's facility, sea and river channels, rail and air transport, the quality of roads and highways, and potential packaging and handling problems created by deficiencies in the transit and communications network. It is crucial for the parties to have an understanding of the time and costs associated with moving goods in the geographic areas where manufacturing and distribution are to occur.
- MARKETING AND DISTRIBUTION Distribution is often a key function of a JV's operations and may be conducted by the enterprise itself or, as is typically the case when the venture is established to distribute the products of one partner into a new market where the other partner has existing sales capabilities, one of the partners. Also, if the JV is formed to develop and market new products, each of the partners may be granted the right to distribute the products in a specified geographical territory, although certain territories might be reserved for the JV. The JV may also be given the right to appoint third party subdistributors in various areas that might lie outside the scope of the business operations of the participants.

Additional Items

Depending on the circumstances and the proposed activities of the JV, various additional items may be included in the business plan. The parties should consider whether any of the following topics might be relevant:

- Technology transfer and protection procedures, assuming at least one party will provide intellectual property and/or technical assistance to the JV.
- Plans regarding acquisition and maintenance of facilities, equipment, and other tangible assets, including procedures for handling anticipated growth in operations.
- Strategies for financing the operations of the JV (see Chapter 12). Financial projections should be developed and accompanied by a description of the key assumptions underlying the projections. The parties should not forget that the plan itself might be used to solicit capital from financial institutions.
- Human resources strategies for the JV should be carefully considered. Management requirements are discussed separately in Chapter 15. The parties must develop a plan for recruiting and retaining all employees necessary for the JV to fulfill its objectives. In that regard, the unique local employment environment, including the role of unions, should be factored into the plan.

CHAPTER 11

Securing Government Approvals

WHEN THE PARTIES HAVE COMPLETED NEGOTIATION of the basic economic and business terms related to the proposed JV, they should turn their attention to the steps required to form the enterprise and launch the business. In most cases, formation cannot occur until the parties have secured approvals from government authorities in their home countries, and in any other countries where the JV expects to be conducting business. If the local government has been involved in the negotiation process, the process of approval can be eased substantially. If not, the parties can expect to expend substantial time and effort dealing with government officials. In so doing, care should be taken not to run afoul of laws such as the United States Foreign Corrupt Practices Act, which regulates gifts made to public officials for assistance in obtaining favorable treatment for commercial transactions, including the creation and operation of a JV.

Foreign Investment Regulations

Most countries have some sort of investment law or an investment code that regulates foreign investment in their country, including investment in a JV with one or more local partners. Foreign investment laws may regulate any type of foreign investment or may be limited to investments in a specified industry sector, such as tourism, agriculture, services, or certain manufacturing areas. Foreign investment laws usually require review of the transaction by at least one, and sometimes more than one, governmental authority.

GENERAL AREAS OF FOREIGN INVESTMENT REGULATION

Foreign investment laws and regulations define the local government's policy regarding foreign participation in the local economy. Although there are a myriad of potential variations in the scope of regulation, in almost every case foreign investment laws and codes will cover the following areas: (1) restrictions on foreign investment in specified industry sectors; (2) limits on the percentage ownership by foreign investors in a project; and (3) controls and conditions.

■ RESTRICTIONS ON INVESTING IN SPECIFIED INDUSTRY SECTORS

In many cases, the foreign investment law will restrict foreign investment in one or more specified areas. At a minimum, foreign investment will be precluded in certain sectors deemed to be sensitive to national security and defense. Thus, it is common to find many countries restricting investments by foreigners in the areas of armaments or telecommunications. Even the United States, which historically has exercised little control over foreign investment activity, has adopted laws and regulations that authorize the President of the United States to review the purchase of certain United States businesses by foreign entities and, if necessary, to block the transaction, either prospectively or retroactively, for national security reasons.

To assist potential investors, the government will generally publish guidelines, with periodic revisions, that specify the areas within the local economy in which foreign capital will be permitted to operate. Often, the law will define such permitted areas in rather general terms, similar to the following: "foreign capital shall be permitted to invest in industrialization, mining, energy, tourism, transportation, and other fields." In other cases, the government will attempt to highlight certain areas in which foreign investment is specifically desired by formulating a separate set of investment laws and regulations that might apply to the chosen industry, such as an agricultural investment law, an industrial investment law, or a tourism investment law.

■ RESTRICTIONS ON PERCENTAGE OF FOREIGN OWNERSHIP

Some countries will limit the percentage of an enterprise that may be owned by a foreign investor, thereby creating the need to form a JV with local partners. JV requirements serve a number of different purposes for the local economy, including: (a) integration of the foreign partner and its assets and resources into the host country economy; (b) creation of local management skills and transfer of technology; (c) reduction in the risk of real or apparent foreign domination of the economy; (d) access by local interests to the foreign partner's international marketing network; (e) responsiveness to government policies; and (f) opportunity to assume control over the entire project, either through nationalization or negotiated purchase.

The exact nature of the JV requirement varies among countries and sectors. For example, some countries require all foreign investments to be made in the form of a JV, and local laws may restrict aggregate foreign ownership to no more than 49% of the equity interests in the project. Other countries adopt different standards with respect to the maximum permitted foreign investment percentage for various economic sectors. Accordingly, the regulations may allow a foreign investor to acquire a majority interest in a JV that will operate in a liberalized business sector, while limiting foreign participation to a minority interest in industries that the government believes must be controlled by local investors.

■ INVESTMENT CONTROLS AND CONDITIONS

Investment codes and related laws often impose certain controls and conditions on foreign investment projects. For example, foreign exchange and repatriation controls are frequently encountered, which may have the effect of limiting the availability of foreign exchange for debt servicing, repatriation of profits, payment of royalties, or the purchase of spare parts. Some investment codes provide for multiple exchange rates and allow certain transactions to take place at a more favorable rate than others. Other types of controls include government price controls, controls on labor and employment, prescribed debt-equity ratios, restrictions on the type of contributions to be made by the foreign investor to the JV (e.g., hard currency and/or absorbable technology), maximum limits on the reinvestment of profits or permissible rates of return, and local content requirements.

INCENTIVES AND GUARANTEES FOR FOREIGN INVESTORS

Countries have used a wide range of incentives and guarantees to induce foreign investment. These include tax and fiscal incentives; customs duty exemptions;

"free trade" zones, where a JV project will be exempt from customs duties and taxes on the condition that it does not service the local market; guarantees that similar foreign investments will not be approved for a certain period of time; government loan guarantees and debt servicing; subsidized factors of production; guarantees against nationalization and expropriation; special dispute settlement procedures; and grants.

■ TAX AND FISCAL INCENTIVES

Foreign investors are often given a choice among various tax and fiscal incentives. For example, one of the most common incentives is a "tax holiday" that effectively creates an exemption from local income and other taxes for a specified time, usually several years. Tax exemptions may also be available for property taxes and taxes on dividends, royalties, and interest payments that might otherwise be payable by the JV, the partners, or contractors of the JV.

■ CUSTOMS DUTY EXEMPTIONS

Customs duties are often quite high in developing countries. Accordingly, one attractive incentive for foreign investors is the right to import capital goods, spare parts, or raw materials at reduced tariff rates or under exemption from duties. In some cases, the exemption may be broad enough to cover personal and household goods of the JV's foreign employees.

■ PROTECTED MARKETS

As with any new business, the foreign party may have concerns about the possibility that imported goods from other countries will create undue competition for sales of products manufactured by the JV. This is a particular concern if low-cost producers are already available and able to funnel goods into the country. Many countries ease the concerns of foreign investors by granting the new JV an effective monopoly over the local market for a certain period of time by imposing quotas or high tariffs on competing foreign goods.

■ GOVERNMENT GUARANTEES

New JVs may be able to take advantage of the economic strength of the central government through the issuance of government guarantees of foreign loans made in connection with the JV. In addition, the government can arrange for assurances from the central bank that it will provide hard currency for use in servicing foreign loans to the JV.

■ SUBSIDIES

Countries often provide various subsidies to new JVs. For example, the government might guarantee the purchase of a certain volume of goods as a means for insuring that the JV will enjoy a minimum level of revenues. In addition, the government might arrange for the JV to purchase electric power at a reduced cost, or acquire undeveloped land at a price substantially below market. Foreign parties should be aware that many countries will not allow JVs with foreign partners to acquire freehold interests in land, although they will permit a long-term lease that may be subject to existing rights of local users.

■ SPECIAL DISPUTE SETTLEMENT PROCEDURES

One of the greatest concerns of foreign investors in considering an international JV is the possibility of becoming involved with an unfamiliar system of dispute resolution. Realizing this, countries are often willing to agree to special dispute settlement procedures that require any investment disputes with the investor to be turned over to international arbitration.

EXEMPTIONS FROM OTHER LAWS

Developing countries, particularly those with a socialist-based legal system, often have a variety of laws that are intended to regulate and control public and private sector activities. For example, it is not uncommon to find that the state has the authority to heavily regulate labor relations and pricing decisions. Many foreign investors might be justly concerned about the impact that these laws might have on the JV's business, and therefore the government may be willing to exempt JVs with foreign participation from these laws. Among the most likely candidates for relief are those rules that require labor participation in management and the distribution of a certain portion of profits to the employees of the enterprise.

PROCEDURAL CONSIDERATIONS

While a number of countries have established a single, centralized agency for the review and approval of proposed foreign investments, developing countries often use interministerial investment boards or commissions to coordinate foreign investment matters. Other structures involve simultaneous review by two or more agencies, such as the country's central bank, the ministry with responsibility for the particular industrial sector, and the agency charged with oversight of trade and business development.

Foreign investors and their local partners will usually be called on to provide a significant amount of data and information during the course of the application and review process. For example, in developing countries, it is common to find that all or most of the following information is needed:

- An investment and financial plan showing the amount of investment in external and local currencies.
- A production scheme indicating the annual volume and value of the production of the proposed JV.
- A services scheme, indicating the creation of services and the volume and value of the services intended to be rendered by the JV.
- An import and export plan indicating the anticipated volume of imports and exports emanating from the JV.
- Local inputs indicating the anticipated volume of raw materials to be used.
- An employment plan and forecast showing a program of training for local persons to acquire the requisite skills in the particular enterprise.
- A description of the industry to be established and the product to be produced.
- A description of the locality where the JV proposes to carry on such industry.
- The date that the proposed JV is to commence operations or the anticipated completion date for the JV project.

In supplying the required information, an effort should be made to demonstrate the anticipated benefits and advantages to the local economy. For example, the application can be used to demonstrate proposed increases in local training and in the level of employment; the active involvement and training of local management personnel; the transfer of new technology to the local company and its personnel; import substitution; and the investment of new capital from overseas. In addition, developing countries are particularly interested in evidence that the JV will increase exports and improve the country's balance of trade.

SANCTIONS

The sanctions and penalties for failure to comply with foreign investment laws are as diverse as the underlying laws and regulations themselves. Country-by-country variations can be found, as well as differences within a single country's laws reflecting the goal that the particular law or regulation is intended to serve. For example, a failure to register an infusion of foreign capital in a particular country may prevent the investor from repatriating any currency from the country in the future. If a technology transfer agreement is subject to investment regulations, failure to comply with registration and review requirements may invalidate the entire agreement. Finally, in some countries, any violation of the foreign investment laws can result in fines and other sanctions against the companies involved, or against individual officers, directors, and other managerial personnel.

PRACTICAL CONSIDERATIONS

A thorough understanding of, and sensitivity to, the administrative process in the host country is a key factor in successfully implementing a JV. Local practice, unwritten laws, administrative decisions, and changing events will all play an important role in this area, and therefore the assistance of local counsel and other local professionals is essential. The local partner should also be able to ease any difficulty in getting the project approved in a timely fashion.

Even with effective assistance, it may take a number of months, even years, for a new JV to finally be approved by each of the local agencies involved in the process. Delays of this type, as well as the possibility that local agencies will require substantial changes in the project, should be anticipated in the agreements between the parties. For example, the foreign party may bargain for the right to withdraw from the project unless approval is received within a specified period of time. Similarly, if the screening authority requires changes in the project that are materially adverse to one party, such changes might also allow that party to withdraw or renegotiate the basic terms of the agreement.

Antitrust and Competition Laws

A proposed JV may well be subject to scrutiny under antitrust and competition laws. The JV arrangement raises special consideration because it has a dual propensity for both procompetitive and anticompetitive effects. For example, joint venturers may be able to realize transactional efficiencies and share the costs and risks of the endeavor, thereby promoting competition by providing a means for new competition by companies that might not have entered the market on their own. On the other hand, if the joint venturers would have entered the market separately without the formation of the JV, then the affiliation might serve to eliminate the competition that otherwise would have existed between them.

Moreover, there are always concerns that the cooperation between the parties in the JV may lead to collusion or collateral restraints that are unrelated to the main purpose of the JV.

REGULATION OF JVS IN THE UNITED STATES

United States antitrust laws apply to the formation of JVs, assuming that the joint venturers acquire stock in the JV and/or the JV acquires assets from one or both of the joint venturers. Based on recent cases and statutory developments, the type of JV that is least likely to pose antitrust problems is a research and development JV, because its activities are typically at least a step or two removed from the level where the most significant amounts of competition might be expected to occur. Production JVs should also be subjected to relaxed treatment, particularly in light of the National Cooperative Research and Production Act of 1993. On the other hand, marketing JVs are the most likely type to raise antitrust problems, regardless of whether the JV is at the same time involved in research and development and production activities. Regulatory concerns may also turn on the scope of activities of the proposed JV, with single purpose JVs that have a limited focus (e.g., a JV to build a multibillion dollar hydroelectric plant) much less likely to raise official questions than a JV in which the venturers integrate all their activities in a particular field.

Depending on the circumstances, a new JV may be subject to the Hart-Scott-Rodino Antitrust Improvements Act of 1976 (the "HSR Act"), which provides that certain acquisitions of voting securities or assets may not occur unless prior notification has been filed with the Department of Justice ("DOJ") and the Federal Trade Commission ("FTC"), and the specified waiting period has expired. The waiting period ordinarily is 30 days, but may be either extended or shortened under certain circumstances by the DOJ or the FTC. The DOJ and the FTC have the right to request additional information or documents regarding the proposed transaction. If such a request is made, the waiting period is extended until 20 days following delivery of all of the supplemental information or documents to the appropriate agency.

REGULATION OF JVS IN THE EUROPEAN UNION

The competition policies of the European Union (EU) are central to the objectives of the EU itself, because they are designed to eliminate practices that interfere with the integration of the separate economies of the EU Member States into a single European market. In recent years, the European Commission, which has primary regulatory responsibility in this area, has appeared to revise its approach to analyzing and processing cooperative JVs. The Commission now seems to be making a more realistic and fact-based economic assessment of potential competition, looking at the extent to which any of the restrictions on competition that may be identified in the arrangement will have an appreciable effect on competition.

REGULATION OF JVS IN OTHER COUNTRIES

Competition regulation outside of the United States and the European Union varies substantially, and the content of those laws is largely dependent on the general industrial policies of the country and the overall competitiveness of its domestic firms. For example, in Japan, antitrust issues are considered under the terms of that country's Antimonopoly Law which, among other things, will prohibit any agreement or contract between foreign and Japanese entrepreneurs that contain any terms that amount to either an unreasonable restraint of trade or an unfair trade practice.

Developing countries are also working to develop laws designed to promote fair and effective competition among autonomous enterprises and ensure that the interests of consumers are protected without the need for direct state management of the enterprises or competition. In developing countries, the specific objectives of competition laws include the prevention of unfair competition in enterprise operations, particularly in market behavior; assurance that enterprise mergers do not create barriers to entry into the market; regulation of monopolies, which in developing countries can include not only natural monopolies but also sectors that remain controlled by the state or its affiliates; and protection of consumers against cartel-like behavior of enterprises.

Regulation of Technology Transfers

Many countries have enacted legislation regulating the content of technology transfer agreements, including license and technical assistance agreements. These regulations may be part of the country's foreign investment laws that deal with JVs, or may be separate laws administered by discrete agencies. In general, technology transfer laws are designed to foster the development of local technical capabilities and, in many cases, monitor the use of foreign exchange and the level of foreign involvement in the local economy. Regulations of this type may take a variety of different forms and are typically focused on the transfer of technology into the country, although a number of countries, particularly those that are more developed, have historically imposed some restrictions on exports that involve certain sensitive forms of technology.

As a general rule, technology transfer regulations operate by requiring the international technology agreement be submitted to, and approved by, a national administrative authority before the agreement becomes enforceable. Governmental bodies charged with reviewing technology transfer agreements often refer to statutory lists of objectionable business practices that must be excised from any agreement as a condition of approval. Among the most common areas of concern are royalty rates and other forms of remuneration, the scope and content of controls that the technology provider seeks to impose on the local transferee, the nature of any implied representations and warranties regarding the quality and performance of the transferred technology, the term of the agreement, governing law, and dispute resolution procedures. Local regulators may also evaluate the terms of the agreement in light of its potential effect on the development of the national economy.

Export Controls

Many countries have adopted statutes and regulations with respect to export controls, all of which are primarily intended to curb the worldwide proliferation of weapons of mass destruction and to prevent certain countries from obtaining goods and technology that may contribute to their military potential. While particular regulatory schemes may vary, they generally rely on a set of licensing procedures that must be satisfied before designated commodities, software, or technology can be exported to other countries, which might be the case when a party seeks to contribute such items to a JV in another country. The definition of technology for purposes of export controls is often broadly construed to include things such as technical assistance. In any event, the application of export controls must be considered before the JV is formed, particularly when the transferred technology might arguably be used for purposes that raise national security issues.

Customs Laws

Countries regulate the inward flow of goods through customs regulations. Customs laws serve a variety of purposes, including revenue collection through tariffs and other import fees, and the enforcement of regulations that have been specifically adopted with respect to imported goods, such as quotas, trade restrictions, antidumping laws, and country-of-origin marking requirements. Enforcement of customs laws also facilitates the collection of statistics on international trade and has become an important part of efforts to control the transfer of intellectual property and related technology. The impact of local customs laws on the ability of the parties to import goods and materials necessary for operation of the JV must be carefully considered. As mentioned above, some countries will grant exemptions for local customs duties as a way of inducing foreign investors to enter into local JVs.

CHAPTER 12

Financing and Insuring the JV

LIKE ANY NEW BUSINESS, a JV will require sufficient funding to conduct its operations. Generally, the primary source of initial financing will be the partners themselves. However, it may be necessary for the JV to borrow money from commercial lending institutions or public financing agencies.

External financing of the JV obviously creates a number of issues relative to the operation of the business. For example, the need to repay amounts received from outside funding sources will create a burden on current cash flow. It will almost always require that the parties agree to a security interest on the assets and properties of the JV, and to various restrictions on the prerogatives of the parties as owners and managers with respect to the business activities of the JV. In addition, external financing may be contingent on the availability of guarantees from each of the parties, a factor that should be taken into account at the outset of the JV. Finally, external financing may impair the ability of the parties to remove profits from the JV in the form of dividends.

Partners' Contributions

A primary motivating factor for forming a JV is the ability to access financing from one party to the JV. In many cases, the operations of the JV could, in fact, be wholly funded by one party; however, such a funding strategy may divert needed capital from other projects and create unacceptable levels of financial risk. The parties inevitably find themselves discussing the amount of equity capital that should be contributed to the JV, and the relative obligations of each of the parties with respect to such contributions. It is worth noting that some amount of equity capital is necessary to induce outside lenders to make loans to the JV. Equity is the cash cushion that lenders look to protect their own funds in the event that cash flow from operations is not sufficient to repay the loans.

A common place to begin the contribution discussions is with the anticipated funding that will be needed to begin operations. As the parties develop their strategic plan, consideration must be given to the amount of cash that will be needed to fund the launch of the JV and to take it through to the point where operations can be funded through retained earnings and bank borrowings. Once this amount is determined, the parties need to decide how the capital burden will be allocated.

The decision of the JV partners cannot be made without taking into account the value of other contributions that the parties might be making to the JV. For example, one of the partners might be providing valuable technology to the JV and, if so, the partner will want appropriate credit for the capital contribution in determining its overall equity interest in the JV. In light of these intangible assets, it is not uncommon for the ratio of cash contributions to vary substantially from the ratio of equity ownership agreed on by the parties for purposes of allocation and distribution of profits.

The timing of capital contributions also needs to be determined. In some cases, only a portion of the required cash will be contributed to the JV at the time of formation. Remaining amounts would be drawn down if and when the JV achieves various operational milestones. A portion of the cash commitment may take the form of a loan, as opposed to permanent equity. If so, the terms of these partner loans need to be determined at the outset. Generally, partner loans are intended to be temporary capital that will be replaced by external financing at some point in the future. Obligations to contribute actual cash to the JV may, in many cases, be supplemented by agreements to act as guarantors for the repayment of loans made to the JV by outside lenders, a topic that is discussed below.

Sources of External Financing

The parties should seriously consider the availability of external financing before entering into the JV. A variety of sources may be available, depending on the business activities of the JV and the geographic area where the JV's operations will be focused. Possibilities may include one or more of the following:

- COMMERCIAL LENDERS One or both of the parties may be able to access existing or new commercial lending relationships to secure a portion of the financing for the JV. While lenders in many developed countries have reduced their international loan exposure over the last few years, this trend is expected to change as companies look for opportunities in emerging markets. The availability of loans from local banks in developing countries depends, in large part, on the ability of the governments in those countries to create a suitable environment for private banking systems.
- EXPORT CREDITS Most developed countries have government-operated programs for loans or guarantees to support its exports. The terms of these programs will vary, and generally do not cover all the expenses of a particular project. Export credit programs typically include some form of political risk coverage for part of any commercial bank debt issued in connection with the particular project.
- MULTILATERAL LENDING INSTITUTIONS Low cost financing might be available through one of several official multilateral lending institutions, including the International Bank for Reconstruction and Development (i.e., the World Bank), the International Development Association, and the International Finance Corporation. Each of these agencies provides direct financing or co-financing for private sector projects, and may even make equity investment. Similar services are provided by several regional development banks, such as the Asian Development Bank in Manila and the Inter-American Development Bank in Washington.
- COUNTRY-ORIENTED DEVELOPMENT INSTITUTIONS These agencies provide project financing with regard to goods supplied from a particular country. In addition, they provide loans and guarantees for business ventures in developing countries involving participation by companies from a specific foreign country. Examples include AID (Agency for International Development) and the Export-Import Bank, both which are used by investors in the United States. These agencies discourage participation by local governments in the projects and typically require substantial developmental benefits.

- PRIVATELY OWNED DEVELOPMENT INSTITUTIONS Recognizing flaws in the policies of many of the publicly managed developmental institutions, a variety of private sector initiatives have been launched to encourage local business development in emerging markets. Examples include PICA in Asia and the ADELA Group in Latin America.
- ISSUANCE OF DEBT SECURITIES Depending on the country and the specific activities of the proposed JV, debt financing might be available through the issuance of bonds or debentures in a public or private offering. The main advantage of a bond issue is that the JV can secure a fixed interest rate and defer repayment to a future date, which is generally much longer than the maturities available through commercial lenders. However, international bond issues are often very difficult to complete, and typically carry substantial underwriting fees and commissions.

Commercial Bank Loans

Commercial bank loans are the most common source of external financing for a JV. Depending on the circumstances, the loan can be secured or unsecured, can involve a single lender or several, and can be designated for different purposes (e.g., construction, working capital etc.) Loans can be for a specific term, or can be in the form of a revolving line of credit subject to repayment and renewal at specified times over the term of the JV. Documents required for a commercial loan include a loan agreement, evidence of the indebtedness (e.g., promissory note), security documents, and guarantees. Key terms in the loan agreement include the amount of the loan, commitment fees, interest, repayment schedules, draw down procedures, representations and warranties, legal opinions, affirmative and negative covenants on the use of proceeds and the conduct of the business of the JV, and events of default.

ADVANTAGES AND DISADVANTAGES

Commercial bank loans have a number of advantages over other external financing sources. First and foremost, they can generally be negotiated quickly and with fewer conditions on implementation of the JV's project and the specific use of funds. In addition, commercial bank loans often contain multi-currency options that can provide the parties with some degree of flexibility in determining the currency used for repayment of the loan.

On the other hand, commercial loans may be more costly than funding from government-supported institutions. After all, banks will charge market rates for their funds and will also insist on a commitment fee. Moreover, commercial lenders generally have special project and country-risk lending limitations that may make it impossible to obtain all the funding necessary for the project to proceed. In addition, most loan agreements have fixed terms shorter than the expected life of the JV, which means that the parties must plan on the need to roll over, or refinance, the loan at least once.

LENDER'S CONSIDERATIONS IN EVALUATING THE PROJECT

While the parties may be convinced of the viability of the proposed JV, they need to consider how the prospective lender will analyze the project. Each of the key factors discussed below should be addressed in the JV's initial business plan and in the presentations made to loan officers.

LENDERS ONLY TAKE CREDIT RISKS

While the parties are willing to take equity risks in launching the JV, lenders are only interested in credit risks. As a general matter, lenders are not willing to accept higher risk in exchange for the possibility of a higher return. Instead, their primary concern is to limit their exposures to amounts that they reasonably believe will be repaid on schedule and with the agreed amount of interest.

The level of credit risk varies with the JV's development stage. During the start-up stage, the JV will be making substantial capital expenditures and incurring a large expense to develop its operational infrastructure. Because the JV may have little or no earnings during this period, and the success of the JV is very much in doubt, the credit risk for lenders asked to make loans to the JV at this stage will be quite high. Accordingly, while the lenders may be willing to defer repayment of principal, it will bargain for a higher rate of interest to compensate for the business risks. In contrast, once the JV is up and running and the JV's ability to meets its goals is clearer, the credit risk will be adjusted appropriately and the JV will find that it may be able to access a broader range of borrowings on more favorable terms.

THE BUSINESS PLAN MUST BE FINANCIALLY VIABLE

The importance of the JV's business plan has already been discussed in Chapter 10. One thing the plan can do is persuade lenders that the JV will be financially viable. While lenders will conduct their own credit analysis of the JV, they will look to the potential borrower to prepare and present appropriate feasibility, engineering, and market studies. The parties should be sure that the financial projections are based on reasonable assumptions regarding the availability and cost of materials and services, including local labor, energy, import and export duties, local materials, and transportation. In addition, the plan should establish that the JV's products and services can and will be produced at the costs, and marketed at the prices and profit margins, contemplated by the parties.

MANAGEMENT MUST BE RELIABLE

Although the primary concern of the lender will be the overall financial viability of the proposed activities, it will also look closely at the background and experience of the persons who will be involved in the day-to-day management of the JV. With respect to the chief executive and operating officers, the lender will want to know whether they have worked and managed in the specific country and industry. The chief financial officer will become a key player because he or she will have responsibility for monitoring use of the funds and fulfilling the periodic reporting requirements that are usually included in the loan documents.

THE TECHNOLOGY MUST BE ESTABLISHED

Lenders are reluctant to make loans for projects that are based on technology that is either obsolete or unproven. Obsolete technology can readily be overtaken by competitors, leading to reduced sales and the need for additional expenditures to develop or acquire technology that can keep pace in the marketplace. At the other end of the spectrum, technology that has not been used and proven in the specific marketplace raises significant concerns for lenders, even when the same or similar technology has been successful in other markets.

THE RIGHTS OF THE PARTIES SHOULD BE CLEARLY DEFINED

Lenders realize that the success or failure of a specific JV depends on the relationship between the owners. Although lenders rarely have an opportunity to observe the actual interactions of the parties during the negotiation of the terms of the JV and the operation of the business, they still can get some sense of the respective rights and duties of the parties by reviewing the venturers' agreement. Lenders are likely to be particularly concerned with the provisions relating to changes in participation percentages, withdrawal of partners, addition of new partners, duties of the partners with respect to service and capital contributions, defaults, dispute settlement, and voting rights and management.

■ REGULATORY AND POLITICAL RISK MUST BE REASONABLE

Commercial lenders are extremely sensitive to regulatory and political risks in the countries where the JV will be active. Banks and financial institutions will limit their exposure in countries where the laws and regulations fail to meet certain minimum standards of consistency and transparency. Beyond that, lenders will attempt to measure the possibility of certain events that might endanger their investment, including expropriation, problems of converting local currency, and political or civil unrest. The level of political risk will depend on the specific activities of the JV and the parties themselves. For example, JVs in natural resources are generally considered to be riskier than JVs in manufacturing because natural resources are depletable and perceived to be of greater importance to the country. On the other hand, the risk of expropriation for a JV based on the transfer of technology from a foreign party is arguably lower because the viability of the technology is dependent on the continued participation of the foreign party.

LOCAL BANKS

The parties need to carefully consider whether to seek a loan from a local bank (i.e., a bank organized and operated in the country where the JV will have its primary base of operations). Obviously, a number of factors need to be assessed, including the loan terms, the range of services offered, and the manner in which local bankers conduct business. In some cases, the range of local banking relationships includes local representatives of multinational banks.

Local banks can offer several advantages to the JV, including better access to information regarding the local economy and contacts among local institutions and individuals. This can be particularly important in those countries where business contacts are based on social relationships. Also, local bankers should have a better understanding of local business practices and the strategies that need to be followed in dealing with governmental agencies. As a general rule, local banks are more interested in providing short-term financing and mortgages, while the branches of multinational banks tend to focus on longer-term financing. In many situations, lending by local banks to approved international JVs is subsidized through the country's central bank.

On the other hand, there are corresponding disadvantages to local borrowing. First of all, the resources of local lenders are generally limited due to shortages of available funds and, in some cases, the local government's preference for restricting loans of local currency to enterprises that are wholly owned by local owners. Local banks are not a good source of foreign exchange borrowing, because they rarely have sufficient foreign currency on hand to meet the needs of the JV. In fact, local governments often encourage foreign borrowing as a way to bring foreign currency into the local economy. Local banks may also not be able to provide the full ranges of services that might commonly be required by an international enterprise, including letters of credit.

GUARANTEES

Guarantees from the JV partners are sometimes required in connection with a loan to the JV. In effect, the lender is advancing funds to the JV on the basis of the credit standing of one or both of the owners of the JV. While the lender will typically look first to the JV for repayment, it is ultimately the responsibility of the "parent" to make sure that the lender is made whole. Among the JV partners, guarantees create the greatest difficulties when one party is unable to provide a guarantee in proportion to its equity interest in the JV. In those situations, the other party may guarantee all or a disproportionate portion of the external financing and, in return, will be entitled to receive a fee from the non-guarantor calculated as a percentage of the outstanding borrowings. Alternatively, the guarantor's fee may be paid out of income generated by the JV and the other party may agree to indemnify the guarantor for losses suffered as a result of assumption of the obligations under the guarantee.

Not surprisingly, the parties generally prefer to keep guarantees to a minimum, even though the guarantee might allow the JV to obtain better loan terms. One reason, of course, is that a JV is often seen as being a riskier undertaking than other projects the party might have going in its home country, and the party may simply prefer to use its credit standing for other purposes. In addition, the need to provide a guarantee is inconsistent with the guiding principle that the JV should be able to stand on its own in order to be a suitable investment choice for the party. That said, some larger firms will provide a guarantee of a portion of the JVs borrowings as a way to avoid including extensive covenants in the loan documents; however, the ability of the parent to provide a guarantee is often limited by covenants in their own agreements with lenders and the need to make disclosures to shareholders.

Insurance

A JV raises the same fundamental insurance issues as any other business. For example, the parties need to consider insurance coverage on the assets and properties used in the business, as well as protection against product liability claims. Business interruption insurance is advisable to cover situations in which the JV is unable to operate. In addition, depending on the circumstances, key person life insurance might be necessary when one or more individuals are considered to be essential to the success of the JV.

A specific issue for the foreign parties is the need to purchase political risk insurance. There are a number of political risk insurance programs available through multilateral institutions such as the World Bank (including the International Finance Corporation), regional development banks, foreign government political risk insurance agencies, and private political risk insurers. Many companies prefer to deal with government-related agencies, such as OPIC in the United States, because of their experience in assistance of foreign parties in disputes with host governments.

In any event, several types of political risk insurance might be necessary in a given situation, including: (1) inconvertibility coverage (against problems with exchange control laws, regulations, practices and procedures), (2) expropriation coverage (against nationalization, confiscation, and material changes in contracts unilaterally imposed by the host government, so-called "creeping expropriation"), and (3) political violence coverage (against physical damage and loss of business income due to war and civil strife).

CHAPTER 13

Forming the Joint Venture

ACTUAL FORMATION OF THE JV will typically occur at a "closing," which occurs at a time specified in the definitive agreement for the JV. At the closing, the parties will make their promised contributions to the JV and deliver various certificates and legal opinions as required by the agreement. It is an event characterized by intense activity and, in many cases, resolution of final issues that had been ignored (or avoided) until just before closing. While it is possible for the transaction to close contemporaneously with execution of the agreement, as a general rule some period of time will pass between signing and closing.

Managing the Formation Process

Successful completion of the formation of a JV requires careful planning and coordination among all the parties. Coordination responsibility typically falls on legal counsel because the other parties lack the necessary training, experience, and overall perspective to identify all the tasks and to ensure their correct completion. Counsel will most often take the following organizational steps:

- Compile and maintain a list of all persons involved in the transaction, including addresses, phone numbers, fax numbers, and email addresses;
- Prepare and circulate a time and responsibility schedule that lists the tasks that need to be completed and assign responsibility for each task, including due dates;
- Schedule periodic "all hands" conferences to review the time and responsibility schedule and discuss potential problems that might impact the timetable; and
- Implement a procedure for monitoring progress on obtaining governmental approvals and third-party consents.

Legal counsel may take several other actions to ensure that the closing goes smoothly. First, a "pre-closing" may be held on a day prior to the closing date to go through all the documents and make sure that nothing is missing or mistakenly recorded. Some documents can even be signed at the pre-closing and held for delivery on the closing date. Second, counsel should prepare a closing memorandum to track the steps needed to complete the transaction.

Venturers' Agreement

The formation of the JV, as well as its operation following formation, is typically driven by a single definitive agreement between the parties that lays out all the essential economic and management terms of their relationship. This document is referred to here generically as the "venturers' agreement." It will actually be a shareholders' agreement if the JV is a corporation, or a partnership

Checklist: Drafting a Venturers' Agreement

The following checklist enumerates information that should be collected to draft a venturers' agreement for a JV. The checklist covers the major areas of negotiation and discussion with respect to a JV, including formation, capitalization, representations and closing matters, management and control, operations, and termination. Each of these topics are discussed in detail in other chapters of this book. A sample Venturers' Agreement can be found in Chapter 18.

Identify the parties, including the venturers, their affiliates, and the entity itself.

Describe the business purpose of the JV. As appropriate, the parties may need to consider business plans for various functional areas, including development, manufacturing, distribution, and marketing.

Determine the JV's legal address, name, principal office, and fiscal year.

Decide on the capital structure of the JV (e.g., a single class of ownership interests, or perhaps a second class with preferential rights). If a corporate form is selected, the parties will need to draft additional documents, such as articles or certificates of incorporation and bylaws.

Establish the procedures for initial capital contributions and the issuance of ownership interests.

Determine the procedures to be followed for raising additional capital, including contributions and/or guarantees from one or both of the venturers, and outside financing from investors and/or banks.

Identify the representations and warranties to be provided by the venturers, and determine the scope of the indemnification obligations of each of the venturers.

Determine the procedures for nominating and electing the members of the management board and the officers of the JV.

Decide which actions will require the consent of both venturers.

Choose a preferred dispute resolution mechanism (e.g., mediation and/or arbitration) and establish appropriate procedures.

Establish procedures for accounting and internal controls, including preparation and delivery of financial information to the venturers.

Determine policies regarding distribution of income and application of funds.

Determine the nature and scope of any restrictions on the outside activities of the venturers, as well as their ability to transfer ownership interests in the JV or to withdraw from the JV.

Determine the JV's anticipated term, events that might cause early termination, and the procedures to be followed at the time of liquidation.

agreement if the JV is organized as a general or limited partnership. Technically, the venturers' agreement starts as a preformation agreement between the parties, and the entity becomes a party to the agreement once it is formed.

The venturers' agreement (see Chapter 18) provides that the parties will take all actions necessary to form the JV entity. It covers capital contributions, management and operation, transfers of ownership interests and dissociation of the parties, dispute resolution procedures, and termination of the JV, all of which are discussed in other chapters. The balance of the discussion here covers items that are most relevant to formation of the JV, including representations and warranties, indemnification, closing conditions, pre-closing covenants, and events that might cause termination of the agreement prior to closing.

REPRESENTATIONS AND WARRANTIES

Representations and warranties are important in any commercial transaction, and are usually supplemented by a legal and commercial due diligence investigation calculated to provide independent verification of statements made by the parties regarding their existing business activities and their plans and intentions regarding the proposed JV. In the commercial context, a representation is a statement of fact on the faith of which the recipient is induced to enter into a contractual relationship, while a warranty is an undertaking that the represented fact is, or will be, true and correct. Covenants are distinguishable from representations in that they usually imply a party's promise of future action.

Representations and warranties may be made in various contexts in the course of a particular transaction. Generally, each party will be required to make a number of representations and warranties to the other party in the documentation relating to the formation and operation of the JV. However, it is not unlikely that additional documents and information, including oral statements, will pass between the parties in the course of negotiations relating to the transaction. To the extent that these items are factual and are made with the intent to induce the other party to enter into the relationship, they will constitute additional representations and warranties.

It will be a condition to closing the transaction that all the representations and warranties made by the parties are true and correct as of the closing. In some cases, the agreement will be signed at or just before the closing, which means that the representations will be fairly current. However, when an extended period of time elapses between the date of signing and the closing, each representation should be carefully reviewed again. If a representation has become inaccurate, the representing party will need to disclose any inaccuracies to the other party. Such disclosures are commonly made through a schedule of exceptions that become part of the agreement. A brief description of some of the more common representations and warranties follows below:

ORGANIZATION AND STANDING

Each party will represent that it is duly organized, validly existing, and in good standing under the laws of its state or nationality of organization, and that it has the requisite legal power and authority to conduct its present business activities and to enter into and perform its obligations with respect to the JV.

- **DUE AUTHORIZATION**

Each party will represent that the consummation of the JV, including each document associated with it, has been duly authorized and approved by all necessary corporation action, which usually includes the approval of the party's board of directors or analogous management body. The parties will further represent that the JV documents will create legally binding obligations on them.

- **NO CONFLICT WITH EXISTING AGREEMENTS**

A party is unlikely to be asked to make a representation regarding its compliance with the terms of various material contracts relating to its preexisting business activities, but each party will usually represent that the transaction does not conflict with or constitute a default under the terms of any material contract to which it is a party or its properties are subject or bound.

- **LEGAL RIGHTS IN CONTRIBUTED ASSETS AND PROPERTIES**

When one or both of the parties will be transferring property or intangible assets to the JV, either in the form of an outright capital contribution or in a separate supply, lease, or license agreement, it is essential to obtain a representation that the party has good and valid legal title in and to the items to be transferred and/or licensed to the JV. Moreover, the party should make a representation that accurately describes the legal rights that the JV will have in the transferred assets, particularly as they might relate to the actual or potential rights of third parties. The representation itself should be expansive and include facts that tend to support the assertion of title in the assets, such as the absence of any litigation or claims relating to the party's ownership rights in the assets and ongoing compliance requirements necessary to perfect its ownership interest in the property (e.g., filing of patent applications).

- **REGULATORY MATTERS**

Each party should make representations with respect to the absence of any violations of statutes or ordinances relevant to their current or proposed business activities. In particular, it is important to ensure that the party will not be precluded from performing designated services on behalf of the JV due to its failure to comply with local laws and restrictions.

- **DISCLOSURE-RELATED REPRESENTATIONS AND WARRANTIES**

A number of documents and oral statements are likely to pass between the parties in the course of negotiations. To ensure that each party is held accountable for any such representations, even those not formally included in the formation documents, it is generally appropriate to include a representation and warranty from each party to the effect that no explicit representation or warranty of the party, nor any exhibit, document, statement, certificate, or schedule furnished by the party in the course of the negotiations, has contained any untrue statement of a material fact or has omitted to state a material fact necessary to make the statements not misleading.

The inclusion of an omnibus representation covering all aspects of disclosure made during the course of negotiations should have a sobering effect on the planning efforts necessary to commence operations of the JV. Because a preliminary business plan will often be incorporated into the formation documents, any projections or assumptions prepared by the parties may become the subject of dispute between them under the guise of misrepresentation after the

Checklist: Closing Procedures for the JV

The actual formation and organization of a JV company generally takes place at a closing coordinated by the lawyers for both parties. The date and time of the closing should be established by the parties in advance, and all necessary documents (e.g., assignments, share certificates, and legal opinions) should be ready for signature well in advance of that date. The obligation of each party to close the transaction will be subject to satisfaction of various conditions set forth in the letter of intent or the venturers' agreement. Other matters that need to be completed at the closing include the following:

If not done prior to closing, execution of the venturers' agreement by all parties, including a representative of the new company itself.

Delivery of a so-called "compliance certificate" from each party that it has satisfied all of its pre-closing covenants.

Delivery of a certificate from each party that its representations and warranties in the venturers' agreement remain true and correct.

Resolution of any litigation relating to formation and operation of the JV.

Delivery of satisfactory opinions from counsel for each of the parties.

Proper composition of the managing board, as provided in the venturers' agreement.

Receipt of all necessary regulatory approvals.

Confirmation that the monetary contributions from the parties have been received in the JV's bank account or in an escrow account.

Executed copy of the documentation necessary to effect any required transfer of technology or tangible assets by the parties to the JV.

Certified copies of the JV's charter documents and organizational minutes.

In the case of a corporation, the completion and delivery of the share certificate(s) for the shares to be issued to each of the parties.

Executed copies of any ancillary agreements required for the formation and operation of the JV, such as a development agreement, license agreement, and services agreement.

JV is formed. Accordingly, it is important for the parties to focus on candor in preparing these documents, with each party achieving an appropriate level of comfort regarding the potential risks associated with making specified representations and warranties.

INDEMNIFICATION

While the representations and warranties from each party are intended to facilitate the appropriate level of due diligence prior to the formation of the JV, they do carry with them the potential for liability between the parties in the event that any of the representations and warranties prove to be false or misleading in light of events that occur following the consummation of the transaction. Although each party would be liable to the other for any fraudulent act or statement made during the course of the formation and operation of the JV, it is often deemed appropriate to include specific provisions governing indemnification obligations with respect to deficiencies in the representations and warranties.

Although an action for fraud will generally survive any time limit imposed in the JV documentation, the parties will usually agree that the representations and warranties will survive for a specified period following the consummation of the transaction. The period may be established to conform with the statute of limitations under applicable law, or may be tied to a specific technical or financial milestone relating to the JV's activities. It is also possible to single out areas of particular concern with respect to which great uncertainties exist, and to establish specific procedures relating to future risks associated with matters covered by one or more representation or warranty.

As a general matter, each party will agree to indemnify the other party with respect to damages, losses, and liabilities suffered by the indemnified party as a result of any material misstatement, error, or omission contained in any of the representations and warranties delivered by the indemnifying party. The documentation will set forth procedures with respect to the indemnification, including notice provisions and, in most cases, the indemnifying party will have the right to assume the defense of any action for which indemnification is available. If the indemnifying party assumes defense of the action and pursues such defense in good faith without materially impairing the financial condition of the other party, the liability of the indemnifying party will usually be limited to the amount of any final adverse judgment.

CLOSING CONDITIONS

The venturers' agreement will typically contain various conditions to the obligations of both parties to consummate the transaction. In many cases, the conditions will be identical, such as the completion of any required regulatory review of the transaction, and receipt of legal opinions and officers' certificates from the other party. One party, typically the foreign party, may bargain for additional closing conditions to protect itself against unforeseen discoveries during the due diligence investigation. For example, the foreign party may have the right to terminate the agreement if its investigation raises uncertainties about the local party's ability to distribute the JV's products. A party will not be obligated to close the transaction if all of the appropriate conditions have not been satisfied, but a party may waive a condition at its discretion.

COVENANTS

In some cases, the parties will not execute the venturers' agreement until just before the scheduled closing. If, however, the venturers' agreement is signed in advance of the closing, it is likely that it will include one or more covenants from the parties regarding activities during the period leading up to the closing. For example, one or both of the parties may undertake to obtain regulatory approvals, and the parties may be obligated to refrain from entering into negotiations with other parties with respect to a transaction that has the same purpose as the proposed JV. A party's failure to perform a covenant may lead to termination of the agreement and/or damages. Each party will be required to certify to the other party at closing that it has complied with all covenants included in the agreement.

TERMINATION

Of course, the parties naturally anticipate that all conditions to closing will be satisfied in a timely fashion, but each party typically reserves the right to terminate the agreement prior to closing on the occurrence of certain events. The most common termination provision allows the parties to call off the deal if the closing has not been completed by a specific date. The "drop-dead" date is selected after taking into account how long it may take to satisfy any conditions to closing, such as completion of regulatory review. The agreement may terminate automatically on the specified date or the parties may be given an option to terminate the agreement if the date passes. Termination also may be available if a specified condition to closing has not been satisfied.

Government Filings

Typically, government filings will be required in connection with the formation of the JV. Procedures vary substantially from country to country, and the parties should obtain competent advice from counsel on the specific requirements and the amount of time that will be required for all approvals to be obtained. If the success of the JV depends on the ability of one or both of the parties to secure various governmental approvals, it is important to develop a schedule setting forth each of the steps that are anticipated to be necessary to complete the regulatory process, including a timetable that can be compared to the amount of other resources that are to be devoted to the JV. Once the procedures are understood, inquiry should be made into the content and quality of the experience that the relevant party has with the subject agency, including prior correspondence and the results of past efforts to secure the same, or analogous, approvals. It is often useful to seek the advice of competent local counsel as to expected difficulties in the regulatory process within the country where the JV will operate.

Ancillary Agreements and Documents

Depending on the size and complexity of the operations of the proposed JV, the venturers' agreement will be supplemented by a number of ancillary agreements and documents attached to the agreement as schedules or exhibits. Key ancillary agreements, such as license agreements, service agreements, distribution agreements, and real and personal property leases are explained in greater detail in Chapter 15. Such agreements are usually included as exhibits to the venturers' agreement and will be signed at the closing.

Other documents that may need to be prepared include a disclosure schedule for each of the parties that set out any exceptions to, or supplemental information for, the representations and warranties made in the venturers' agreement; promissory notes and security documents if part of the capital contribution will be made in the form of a deferred payment obligation; and any internal rules and procedures for operation of the JV (e.g., bylaws for a corporation).

Cash Contributions

The parties need to establish a bank account for the JV prior to closing, to receive cash contributions to be made by the parties. As appropriate, wire transfer instructions should be issued to the parties. In some cases, funds may be wired into an escrow account opened and held by counsel for the JV pending resolution of all issues and satisfaction of any conditions to closing.

Closing Documents

At closing, the parties will exchange the documents necessary to form the JV, including signature pages to each of the documents, certifications from officers of each of the parties, and legal opinions from counsel to one or both of the parties.

CLOSING CERTIFICATES

The closing will include deliveries of a number of different certificates from the principals of each of the parties and public officials. The forms of these certificates have become standardized over the years, but counsel may have some special requirements regarding drafting that should be brought up prior to the closing date. Common certificates from public officials include:

- Legal and tax good standing certificates from the jurisdiction where each party's entity is organized.
- Certified copies of organizational documents on file with the appropriate regulatory authority for each of the parties.
- Notices from each governmental authority having jurisdiction over formation of the JV.

Because it may take some time to gather the certificates from public officials, they should be ordered well in advance of the closing. It is common to accept certificates that have been issued within three to five days prior to the closing provided that the officers certify that no changes have been made since the date of the certificate from the public official. Information in public official certificates is often updated by telegram or telephone call as of the date of the closing.

THIRD PARTY CONSENTS AND PERMISSIONS

Consents or permissions from third parties may be required in connection with the formation of the JV. For example, whenever a party is transferring any property rights to the JV, consents may need to be obtained from landlords, licensors, and creditors. Approval of the JV may be required from a third-party lender, even if a party is not transferring assets, because the operation of the JV may constitute a material change in the party's business. In any event, both of the parties should examine all the material contracts and agreements, including leases, government contracts, collective bargaining agreements, permits, and consent decrees, to determine whether a third party's consent or approval is required.

TRANSFER DOCUMENTS

Legally sufficient documents of transfer should be delivered to complete the contribution of assets from the parties to the JV. For example, a bill of sale will be used to transfer ownership of personal property, deeds of trust will be necessary to transfer real property, and assignments will be used for transfers of leases, contract rights, and intangible property. The parties should be sure that all recording and publication requirements associated with the transfer are satisfied.

LEGAL OPINIONS

It is customary for each party to request an opinion of counsel from the attorney for the other party with respect to various matters relating to the other party and the proposed transaction. The scope of the opinion should be agreed on in advance, and parties need to take into account differences among lawyers around the world with regard to the form and content of legal opinions. Typically, the legal opinion will cover the legal good standing of the party, its power to enter into the transaction, the validity and enforceability of the party's obligations under the terms of the various agreements relating to the JV, the party's title to assets that it will contribute to the JV, and the absence of any litigation relating to the JV, or conflicts with other agreements to which the party is subject. A party may also request a tax opinion covering the tax treatment of contributions to the JV and distributions that the party expects to receive from the JV in the future.

Postclosing Actions

Once the closing is completed, formal operation of the JV begins. For this process to proceed smoothly, the parties should be sure that all documents are recorded, and that timely notice is provided to regulators, lenders, and others having an interest in the launch of the JV. Arrangements should be made to complete the full transfer of ownership and control of contributed assets, including shipping, storage, installation, and training of local employees. The parties will need to organize all their files, document any last minute oral agreements between them that may have been made at the closing, and distribute definitive copies of all the documents so that each party has a record of the proceedings.

CHAPTER 14

Management and Control of the JV

ONE OF THE MOST IMPORTANT MATTERS to be negotiated between JV parties is the devising of an appropriate structure for management and control of the entity. The relative interests of the parties in the JV's profits need not dictate the degree of actual control exercised by the parties. Although a majority interest in the profits of the enterprise might well mandate the assumption of control, in some situations the nature of the party's contribution to the enterprise, or local laws, may require that the party with a minority interest in the profits of the JV will be in control of certain of the JV's activities.

Generally, each party is given the right to designate one or more representatives to act as members of a managing board (e.g., a board of directors if the JV is organized in a corporate form). In addition, either as a matter of law or by contract, each party will have voting rights on matters of importance to the JV. The JV, as a separate entity, may contract with one or both parties to conduct specific functions or services; this can include research and development, manufacturing, or distribution. As a result of these contractual arrangements, one party effectively assumes control over a material aspect of the JV's operations, even though nominal authority remains in the JV's managing board.

Factors for Consideration in Allocating Control

Several different factors need to be considered in the course of allocating control of the JV, including the functional and operational objectives of the JV, the level within the organizational structure at which decisions should be made and responsibilities placed, the degree to which the success of the JV is depending on the use of "shared control," or unanimous voting requirements, the key commitments of each of the parties, and the major business and technical milestones that must be achieved for the venture to prosper.

FUNCTIONAL AND OPERATIONAL OBJECTIVES

The parties should focus on the key functional and operational objectives of the JV and attempt to allocate responsibilities in a manner that takes into account which party possesses the requisite expertise necessary for achieving those objectives. In most cases, control should be allocated in relation to the respective substantive contributions of the parties to the venture, but the nonexpert party must be given the opportunity to review major actions proposed by the controlling party. Therefore, a party contributing technology to the enterprise should have the primary right to control its use in development efforts, and a party with responsibility for sale and distribution should be given primary authority over various marketing matters, with an overall review and approval procedure.

LEVEL OF DECISION-MAKING

Serious consideration must be given to the appropriate scope of authority to be exercised by the venturers, members of the managing board (refereed to as directors), and the officers and managers of the venture. If the success of the venture depends on its ability to move rapidly to exploit opportunities in the local marketplace, it probably makes sense to delegate a good deal of discretion to the officers and managers of the venture, with the role of the directors and venturers being confined to periodic performance reviews. Alternatively, if development of the venture involves completion of a series of tasks or the purpose of the venture is the exchange of functional knowledge and expertise, an effort should be made to establish shared decision-making procedures.

NEED FOR SHARED CONTROL

The parties must consider the affect of shared control requirements (that is, provisions that require that both parties must approve specified actions) will impact the day-to-day actions of the venture and its ability to achieve the goals and objectives specified in its business plan. While shared control might appear to be an attractive means for easing concerns that might exist at the commencement of the relationship, the practical effect of such an arrangement might be to divert attention from the objectives of the venture to burdensome procedural measures that are of little consequence to effective management of the business. As a general rule, it is probably better for the parties to limit the areas in which the shared control requirement will apply to those that have a material impact on their ability to protect their interests in the JV.

KEY COMMITMENTS AND PERFORMANCE MILESTONES

Control is best understood in the context of identifying the crucial financial and technical commitments of the venture, as well as the manner in which the performance of the venture is to be monitored and assessed. In the course of developing the overall strategic business plan for the venture, care must be taken to identify material and largely irreversible commitments of cash and other resources, as well as the key technical and financial objectives of the venture. Each item provides an opportunity to assess the management and control of the venture and should require close consultation and agreement between the parties. In some cases, it may be appropriate to abandon or modify the original business plan, or transfer control of the venture from one party to another.

Allocating Control in "50-50" JVs

The parties are free to establish and maintain any appropriate distinctions between their interest in the assets and profits of the venture on the one hand and their right to exercise control over the operations of the venture on the other. For example, parties that each contribute a relatively equal amount of cash and assets to the JV and that agree to share profits and distributions equally (i.e., "50-50") may nonetheless allocate control over certain decisions in a manner that departs from shared control.

Seven Principles for Successful Meetings

At this point in the JV formation process, additional members of the management team are likely to be invited to participate in the discussion and decisions. Assuming the JV has international partners, the room will be full of distinctly different personalities from disparate cultures and business traditions. It will be important to build a successful JV management team quickly and efficiently, a process that can be facilitated if you know and practice the following principles:

1. DEFINE A SPECIFIC PURPOSE The purpose of a meeting should be clearly and specifically defined in advance so that the discussion is organized and focused, the attendees can be adequately prepared, and positive results can be realized and implemented. Most likely, you will need to have a series of meetings, starting with introductory briefings and then progressively dealing with the management issues relevant to the particular JV.
2. SCHEDULE SUFFICIENT TIME A meeting is not productive if discussions are rushed, and even cut off, for lack of time. Set the time for each agenda item in advance. Keep discussions on point and table issues if the flow becomes circular. If attendees speak different languages, add extra time to account for translators. If there is not enough time, you have probably not defined the purpose with sufficient precision.
3. PREPARE AND DISTRIBUTE A WRITTEN AGENDA IN ADVANCE Request the key attendees to contribute to the meeting agenda. Develop a written agenda and distribute it to all attendees well in advance of the meeting. Place issues that require creativity at the top of the agenda and those that take less thought at the end.
4. LEARN ABOUT THE PEOPLE ATTENDING Take time to get to know the attendees and their local cultures and customs. Find out their names and titles. Observe their personalities in advance and prepare strategies to preclude potential clashes at the table. Be certain to acknowledge the principals or department heads, because they will tend to set the tone for communications. Progress in the meeting is likely to depend on their support.
5. KEEP THE VENUE COMFORTABLE Provide a comfortable meeting place. Avoid violating basic cultural taboos about food, flowers, or colors. Eliminate potential distractions, hardships, and hazards to keep the attendees more attentive, peaceful, committed, and productive. Use place cards to assign seats, and make sure that the names are clearly readable to facilitate introductions and discussions.
6. PRECLUDE DELAYS AND DISTRACTIONS Passing out reference materials during a meeting is a distraction. Prepare a packet for each attendee in advance, and be certain to include common supplies such as pencils, pens, and paper pads. Test equipment in advance and plan to have extra parts, and even replacement equipment, immediately on hand.
7. PROVIDE IMMEDIATE SUPPORT STAFF Have a reliable administrative assistant on hand, specially selected for cultural awareness, quiet proficiency, and quick trouble-shooting. Prior to the meeting, train that person in protocol, professional demeanor, and expected duties. Establish a set of signals to allow for silent communication that will not disturb the meeting.

SEPARATE CLASSES OF OWNERSHIP INTERESTS

For a corporate JV, each party might be issued a separate class of stock with distinct rights to vote on the election of directors, as well as on other matters relating to the business entity. For example, one party might be issued a class of stock with the right to elect a majority of the members of the board of directors, while the other party might be issued a class of stock with rights to elect the remaining board members and to approve specific corporate actions. Alternatively, some parties may hold nonvoting stock, while others may hold a different class of voting stock, but the proportional economic interest in the profits of the venture can nevertheless reflect the value of each party's contribution. Local corporate law may well require separate class votes on a number of matters, although the parties are usually free to expand the list provided by statute. Similar devices might be used when the JV is organized in another entity form, as long as applicable law permits creation of two or more classes of ownership interests.

DESIGNATION AGREEMENT

The parties might enter into a contractual agreement providing for the right of each party to designate specific officers and managers of the JV. For example, one party might be given the right to designate the chief executive officer, and the other might be given the right to designate the chief financial or technical officer.

BOARD SUBCOMMITTEES

Even if the parties share nominal control of the management board, they might agree to delegate decisions in specified areas to a subcommittee of the board controlled by the party having expertise in that area. For example, decisions regarding research and development might be left to the chief technical officer of the JV, who in turn is appointed by the party with expertise in that area, together with a board subcommittee of representatives of the appropriate party.

Allocating Control in "Non-50-50" JVs

While we have assumed that the parties have an equal interest in the profits of the JV, often one party will have a greater interest in the profits. If three or more parties own the JV, at least one may have a profit interest that is less than that of the others. Nevertheless, the same mechanisms used in 50-50 JVs can be used to permit a party with a minority profit interest to exercise effective control of the JV. Likewise, local law may provide certain voting rights to minority owners that effectively grant them the right to veto actions taken by the majority owner, either directly or by virtue of the right of the minority owners to demand an appraisal of the value of their ownership interests and the repurchase of their interest at that value by the JV.

Size and Composition of the Management Board

If the JV is formed as a corporation, responsibility for the overall management of the business will lie with a board of directors as a matter of corporate law. But, even if the parties do not elect to use the corporate form, it is common to create a body similar in form and authority to a board of directors, perhaps referred to as a management board, board of managers, or even a board of directors. The venturers will each appoint at least one member of the board, and the venturers' agreement will specify the basic structural elements of the board, including the number of members, quorum requirements and, if appropriate, any special requirements with respect to the composition of the board.

The appropriate size of the managing board will depend on the need to comply with legal requirements, as well as the intent of the parties as to the optimal composition of the body. The parties should try to ensure that each board member can make a specific contribution to the operation of the enterprise. The number of members should be set at a level that permits meaningful communication plus effective and timely decisionmaking.

SENIOR EXECUTIVES OF VENTURERS

It may be appropriate to require one or more senior executives of each party to serve on the board, at least during the sensitive start-up stage. The presence of senior management develops a sense of commitment on the part of the parties, and ensures that the activities of the venture are given proper attention within the organizational scheme of the parent companies.

FUNCTIONAL AND GEOGRAPHIC EXPERTISE

Each party should make an effort to ensure that its designees have specific experience in the functional or geographic areas where the venture will be operating. For example, a party that is contributing technical knowledge to the venture might consider designating a member who is conversant with the technology and who can assess the success of the technology transfer. Similarly, a member with experience in the local market or with local customs can ease the burden of communication with managers and directors of the local party.

PRIMARY BUSINESS ACTIVITIES OF VENTURE

As the venture develops, the composition of the board should reflect its changing business activities, as well as any changes in the structure or organization of the parent companies. A shift in emphasis from development to distribution may create a need for different personnel on the board. Also, one party may reorganize its own internal structure, thereby causing responsibility for a given product or function to change. For example, a shift in organizational focus from geographic markets to product line may diminish the autonomy of foreign JVs. In those cases, it is important to ensure that the board members selected by that party continue to be able to articulate the needs of the venture within the new organization.

LOCAL REPRESENTATIVES

If required by law or local custom, it may be necessary or appropriate to appoint members of the local business community or government representatives to serve on the board. The presence of unaffiliated board members obviously raises the need to consider the effect on the control of the board. If such a member is appointed, an effort should still be made to assess the contribution that he or she might make to the resources and activities of the venture.

KEY MANAGERS OF THE VENTURE

Consideration should be given to selecting key managers of the JV to serve on the board. For example, the chief executive and operating officers of the JV might be included as board members, because these persons have also previously been selected by the joint venturers themselves. It may also be useful to appoint a representative of local factory suppliers, particularly if heavy dependence is to be placed on the availability of the local labor force.

CHAIRMAN OF THE BOARD

In determining the composition of the board, consideration should be given to the designation of the chairperson. If a chairperson's position is created, thought should be given to rotating the authority to designate the chair between the parties. The authority of the chairperson is usually limited to certain ceremonial matters, such as presiding at the various board meetings. However, it may be appropriate to expand the role of the chairperson to include responsibilities relating to key aspects of the overall planning and management of the enterprise, including the development of the strategic business plan, and the coordination of functional activities delegated to each of the parties.

Control of the Management Board

Although the parties may impose supermajority voting requirements as to certain matters, actions by the board generally require the vote or consent of a majority of its members. Accordingly, the ability of one party to designate a majority of the members of the board in effect allows it to control the JV's daily operations. Any number of mechanisms exist for allocating effective control of the board, including the following:

1. One party is given the right to designate such number of members as might be necessary to control the board. For example, the party would have the right to designate three members of a five person board.
2. One party is given the right to control the board, subject to the requirement that certain actions cannot be taken without the consent of all board members. This may be the most appropriate structure for a JV, because it vests in one party the ability to initiate actions and manage the venture, while preserving appropriate protection for the non-controlling party.
3. One party is given the right to control the board pursuant to one of the above procedures, but provision is made for a shift in control on the occurrence of one or more events specified by the parties.
4. The parties share control of the board, but provision is made for a shift of control to one party at some point during the development of the venture.
5. The parties provide for one or more mutually selected independent board members, and implement a voting procedure that vests final decision-making authority in those members when the parties are unable to reach a consensus. However, finding persons who are willing to arbitrate disputes between the parties may be difficult, and the parties may have to resort to third-party arbitration procedures.

Shifting Control of the Management Board

The JV's changing needs mandate that the parties give serious consideration to providing for a mechanism to shift effective control of the board to one party after the passage of a specified period of time or on occurrence of one of several specified events. While such vote switch procedures will allow one party to elect a majority of the board, they need not necessarily alter the respective interests of the parties in the profits of the JV. Depending on the circumstances, a change in control of the board may be accompanied by corresponding changes in the scope of authority provided to the body in the organizational documents of the JV.

A change or assumption of control of the board on a certain specified date is not necessarily a punitive action, but may simply recognize the development and maturation of the JV and its activities. For example, if the business plan contemplates an initial period of joint development activities, it would seem logical that the parties should share in the control of the JV during that period, particularly if one of the objectives of the enterprise is to ensure appropriate transfer of technology. However, on completion of the development stage the activities of the JV will shift toward sales and distribution, at which time it may be appropriate for the party with the specific distribution capabilities to assume responsibility for the day-to-day operations of the JV.

Whenever a change in control might occur, the parties must carefully consider the circumstances, if any, under which they will revert to the management and control structure that existed prior to the specified event. The ease of accomplishing this transition depends, in large part, on the type of default and the degree of authority being exercised by the parties with respect to essential functions of the enterprise. Moreover, many of the events that trigger a shift in control may be so serious that it may be more appropriate for the parties to restructure, or even terminate, the activities of the venture.

Selection of Officers

Responsibility for management of the day-to-day affairs of the JV lies with the officers selected by the board, subject to any obligations that might be imposed on them to report to the board. A variety of methods can be used for selecting the JV officers. One procedure that is sometimes used for international JVs is to alternate various positions between the parties, such that a representative of one party serves as the president and chief executive officer every other year. In those years when a party does not have the right to elect the president, it will usually be allowed to name the executive vice president or chief financial officer.

It often makes sense to allocate officer positions in a manner that reflects the anticipated functional contributions of each party. For example, if one party has responsibility for research and development, the chief management officer in the technology area should be a representative chosen by that party. Similar appointments should be made in the areas of manufacturing, distribution, and service. Obviously, in each case the party who does not have the right to select a given officer position should still receive reports and other information that allows it to evaluate performance in that area.

Matters Subject to Unanimous Approval

The parties need to strike an appropriate balance between permitting the officers and managers of the JV to make appropriate decisions regarding the operation of the enterprise and reserving the right, as the owners of the venture, to review and approve certain matters. The matters that are subject to the shared control of the owners, thereby requiring approval of both partners, should be limited to those items that are material to the performance of the venture, because making numerous actions subject to a unanimous vote will diminish, or even eliminate, the ability of the venture to quickly respond to appropriate business opportunities and changes in competitive conditions.

Sample Contract Provision: Vote Switch Procedures

The following provision is an example of vote switch procedures that provide a mechanism for shifting effective control of the corporation's (the JV's) managing board on the occurrence of one of several events to be agreed by the parties. It assumes that one party has the right to elect a majority of the managers. Depending on the circumstances, a change in control of the board may be accompanied by corresponding changes in its scope of authority as provided in the JV's charter documents.

If, at any time prior to [*date*], any of the following events ("Voting Right Event") shall have occurred:

(a) Any material breach by Partner A of this Agreement or the Ancillary Agreements;

(b) Default by the Corporation on a material financial obligation;

(c) Breach or default by the Corporation under the Certificate, Bylaws, or this Agreement;

(d) Breach by Partner A, the Corporation or any of their respective directors, officers, employees, or consultants of any confidentiality obligations imposed by this Agreement or under any other related agreements;

(e) The initiation of material patent actions or other litigation against the Corporation by a third party;

(f) Failure of Partner A and/or the Corporation to meet certain technical milestones in the development or registration process in their respective Territories or failure of Partner A and/or the Corporation to meet certain revenue goals; or

(g) The occurrence of one of the events specified in Section [*number*], which triggers an option to purchase Partner A's interest, with respect to Partner A; or

(h) The bankruptcy of the Corporation,

then Partner B shall thereafter have the right to elect a majority of the Board of Directors until such Voting Right Event has been cured.

Protective Provisions for Minority Venturers

Minority owners of a JV will usually require that certain restrictions be placed on the ability of the majority owner to take certain actions without the consent and approval of the minority. While no single list of restrictions can address all the possible concerns, the following are among the most common areas of regulation in a JV agreement:

1. The agreement might restrain or restrict the sale of a substantial part of the JV's assets and its liquidation, dissolution, or merger with another company. This protection may not be necessary in jurisdictions where local law requires approval of all owners for a sale or change in control of the JV.
2. Frequently, a limit is imposed on the amount of debt the JV might undertake without the consent of both parties.
3. In many cases, both parties must approve capital expenditures that exceed an agreed amount or percentage of assets, sales, or income. The leasing of equipment or real estate may be similarly restricted.
4. If employees or executives of a party are likely to be employed by the JV, the minority may seek to impose a limit on compensation paid to such personnel.
5. The agreement may restrict the ability of the JV, without the consent of the minority, to enter into a contract with the majority owner or any related entity. On the other hand, if an existing and mutually agreed arrangement with the majority owner is material to the success of the JV, the agreement may prohibit any modifications to the arrangement without consent of the minority owner.
6. The hiring and firing of key personnel may be matters that require the consent of both parties. While such clauses are generally not intended to interfere with the JV's daily operation, the qualifications and performance of the chief executive officer of the JV are of great importance to both parties.
7. Unanimous consent should be required before the JV can undertake a fundamental change in the nature of its business objectives or its field of operations. A restriction might be added on the JV's ability to manufacture or distribute additional or different products or to change the JV's target markets.
8. The agreement may attempt to address the question of distributions of earnings, reflecting a compromise in different interests and philosophies of the parties. Clauses may range from veto rights to mandatory distributions based on earnings.

CHAPTER 15

Operating the JV

ALTHOUGH A GOOD DEAL OF THE EMPHASIS during negotiation of the JV's terms is placed on issues relating to capitalization and management, it is important for the parties to remember that the JV will become an independent operating entity with a life of its own. As such, the parties should be sure that the documents cover the key points relating to the actual operation of the JV, including the responsibilities for the functional activities of the JV (e.g., research and development, manufacturing, or distribution); operational matters, such as legal compliance, insurance, staffing and other similar issues; accounting and financial reporting matters; and other covenants relating to operation of the business and the activities of the partners.

Functional Activities

The key functional activities of the JV—such as research and development, manufacturing, marketing, distribution, or services—may be conducted by personnel employed directly by the JV, by one or both of the parties pursuant to ancillary agreements between them and the JV, or by third parties. For example, one party may agree to contribute part of its existing technology to the JV as consideration for its ownership interest, and then may enter into a research and development agreement with the JV to perform the additional work required to create new products that can then be marketed by the JV. Similarly, one or more of the partners may enter into a distribution agreement with the JV relative to the sale of the JV's products.

When the JV structure uses ancillary agreements with the parties to fulfill the functional needs of the JV, the negotiation of each agreement generally raises the same sorts of issues as would arise in any other context. However, if the functions are to be performed by JV personnel, many of whom may be loaned or assigned to the venture by the parties, it becomes important for the parties to lay out their expectations in the JV documents, including the business plan. For example, if JV employees are to be involved in development work, it is usually a good idea for the parties to agree on a development plan and to include covenants in the JV agreement regarding those matters that typically arise in a technology agreement, such as ownership of inventions, and duties to perfect and protect all of the legal rights of the JV in the technology.

LICENSING ARRANGEMENTS

A license facilitates the transfer of valuable legal rights and technology or other intellectual property from one party to the other to further the purposes of a strategic business relationship, including a JV. A licensing arrangement is created when one party (the "licensor") owns or otherwise controls the right to use a valuable legal right and grants to the other party (the "licensee") the right (or license) to utilize the legal rights for the purposes specified in the contract between the parties. In consideration for the grant of the license, the licensee agrees to compensate the licensor, by the payment of a flat fee or by payment of an amount determined by reference to amounts received by the licensee from the use of the licensed rights. However, in some cases, the compensation may be in-kind, such as when the licensee agrees to deliver finished goods to the licensor for resale.

In the JV context, a license agreement is generally used whenever a partner is contributing intellectual property rights to the JV for use in the JV's field of activity. In most cases, the license is exclusive, and the licensor may be entitled to royalties based on the revenues derived by the JV from the use of the licensed technology. Alternatively, the anticipated stream of income to the JV from the use of the licensed technology may be factored into the valuation of the partner's contributions to the JV in exchange for its interest in the profits of the JV. A license agreement will also be used when the JV licenses technology to a partner, which might occur once the JV has completed the development work and wishes to have a partner manufacture or distribute products embodying the technology produced by the JV. Although the intellectual property rights requirements of a JV are commonly satisfied through internal development or licensing from the partners, the JV itself can enter inbound licenses to gain the right to use intellectual property rights of third parties, or outbound licenses that permit third parties to use the JV's technology for specified purposes, such as the manufacture of parts or the distribution of products in a different geographical region or market sector.

RESEARCH AND DEVELOPMENT

Research and development activities are usually confined to JVs between partners with sufficient capital to fund the extensive amount of work usually required to complete the development and testing of new products. However, some amount of development work may be necessary in smaller JVs, even if it is limited to insubstantial changes to adapt a generic product to the requirements of the local market. As discussed in Chapter 10, careful attention should be given to the business development plan, including the research budget and the staffing requirements for the research work. Beyond that, however, the actual research contract should also cover the scope and content of the research program, including any agreed milestones, and the allocation of ownership and usage rights with respect to the technology that may be developed during the course of the research program.

MANUFACTURE AND SUPPLY

Manufacture and supply arrangements are always an important part of a JV's functional portfolio. In some cases, the JV is created to manufacture products or to supply raw materials for the partners. If, however, the JV's operations focus on sales and distribution, the JV may need to obtain manufacturing resources from an outside source, whether a JV partner or a third party.

A contract for manufacture and supply is similar to that used in a sale of goods relationship, the distinction being that a manufacture and supply agreement contemplates that a number of orders and deliveries of the specified goods will be made over an extended period of time. Such an agreement should always include:

- A clear description of the goods, including any special needs with respect to performance and quality;
- The manner in which the goods are to be priced and delivered;
- Any requirements with respect to shipping and insurance;
- The form and timing of payment and related credit arrangements; and
- Warranties and limitations on the respective liabilities of the parties to the agreement.

MARKETING AND DISTRIBUTION

A common practice is for the JV partners to perform some sort of marketing and distribution function on behalf of the JV. The partner may supply all of some of the following services: market research, application engineering, ordering services, communications with regard to marketing forecasting and sales, advertising, distribution, and transport. If the marketing and distribution partner is going to function as an agent of the JV, a separate agreement should prescribe the commission to be paid, generally expressed as some percentage of sales. If, on the other hand, the partner is to operate as an independent distributor, then the provisions must be carefully drafted to avoid any antitrust concerns that might arise because two companies have formed an agreement relating to the prices at which the JV products will be sold to end users.

Operational Activities

Like any other business, a JV requires careful attention to a broad range of day-to-day operational issues. In fact, this issue is one of the main distinctions between a JV and each of the other contractual alliances available to the parties (e.g., distribution arrangements), which are carried out without the need for creating a new infrastructure. Specific operational requirements can include management support, administrative services, technical assistance, real property arrangements, and the acquisition of equipment and machinery. Each of these requirements can be satisfied in several ways. The JV itself can fund the necessary operational services, or one or both of the parties can enter into contractual arrangements with the JV to provide the required services. In rare cases, a third party may be the vendor to the JV.

SERVICE AGREEMENTS

A JV may employ its own personnel to provide administrative services (e.g., financial, legal, personnel, and public relations) in connection with the operations of the JV, but it may be more cost-effective to have the JV enter into a contract with one or more of the JV parties to provide some of those services. Such a management services agreement can be particularly attractive if all or part of the JV's operations are to be conducted at or near the facilities of one of the JV parties. In any event, a management services agreement should describe the types of services to be rendered and should establish the fees to be paid to the provider. In addition, the agreement should make it clear that the provider's undertaking to provide services and advice to the JV is not a guarantee of the JV's success.

Human Resources

Staffing requirements for the JV should be carefully considered in the business plan. The JV may satisfy its human resources requirements by independently hiring, or by borrowing one or more employees from the partners on a temporary or permanent basis. The employment relationship for an international JV usually raises challenging issues of reconciling different values and cultures. Beyond that, however, the parties may want to use a variety of legal instruments to maintain commitment and loyalty among its workers. For example, employment contracts should be considered; however, caution should be used to ensure that such agreements conform to applicable local requirements. In addition, the JV might establish employee benefit plans, including profit sharing arrangements. The effect of local securities laws and the role of local unions must be taken into account, as well as the requirements of any governmental agencies with authority to regulate the employment relationship.

Accounting Matters and Financial Reporting

Accounting and financial reporting is an essential part of monitoring the progress and management of the JV. The parties must reach agreement on the establishment of accounting and internal controls, including the selection of an independent public accountant to audit the JV's books and records. In addition, the JV agreement should describe all of the financial information that is to be prepared and distributed to the parties during the term of the venture. These reports will provide the basis for budgetary and capital allocation decisions, permit discovery of deviations from goals and objectives specified in business plans and, finally, allow the parties to evaluate the performance of product and marketing strategies, or the progress of technology development efforts.

MAINTENANCE OF BOOKS AND RECORDS

The parties should agree that each of them will cause the JV to maintain full and accurate books and records of account. In addition, the managers of the JV should be required to devise and maintain a system of internal accounting control such that: (i) transactions are executed in accordance with general or specific internal authorizations, and recorded in a manner that permits the preparation of financial statements and tax return information; (ii) access to specified assets is tightly regulated; and (iii) internal audits are conducted regularly to ensure that the internal records with respect to various assets conform to actual inventories. Each of the parties should have the right to review the books and records of the JV and, if necessary, to conduct their own independent audit.

INDEPENDENT PUBLIC ACCOUNTANT AND LEGAL COUNSEL

The appointment of an independent public accountant is an important part of the internal controls for the JV. Usually, the parties agree on the initial independent accountant at the time the JV is organized, and any changes in the independent accountant require the consent of both parties. Similar procedures should be followed for the selection and continued engagement of legal counsel

Cross-Cultural Team Building

Cross-cultural team building is one of the most difficult tasks confronting managers of an international JV. Managers should carefully study the composition of the group or team and consider how their cultural backgrounds may impact day-to-day operations of the JV. The following summarizes some of the key issues.

LEADERSHIP STYLES

Leadership styles vary widely among different cultures. In Latin America and in many Asian cultures, the preference is for a hierarchical type of leadership in which the leader takes full responsibility for all major decisions of the group. On the other hand, some cultures expect their leaders to be participative, and prefer a team facilitator rather than a leader. Clashes over leadership style in a cross-cultural group might be avoided by assigning separate tasks to different groups and using different leadership styles to complete them.

COMMUNICATION

Poor communication is one of the main reasons that a JV fails. Often this is the result of cultural differences in preferred communication style. While group members from Germany and the United States would expect good communication to be precise, direct, and detailed, individuals from Saudi Arabia, Brazil, and Japan would define good communication as indirect and full of non-verbal cues. Cross-cultural teams often let these differences fester. The best way to resolve this dilemma is to clarify to the team at the very start what good communication within the team means.

HANDLING CONFLICT

Different cultures view and resolve conflicts in very different ways. Some cultures prefer to deal with conflicts head-on, while others are embarrassed or disturbed by a direct approach. A good way to deal with such problems is to use an intermediary who is sensitive to the concerns of both parties.

GOALS AND OBJECTIVES

Distinctions can be made between task-driven cultures and relationship-driven cultures. Group members from the former tolerate a shorter time horizon for achievement, while group members from the latter tend to view time less urgently and take a longer-range view of achievement. Managers should consider setting up a combination of short-range task-driven goals combined with goals achievable in a longer, less intense timeframe.

DECISION MAKING

Managers need to achieve a balance between consultation and authoritarianism in making decisions about team activities. For example, while workers from many of the Middle Eastern countries would not expect to be consulted about various decisions, other workers come from backgrounds where consensus building is both expected and essential.

to the JV, bearing in mind that each of the parties may need to secure their own legal counsel with respect to certain matters relating to their separate interests in the JV.

FINANCIAL INFORMATION

The parties need to agree on the scope and content of the financial information regarding the enterprise that will be generated and distributed by management in cooperation with the JV's independent public accountants. Much of the information may be readily available to the parties involved with the activities of the JV on a daily basis. However, if one party is removed, either geographically or otherwise, from the physical facilities of the JV, financial information becomes a key part of that party's ability to assess the viability of its investment. Among the financial information that might be required is the following:

- Audited annual balance sheets and statements of income and changes in financial position.
- Quarterly unaudited balance sheets, and statements of income and changes in financial position, prepared in accordance with generally accepted accounting procedures.
- Monthly balance sheets and statements of income and changes, prepared in accordance with generally accepted accounting procedures and in a manner that permits comparison to key objectives and milestones for the period in which the monthly information is prepared.
- A detailed annual plan that includes monthly capital and operating expense budgets, cash flow statements, projected balance sheets, and profit and loss statements for each month and for the end of the year, itemized in such detail as each of the parties may consider to be necessary.

Covenants

The formation and operation of a JV requires a significant amount of documents and regulations. While the parties should make every attempt to establish concrete guidelines on all material aspects of the operation, some issues simply don't lend themselves to detailed agreement. In those cases, the parties must be content to reach agreement on certain overriding principles that will bind their relationship, generally in the form of covenants relating to operation of the JV and certain activities of the partners.

OPERATION OF THE JV

Covenants regarding the internal operations of the JV serve several purposes. Most importantly, they cause the parties to focus on the day-to-day operations of the venture and the resources that will be required for successful operation. Also, if one party is given control over the management of the enterprise, covenants of this type ensure the non-participating partner that due care and attention will be paid to the business, and will provide certain standards for measuring the performance of the manager. Typically, a breach of any of the aforementioned covenants will trigger a vote switch, in which either control of the JV reverts to shared management responsibilities, or the existing management is entirely replaced by agents and representatives supplied by the other partner.

ACTIVITIES OF PARTNERS

Generally, the partners in a JV will have certain fiduciary duties to one another with respect to their actions in relation to the JV. In addition, it is common for the partners to negotiate various limits on activities that, while outside the current scope of the JV, nonetheless may have some impact on the relationship of the parties and the ultimate success of the collaboration. Care must be taken, however, in drafting these limitations so as not to raise the concerns of regulators charged with reviewing the JV for potential adverse effects on competition.

- COMPETITIVE ACTIVITIES The parties may include various agreements relating to their other business activities, such as a covenant not to engage in any activities that might compete with those of the JV for a specified time that extends for some period after expiration of the contemplated term of the enterprise.
- FUTURE BUSINESS OPPORTUNITIES One or both of the parties may have an interest in establishing a formal mechanism by which the parties might discuss future business opportunities of mutual interest. For example, the parties may agree to include a "right of first negotiation" with respect to the exploitation of new product opportunities in a specified technical or geographic area, either through the formation of a new JV, or by expanding the scope of activities of the existing entity. The wisdom of expanding the original scope of the JV should be considered when the initial business plan for the JV is prepared.

Sample Contract Provision: Administrative Services

This provision illustrates the scope of administrative services that one or both of the parties may provide to the JV while the new entity is launching its activities and looking for personnel to take on some of the listed tasks.

1. FINANCIAL SERVICES

[*Identity of provider*] shall make available to the Company the services of its treasury, control and planning departments, or the equivalent thereof, to assist the Company with respect to accounting, control, and other financial matters as the Company requests. Such services shall include assistance and advice with respect to external financings, bank relations, cash management, investments, public reporting, accounting, credit and collection, and such other matters as such departments generally handle for [*identity of provider*].

2. TAX AND AUDIT

[*Identity of provider*] shall make available to the Company the services of its internal audit and tax departments, or the equivalent thereof, for consultation and advice with respect to the establishment, execution, and control of accounting policies, financial budgets, administrative procedures, and systems as the Company requests. [*Identity of provider*]'s tax department shall also assist the Company in the preparation and filing of all required tax returns and other tax-related reports, and shall advise the Company with respect to tax matters generally.

3. LEGAL

[*Identity of provider*] shall make available to the Company the services of its legal department to provide such services to the Company as the Company requests and as are usually provided by such department to [*identity of provider*]. Such services shall include counsel, advice, and assistance with respect to contracts, litigation, government regulatory matters, products liability, distribution practices, corporate record keeping, patent and trademark applications and prosecutions, selection and general supervision of outside legal counsel engaged by or on behalf of the Company, and such other matters as [*identity of provider*]'s legal department generally handles for [*identity of provider*].

4. PERSONNEL

[*Identity of provider*] shall make available to the Company the services of its personnel division, which shall provide to the Company such services as the Company requests and as it generally provides to [*identity of provider*]. Such services shall include advice and information concerning the recruitment, hiring, training, and retention of personnel, as well as the setting of standards for performance and efficiency for such personnel; assistance in the accomplishment of wage and salary programs, and the compliance of such programs with all applicable regulations; assistance in the development and establishment of pension and other employee benefit programs; and the conduct of negotiations for and assistance with respect to all general labor matters.

5. PUBLIC RELATIONS

[*Identity of provider*] shall make available to the Company the services of its corporate communications department, or the equivalent thereof, for handling internal and external business communications and other matters as the Company requests and as is usually handled by such department for [*Identity of provider*]. Such services shall include assistance in the preparation of internal and external news releases, relations with local and national trade and general press organizations, the organization of news conferences, the preparation of product literature for distribution to the general public and the trade, the organization and implementation of advertising and promotion campaigns, and such other similar matters as [*identity of provider*] and the Company may mutually agree.

6. MISCELLANEOUS SERVICES

[*Identity of provider*] shall make available to the Company as the Company requests, the services of its purchasing department, corporate physical distribution department, insurance department, real estate department and other miscellaneous administrative staff groups, or the equivalents thereof, to advise and assist the Company with respect to matters falling within the areas of expertise of these various departments.

Sample Contract Provision: Charges for Services

Although a party may provide certain services to the JV without charge, it is common to provide in the agreement for some reimbursement. Charges for services should be addressed in advance through a provision similar to this one.

1. SERVICES FOR INTERNAL DEVELOPMENT

Services supplied to the Company by [*identity of provider*] under this Agreement for the purpose of the internal development of the Company as a business, which is deemed to include the training of technical personnel but exclude the development of new technology, shall be charged on a fully-loaded cost basis plus a [*number*] percent administrative surcharge.

2. FULLY LOADED COSTS

For purposes of Section X.1, "fully-loaded cost" shall be computed at the same rates and in the same manner as the amount that [*identity of provider*] charges or would charge, in accordance with its usual practices and policies as in effect from time to time, to its internal divisions and subsidiaries for identical or similar services rendered contemporaneously with services to be provided to the Company under this Agreement, together with all out-of-pocket expenses incurred by [*identity of provider*], including without limitation, all travel, housing, relocation, and subsistence expenses of [*identity of provider*]'s personnel directly related to the rendering of services to the Company under this Agreement.

3. SERVICES FOR CLIENT-BILLABLE WORK

Services supplied to the Company by [*identity of provider*] under this Agreement for work that is billable by the Company to a client or clients shall be charged on an arms-length basis. In the alternative and at the option of the Company with the concurrence of [*identity of provider*], such charges shall be billed on the basis of a pro rata share of the revenues of the respective project, with the pro rata basis calculated by the relative independent contribution of [*identity of provider*]'s employees to such project in comparison to that of employees of the Company, while taking into account fully-loaded costs. Determination of the relative independent contribution of employees of [*identity of provider*] and the Company to a particular project shall be made by the Board of Directors of the Company after consultation with the Chief Executive Officer and Chief Technical Officer of the Company.

4. REIMBURSEMENT AND RECORD KEEPING

For all services supplied to the Company by [*identity of provider*] under this Agreement, the Company shall make reimbursement to [*identity of provider*] quarterly within [*number*] days of receipt of [*identity of provider*]'s invoice therefor. [*Identity of provider*] shall keep reasonable records as evidence of the above costs for periods of not less than [*number*] years, and shall allow the Company to examine such records at reasonable times.

Sample Contract Provision: Development Program

When the JV involves research and development activities, the parties should reach agreement on the scope and purpose of the development program. This contract provision lays out the procedures for creating a development program, and sets out the rules for reimbursement of expenses incurred by the parties. Supplemental provisions should cover exchange and protection of confidential information and other results of the development program, and ownership and use of the new technology.

1. DEVELOPMENT PROGRAM

Partner A and Partner B agree to conduct on behalf of the Company, on an accelerated and coordinated basis, [*description of research*] for the purpose of securing all approvals (governmental or otherwise) necessary for the Parties to engage in the Field of Activity and manufacture and to sell (*New Product*) in their respective Territories, as defined in the Shareholders' Agreement. During the Term of Support, each of the Parties shall make reasonably available to the Company its technical personnel and facilities required to perform such scientific, research, and development projects relating to the Field of Activity as the Company requests and as the Parties may agree from time to time. The Parties may each have others perform or assist in performing the work under the Development Program, provided, however, that each of the Parties shall cause such other parties to be bound by the provisions of this Agreement as if they were parties to it.

2. DEVELOPMENT PLAN

On commencement of the Development Program (no later than thirty (30) days after the date of this Agreement), and no less frequently than quarterly thereafter, the Parties shall meet to formulate a detailed plan for development projects to be performed by the Parties during the course of the Development Program. The plan shall identify the technical problems involved and the general outline of experiments to be carried out, an estimate of the personnel and equipment to be contributed by each Party, a detailed budget setting forth the total estimated costs of each Party required to perform the work and, where possible, the nature of the work to be performed by each. Once the Parties have agreed to such plan, a copy of the plan shall be made a part of this Agreement; provided, that such plan may be modified or amended at any time by written agreement of the Parties. Each Party shall diligently conduct the agreed development projects and shall use their best efforts to reach the agreed goals of the such projects. Each Party shall prepare and supply to the Company written progress reports at the end of every three (3) month period.

3. EXPENSES

The Company shall pay to each Party an amount equal to that Party's respective total costs incurred in conducting work under the Development Program. Such total costs shall be determined in accordance with generally accepted accounting principles. At the end of each calendar month each Party shall each submit a written statement to the Company setting forth the total costs incurred by the Party during that calendar month. On receipt of such statement, the Company shall promptly pay the Party an amount equal to the total costs incurred by the Party in conducting the development projects for that month. Each Party shall keep correct and complete records containing all information required for determination of costs to be paid hereunder for periods of not less than three (3) years, and shall permit such books and records to be inspected by the Company during reasonable business hours.

Sample Contract Provision: Technical Assistance

A common purpose of many international JVs is the transfer of know-how from one party to the other. Technology transfer procedures should be laid out in detailed technical assistance provisions similar to the one set out below.

TECHNICAL ASSISTANCE

1. Partner A shall furnish to Partner B, at Partner B's request, the services of Partner A's personnel or of its agents (hereinafter "Partner A's personnel"), to give technical assistance and information for the start-up of a manufacturing facility for New Product. Such facility shall be constructed and said New Product shall be manufactured by Partner B with the use of Manufacturing Information furnished to Partner B under this Agreement, the use of which is authorized by this Agreement. It will be Partner B's responsibility to provide Partner A's personnel with suitable working quarters and adequate clerical and other assistance to facilitate the performance of the services.

2. Such services shall be available to Partner B at reasonable times and for reasonable intervals agreeable to Partner A during a two (2) year period commencing one (1) year prior to the expected start-up date for the manufacturing facility. Unless otherwise agreed to in writing by Partner A, the total of services to be provided by Partner A's personnel, exclusive of travel time, shall not exceed [*number*] person-days, based on an eight (8) hour workday schedule.

3. Such services usually shall be furnished at one or more locations of Partner B designated by Partner B and will involve consultation between Partner A's personnel and Partner B's personnel, either by telephone or by visits of Partner A's personnel to such locations. At the sole discretion of Partner A, such services may also be furnished at locations designated by Partner A, and may involve one or more visits of Partner B's personnel to such location(s).

4. Partner A shall provide training relating to the subject of this Section at Partner A's plant to personnel of Partner B. Such training shall be provided without charge, in addition to other services provided in this Section, and at Partner B's request. Such training shall be available to Partner B, at reasonable times and for reasonable intervals agreeable to Partner A during the two (2) year period commencing one (1) year prior to the expected start-up date for the manufacturing facility. Partner B's personnel to be trained shall be limited to no more than two (2) persons at any one time and their cumulative training shall not exceed [*number*] person-days in each year of the two (2) year period referred to above, based on the regular workday schedule at said plant.

CHAPTER 16

Crisis Management: Saving the Troubled Relationship

AN INTERNATIONAL JV FACES SUBSTANTIAL OBSTACLES to success. Not only must the parties deal with the same risks and uncertainties that confront any new business, regardless of form, but they must also grapple with integrating disparate management styles and business cultures. As such, it is important for both parties to keep a sharp eye out for the common signs of potential JV trouble, as described in Chapter 5. In addition, although it may be somewhat awkward to spend inordinate amounts of time before the JV is even formed in debating the consequences of failure, some of the procedures described in this chapter should be considered as strategies for resolving disputes between the parties without their having to resort to the costs and aggravations of litigation.

Dispute Resolution Mechanisms

When an event occurs that is considered to be a deadlock under the terms of the agreements between the parties, a number of different dispute resolution mechanisms can be used. Among the more common methods are mandatory bilateral discussions, mediation and arbitration, swing-vote directors, put-sell options and, in extreme cases, termination and dissolution of the JV.

BILATERAL DISCUSSIONS

The best way to deal with actual and potential trouble is for the parties to get together to talk through problems and attempt to arrive at solutions in a way that falls short of some of the more formal dispute resolution mechanisms discussed below. The parties may agree that any dispute among representatives of the parties at the JV level will be passed up successive levels of the internal ladder of each organization, eventually reaching the office of the chief executive officer of each party. Hopefully, the hassle or embarrassment of bringing more and more people from the parent organization into the affairs of the JV will encourage the officers and directors of the JV to reach some accommodation. This type of arrangement also has the benefit of exposing the dispute to a larger pool of managers, with the potential of bringing more creative resources to bear on the problem.

MEDIATION AND ARBITRATION

Some parties will rely on mediation and arbitration involving independent third parties as a means for resolving disputes. This procedure may work fairly well when the dispute involves questions of fact or law, or can be resolved by reference to the precise terms of the definitive JV agreement itself. However, when the dispute arises over issues of policy or business judgment, mediators or arbitrators can only assist the parties in communicating, but are not competent to hand down a decision as to the proper business strategy.

SWING-VOTE DIRECTORS

One easy method of resolving a deadlock is to provide for the presence of a tie breaking vote at meetings of the directors and shareholders. The tie breaker can be an officer or director elected by one party and then the other in alternate years under a bylaw requirement that the officer be elected from among the directors representing a different class each year. The swing-vote director may also be a third party in whom the JV partners have confidence.

PUT-SELL OPTIONS

Both parties may be given a right to "put" their shares to the other party at a fixed price, and the other party must either agree to purchase the shares at the price fixed by the party making the put or sell its own shares to the first party at the same price. Options of these types are more fully discussed below in the context of termination, however, they are usually only viable when both parties have the financial resources to fund a purchase, or when the parties are able to reach some agreement for extending credit on the transaction.

TERMINATION AND DISSOLUTION

In extreme cases, the parties may agree to terminate the JV, dissolve the company, and liquidate and distribute the assets in the manner provided in the articles of incorporation.

Mediation Procedures

In some situations, the parties may have difficulty resolving problems because they don't know how to structure the discussions in a way that is calculated to produce good results in a timely fashion. If so, consideration should be given to engaging a professional mediator to work with the parties, often as a condition to moving on to the more formal dispute resolution mechanism of arbitration. A mediator should be appointed before mediation is needed. If that's not possible, the parties should agree on a procedure for selecting the mediator, including use of a recognized mediation group to locate qualified persons. Each mediator has his or her own style, and the parties are always free to suggest their own procedures. However, experience has shown that the following steps are usually part of the mediation process:

- SETTING THE STAGE AND THE GROUND RULES The mediator should hold one or more meetings with both parties to set up the ground rules for the mediation sessions. The mediator should allow each party to air its grievances in front of the other party and gather information on what, if any, steps the parties have taken on their own to resolve the problems.
- PRIVATE MEETINGS The mediator should then hold a series of private meetings with each party to get a better idea of how each side sees the problems and the solutions that each is willing to suggest to move forward. If possible, the mediator should determine which issues have the highest priority for each party, and identify any issues that threaten the entire relationship. The mediator's job is to

be a good and sympathetic listener, but the mediator should also try to educate each party about the basis for the concerns of the other party.

- SOLICITATION OF PROPOSALS FOR RESOLVING THE DISPUTE Once the issues have been identified, the mediator should meet with each party privately, and secure a formal proposal from each on what they think might be a fair basis for solving the problems. The mediator should probe each proposal carefully to determine where the party might be willing to compromise. Based on the mediator's discussions with the parties, he or she should be able to reconcile the proposals of the parties and come up with a single solution that can be presented to the parties for consideration.
- SHUTTLE DIPLOMACY Once the initial solution has been presented to the parties, the mediator should listen carefully to their criticisms, and shuttle back and forth between them to try and reach accord on specific issues. In these meetings, the mediator will not only try to present the positions of each side, but will also offer his or her own opinions regarding which proposals will, in fact, be acceptable.
- THE END GAME The final step includes drafting a written agreement or other document that sets forth results of the mediation, including a record of those points on which the parties have reached agreement and, if necessary, those issues that remain in dispute. If appropriate, the mediator can assist the parties in modifying their existing agreement to accommodate the changes that follow from the mediation. If mediation has not been successful, the mediator should recommend further dispute resolution procedures, including arbitration.

Arbitration Procedures

Binding arbitration is an alternative dispute resolution procedure. It has gained great popularity in the context of international business relationships, particularly when the participants are concerned about conducting litigation in one of the jurisdictions where a participant is domiciled. Although arbitration can be slow, and enforceability of an arbitration award can be a concern, this procedure allows the participants to pursue solutions to complex problems without the need to allocate fault, as will happen if the matter is brought to the courts.

Generally, arbitration is conducted by a panel of one or more arbitrators chosen by the parties. The original JV agreement should stipulate the applicable law or rules for the arbitration procedure, which may be selected from a number of different alternatives. In each case, commercial arbitration is intended to place the dispute before a group of impartial experts, who will limit their inquiry to facts and circumstances relevant to interpretation of the specific portion of the contractual agreement and who will render a decision that conforms to the standards of international commercial practice.

Arbitration allows the parties to seek an orderly resolution to disputes without the need to terminate what is otherwise a profitable and successful business relationship. In many cases, honest differences will arise when the parties are unfamiliar with various customs and the meaning ascribed to contractual undertakings under the laws governing the actions of the other participant. Moreover, the use of experts can be extremely valuable in resolving thorny valuation issues, particularly if a material portion of the JV's assets consists of intangible property.

Ten Steps for Effective Arbitration

Advance preparation for an event that may never happen may seem like wasted resources, but such planning can actually bring the parties closer together at the start by giving them control over their future regardless of what might occur. It is also essential that you understand the resolution process from the beginning, because it will be easier to collect and categorize the data as you go along in a calmly running operation, rather than at the end while emotions are interfering with issues and you just want a quick escape.

1. Negotiate the dispute resolution procedures before they are needed. Once problems have arisen in the relationship, it becomes much more difficult for the parties to think clearly about the best way to resolve the dispute.
2. Choose a well-recognized set of rules to govern the proceedings. Major arbitration organizations can provide materials that explain how their rules work.
3. Appoint an arbitrator who understands the process, is familiar with the matters in dispute, has technical expertise in the particular industry, is knowledgeable in the law governing the JV, and actively manages the process. If a panel of arbitrators is used, make sure that the chair of the panel fits this profile.
4. Obtain the advice of legal counsel who is familiar with the arbitration process and international trade practices.
5. Adhere to the time limits that the arbitrator imposes before and during the hearing. The JV must continue during arbitration, and every effort should be made to keep the process moving and get the problems resolved as soon as possible.
6. Arbitration is supposed to be a cost-effective alternative to lengthy court proceedings. Try to limit requests for procedural and evidentiary decisions to those that are truly necessary to resolving the underlying dispute.
7. Do your best to cooperate in making documentary evidence and witnesses available. The arbitrator needs to have all available information, and will usually make an effort to limit the burden of producing documents and witnesses.
8. The relative informality of arbitration sometimes leads the parties to greater showings of emotion than if the matter was before a judge. However, it's best to avoid emotional overtones and simply focus on the issues.
9. Present an organized, strong argument (whether through counsel or on your own). And, in turn, listen carefully to the other party and be sure that your responses clearly address the other party's specific concerns.
10. Be prepared to accept the arbitrator's decisions and move on. Before the proceedings are completed, make sure that you understand the decision and that there are no particular ambiguities that may lead to misunderstandings later.

SUBJECTS COVERED IN ARBITRATION CLAUSES

In drafting an arbitration clause, the parties must establish the shape and character of the dispute resolution process, including the length, complexity, fairness, and cost of the proceedings. The relevant arbitration rules should be selected, the forum should be chosen, the language in which the proceedings are to be conducted should be stipulated, and the parties should clearly state their intent that the decision of the arbitrator will be final and binding on them. Moreover, it is important to specify clearly those matters that must be taken to arbitration and the scope of remedies that are to be made available to the arbitrator, including the power to dissolve the JV or to terminate licenses or other rights in situations where money damages are not sufficient and continued breaches will undermine the intent of the participants in conducting the JV.

SELECTION OF ARBITRATION RULES AND ARBITRATION FORUM

Parties face a choice between an administered proceeding before one of the many organizations that have been established to serve as arbitration forums, or an ad hoc arbitration proceeding, in which the parties essentially attempt to develop their own rules for dealing with disputes. Obviously, ad hoc arbitrations offer the opportunity for more flexibility and cost savings. However, they are generally more difficult to design and conclude, because the success of the procedure depends on cooperation among parties who are otherwise at odds with respect to some material matter under their contract. Detailed arbitration provisions are especially important in ad hoc proceedings because there are no agency or forum rules to fill in any gaps or questions in the agreement. A thorough review of local rules is also critical whenever ad hoc proceedings are contemplated, and local courts may be used to assist the parties in starting the proceedings or selecting the arbitrators.

If the parties prefer administered proceedings, there are a wide number of arbitral bodies and rules from which a selection can be made, including the Rules of Conciliation and Arbitration of the International Chamber of Commerce ("ICC"), the Commercial Arbitration Rules of the American Arbitration Association ("AAA"), and the Rules of the London Court of International Arbitration ("LCIA"). Each of these bodies will administer arbitrations under their own rules, or will serve as arbitrators in proceedings that are to be conducted under the arbitration rules of the United Nations Convention on World Trade Law ("UNCITRAL").

■ ICC COURT OF ARBITRATION

The ICC's Court of Arbitration, which is headquartered in Paris, is probably the best known arbitral body with respect to international arbitration matters. The ICC rules are less detailed than those used by arbitral bodies. However, they are distinguished by their requirement that the parties prepare a detailed "Terms of Reference," which is similar to a pretrial order and summarizes the claims of the parties and the issues to be settled as part of the arbitration proceedings. While the Terms of Reference can greatly assist the parties in framing the issues, and may even facilitate an early settlement of the dispute, the exercise can be somewhat time consuming and expensive. The Terms of Reference, as well as the arbitrators' appointment and ultimate award, are reviewed by the ICC Court, which meets monthly, and while the ICC Court has no authority to override arbitrators, it can modify the form of the award, review computation of damages and interest, and draw the arbitrators' attention to other points of substance.

■ AAA RULES FOR COMMERCIAL ARBITRATION

The AAA's Rules for Commercial Arbitration are another excellent set of rules that are based largely on common law elements. The AAA is able to administer international arbitration proceedings abroad or through its regional offices throughout the United States. The AAA has supplementary procedures for, among other things, the selection of arbitrators from a neutral country (rather than the AAA's national panel), payment of costs, and the language of the proceedings (which the AAA determines, in the absence of agreement between the parties, after considering the nationality of the parties, their counsel and witnesses, as well as the place of the proceedings). If applicable law permits, the arbitrators in an AAA proceeding may subpoena evidence, either on a party's request or their own initiative. Equitable relief, such as specific performance, is also available in AAA proceedings.

■ LONDON COURT OF INTERNATIONAL ARBITRATION

The LCIA's rules represent a combination of common and civil law traditions. In most cases, the arbitration hearings will take place in London, but the parties may agree to hold the hearings elsewhere, and the arbitrators may themselves determine that another place is more appropriate. Until 1979, when the English Arbitration Act of that year placed severe limitations on appeals to the English courts on international arbitrations, many parties were reluctant to arbitrate in London due to the relatively liberal rights of appeal to English courts on a number of arbitration matters, including preliminary points. Fees for LCIA arbitrators and administration are based on the time expended, at hourly or per diem rates.

■ UNCITRAL RULES

The UNCITRAL rules were developed by the United Nations Commission on World Trade Law. The UNCITRAL does not actually administer arbitrations, instead the rules provide for designation of a neutral agency or court to act as the appointing authority to nominate arbitrators and perform certain other functions. The ICC, AAA, and LCIA, as well as other leading arbitral groups, are willing to act as an appointing authority for arbitrations to be conducted under UNCITRAL rules. The UNCITRAL rules provide the arbitrators with wide latitude and authority on procedural matters, and the rules reflect a number of civil law elements, including a preference for deciding cases on documents rather than testimony, and independent inquiries by judges.

JUDICIAL REVIEW

The parties should consider addressing the availability and scope of judicial review for decisions rendered during the course of the arbitration. If the right to judicial review is not addressed by the parties in the contract, reference will be made to local law. In the United States, judicial review is limited under the terms of the Federal Arbitration Act ("FAA"), which provides that mere errors of law or mistakes of fact are not ground for vacating an award. However, an award may be vacated on more narrow grounds, including a finding that the arbitrators exceeded the scope of their jurisdiction. It is important to note that there is authority to support a contractual waiver of all judicial review of arbitrations governed by United States law provided that the waiver is clear and unequivocal. On the other hand, there also is some authority that the parties can contract to grant greater judicial appellate review power than provided under the FAA.

Sample Contract Provision: Dispute Resolution Procedures

X.1. NEGOTIATION AND MEDIATION

Except as provided in Section 11, neither Party shall institute a proceeding in any court or administrative agency to resolve a dispute between the Parties before that Party has sought to resolve the dispute through direct negotiation with the other Party. If the dispute is not resolved within [*number*] days after a demand for direct negotiation, the Parties shall attempt to resolve the dispute through mediation. If the Parties do not promptly agree on a mediator, either party may request [*name of appointing entity*] to appoint a mediator certified by [*name of certifying entity*]. All mediation proceedings shall be held in [*location*]. Nothing in this Section precludes the Parties from agreeing to submit the dispute for resolution by arbitration under conditions and procedures set forth below. The fees and expenses of the mediator shall be paid one-half by each Party.

COMMENT: The parties should attempt to resolve disputes through informal discussions before resorting to formal mediation and arbitration. This provision requires that the parties must enter into direct negotiations if a dispute arises. If those negotiations are unsuccessful, then mediation is the next order of business. Because differences of opinion between the parties can arise in a number of different contexts, consideration should be given to coming up with a list of the matters that might trigger the formal dispute resolution procedures. Possibilities include a failure of the parties to reach agreement on amendments to the charter documents of the entity, material changes in the JV's line of business, or declaration of dividends or selection of managers.

X.2. RESOLUTION OF DISPUTES BY ARBITRATION

If the mediator is unable to facilitate a settlement of the dispute within a reasonable time, as determined by the mediator, the mediator shall issue a written statement to the Parties to that effect. The dispute shall thereafter be determined by binding arbitration as provided below in accordance with the UNCITRAL Arbitration Rules [*specify either* as now in effect *or* as amended from time to time]. Notwithstanding the foregoing, the Parties shall not be required to submit a dispute to binding arbitration as provided herein if the nature of the dispute falls within the scope of Section 11 below.

COMMENT: This provision triggers the arbitration procedures if the mediation conducted in accordance with Section 1 above is unsuccessful. Exceptions to required arbitration are set out in detail in Section 11 below. The key decision for the parties is the selection of the arbitration rules, and the parties need to consider whether they want to apply the arbitration rules as they exist at the time of the original agreement or accept modifications that may be adopted by the arbitration group over the term of the relationship.

X.3. NUMBER AND SELECTION OF ARBITRATORS

The arbitration shall be heard and determined by three (3) arbitrators. Each Party shall appoint an arbitrator of its choice within twenty (20) days of the submission of a notice of arbitration. The Party-appointed arbitrators shall in turn appoint a presiding arbitrator of the tribunal within fifteen (15) days following the appointment of both Party-appointed arbitrators. If the Party-appointed arbitrators cannot reach agreement on a presiding arbitrator of the tribunal and/or one Party refuses to appoint its Party-appointed arbitrator within said fifteen (15) day period, the appointing authority for the implementation of such procedure shall be the American Arbitration Association (AAA). The AAA shall appoint an independent arbitrator who does not have any financial interest in the dispute, controversy, or claim. If the AAA refuses or fails to act as the appointing authority within thirty (30) days after being requested to do so, then the appointing authority shall be the Court of the International Chamber of Commerce ("ICC"), who shall appoint an independent arbitrator who does not have any financial interest in the dispute, controversy, or claim. In no event shall the presiding arbitrator be of the same nationality as any of the Parties or their ultimate parent entities. All decisions and awards by the arbitration tribunal shall be made by majority vote.

COMMENT: In most cases, the parties will opt for a single neutral arbitrator or, in larger or more complicated disputes, will settle on a panel of three arbitrators, with final awards or decisions generally being made by a majority vote. If three arbitrators are used, each party will generally choose a single arbitrator and then those two will select the neutral third arbitrator. However, if the parties are not able to agree on third, recourse to the local courts may be necessary to break the impasse. AAA and ICC rules presume one arbitrator, while the UNCITRAL rules presume three arbitrators unless the parties agree otherwise. In the case of the ICC, the presumed number may be increased by the ICC if the dispute warrants three arbitrators. The ICC requests nominations of the neutral arbitrator from the national committee at the seat of arbitration, while the AAA and UNCITRAL rules provide for the appointment from a list previously sent to the parties from which they could have selected their own neutral third arbitrator.

X.4. PLACE AND LANGUAGE OF ARBITRATION

Unless otherwise expressly agreed in writing by the Parties to the arbitration proceedings, the arbitration proceedings shall be held in [*location*] and shall be conducted in the [*description*] language by arbitrators fluent in that language.

COMMENT: The designation of the place for the arbitration hearings clearly is one of the most important choices that must be made in structuring the arbitration provisions. While obviously the situs of the arbitration will have a bearing on such practical matters as the convenience of witnesses and access to evidence that might be germane to adjudicating the dispute, the location will also have an effect on the enforceability of the award and on various important procedural matters. For example, under the New York Convention, the place of the arbitration, not the nationality of the parties, determines where it is enforceable. As to procedural matters, usually local law, in the absence of a contrary provision in the clause relating to arbitration, will govern such things as conflict of laws issues, appellate rights, the right of foreign lawyers to participate in arbitration hearings, and access to local courts for provisional remedies (e.g., temporary restraining orders).

X.5. GOVERNING LAW AND PROCEDURES

The Parties expressly agree that the provisions of this Agreement, including the rules of the [*name of arbitral institution*] and the laws of [*arbitral location*], as modified by the terms of this agreement, shall govern the arbitration of any disputes between the Parties. In the event of any conflict between the law of [*location*] and the law of the arbitral location with respect to any arbitration conducted pursuant to this Agreement, to the extent permissible, it is the express intent of the Parties that the law of [*location*], as modified by this agreement, shall prevail.

COMMENT: Each of the major arbitration rules allow the parties to select in their arbitration provisions the governing substantive and procedural laws that will apply to the arbitration. A choice of law provision should always be included in the arbitration clause, because forcing the arbitrators to decide which law should apply before adjudicating the underlying dispute can add tremendous uncertainty and unpredictability to the outcome. In most cases, foreign parties will want to elect their own substantive law. Alternatively, the foreign party may be willing to agree on a foreign law based on concepts (i.e., common or civil) that are somewhat similar to those that apply in the foreign party's own country.

X.6. DISCOVERY RIGHTS

For good cause shown, and after objections are considered, the arbitrators may compel: (1) the production of relevant, non-privileged documents or other evidence within the possession, custody, or control of a Party; (2) the inspection of any goods, real estate, samples, or any other thing whatsoever if relevant and non-privileged; and (3) the disclosure of a list of witnesses who may testify at the hearing. The arbitrators may order the Party seeking disclosure to pay the reasonable costs of the production of the information sought. Failure to abide by the arbitrators' production orders may lead to sanctions, monetary or otherwise, and if the disobedience substantially prejudices one side, the arbitrators may issue a total or partial award in favor of that party on the issue or issues to which that Party was so prejudiced.

COMMENT: As a general rule, discovery rights are not available in an international arbitration unless the parties specifically provide for them. A party from the United States or any other country with a common law legal system may encounter some difficulty in negotiating with a foreign party from a developing country for discovery rights, because extensive discovery is not the norm in many foreign countries, particularly those with strong civil law histories.

Arbitration rules will provide for at least limited exchange of evidence. For example, under the UNCITRAL rules, the arbitrators may require that the parties provide a summary of the documents and evidence to be used at the hearing to prove the issues asserted in the claim or defense, and AAA rules also provide for the disclosure of evidence, such as an exchange of witness lists and documents. ICC rules require submission of relevant documents with the claim or defense, but they otherwise have no provision for discovery.

X.7. INTEREST AND COSTS

The costs of the arbitration proceedings (including attorneys' fees and costs) shall be borne in the manner determined by the arbitrator(s); the award shall include interest from the date of any breach or violation of [*description of*

agreement], as determined by the arbitral award, and from the date of the award until paid in full, at [_interest rate_].

COMMENT: The arbitration provisions should include procedures dealing with interest, currency, costs. and legal fees. This may be particularly important in an arbitration proceeding conducted in a developing country because you may encounter significant delays in enforcing the award. Moreover, local law may provide that the losing party must pay the legal fees of the prevailing party. AAA and UNCITRAL rules permit the arbitral tribunal to fix costs and assess them as it deems appropriate, usually against the losing party. Proceedings under the ICC rules require that reference be made to local law as to the award of fees and costs.

X.8. FORM OF ARBITRAL AWARD

The decision of the sole arbitrator or a majority of the arbitrators, as the case may be, shall be reduced to writing. It shall be final and binding without the right of appeal, and it is the sole and exclusive remedy regarding any claims, counterclaims, issues, or accountings presented to the arbitrator. It shall be made and promptly paid in [_type of currency_] free of any deduction or offset, and any costs or fees incident to enforcing the award shall to the maximum extent permitted by law, be charged against the Party resisting such enforcement.

COMMENT: As a general rule, arbitrators are not required to provide written explanations for their awards unless the parties provide otherwise or the rules of the arbitration agency so require. The ICC rules do not require opinions, although ICC arbitrators will usually issue a written explanation so as to facilitate a more beneficial review of the proceeding by the ICC Court. The AAA, LCIA, and UNCITRAL rules all require that arbitrators supply an explanation for their decisions. Written awards are essential for a judicial challenge to the decision, and also provide a means for the parties to structure their future behavior in the areas in which the dispute originally arose. Also, a written award allows the parties to verify that there have been no computation or other types of errors that need to be corrected.

X.9. CONSEQUENTIAL DAMAGES

Consequential, punitive, or other similar damages shall not be allowed; provided, however, the award may include appropriate punitive damages if a Party has engaged in delaying and dilatory actions.

COMMENT: The parties may place limitations on the scope of relief that can be awarded by the arbitrator. In this case, the arbitrator is precluded from awarding consequential or punitive damages unless a party has purposely delayed the proceedings.

X.10. ENFORCEMENT OF AWARD

Judgment on the award may be entered in any court with jurisdiction over the person or the assets of the Party owing the judgment, or application may be made to such court for a judicial acceptance of the award and an order of enforcement, as the case may be.

COMMENT: The enforceability of the award should be specifically addressed in the contract to ensure that there will be no uncertainty as to whether a court will have jurisdiction to confirm an award made in arbitration. The New York Convention on the Recognition and Enforcement of Foreign Arbitral Awards of 1958 provides each party with comfort that foreign arbitral awards rendered in any jurisdiction that is a member of the New York Convention will be honored in any other jurisdiction that is also a member of that Convention.

X.11. DISPUTES NOT SUBJECT TO ARBITRATION

Notwithstanding anything herein to the contrary: (1) disputes, claims. and controversies regarding the breach or threatened breach of [*name of agreement*] on trade secrets and confidential information shall be decided by a court of competent jurisdiction in [*location*]; and (2) no Party is barred from seeking a temporary restraining order in [*location*] involving [*description*]. If court action has been reserved, the Parties irrevocably consent to the jurisdiction of the court of [*description*]. The Parties appoint [*name*] as agent for service of process and waive the provisions of all international conventions on service of process (or other applicable service of process laws).

COMMENT: Although some issues may not be arbitrated in certain jurisdictions as a matter of statute or public policy, for most conflicts the parties have wide latitude as to which disputes might be brought before an arbitrator. They may simply provide that any dispute, controversy, or claim arising out of the contract will be settled through arbitration. However, in some cases, one party may want to reserve a few potential disputes for the courts. If so, those matters should be specifically described in the provisions covering dispute resolution. Among the areas in which a party may want to make a reservation are disputes involving the nondisclosure of trade secrets or confidential information and other conflicts that might require immediate judicial assistance through, for example, a temporary restraining order or preliminary attachment.

Sample Contract Provision: Option To Purchase

The following provision is an example of procedures that might be included to facilitate a party's withdrawal by means of the other party's purchase of its interest in the JV. Such a provision is especially useful when the relationship has soured but it makes sense to continue the business. In negotiating this provision, the parties should consider the events that will trigger the option and the price to be paid in the transaction.

OPTION TO PURCHASE

1. On the occurrence of any of the following events:

(a) The insolvency or bankruptcy of one of the Parties;

(b) Any liquidation, dissolution, merger, consolidation, or reorganization of any of the Parties, or any transfer of more than [*number*] percent of the [*specify type of interest*, e.g., issued and outstanding stock *or* partnership shares] of any of the Parties;

(c) Any Party's material breach of this Agreement that is not cured within [*number*] days following written notification to the breaching Party from the other Party, which notice shall specify the nature of the breach and shall refer to the rights of the nonbreaching Party as provided in this Agreement; or

(d) The accumulated losses of any Party during the [*number*] year period ending on [*date*] exceeds the paid-in capital of that same Party as of that date, then, in the case of items (a) - (c) above, any Party that has not suffered the event or materially breached this Agreement, or in the case of item (d) above, any of the Parties, shall have the right to purchase all of the Venture Interest held by the other Party on the terms set forth in this Section. This purchase right shall be exercisable in writing within [*number*] days after the later of the date on which (1) a Party receives written notice of the occurrence of such event, or (2) an appraisal, as contemplated in #2. below, is concluded. Each Party specifically agrees to notify the other Party promptly in writing of the occurrence of any of the events specified in this Section.

2. The purchase price for any Venture Interests to be purchased under this Section shall be computed as follows. Within [*number*] days after the occurrence of an event described in #1. above, the Parties shall jointly appoint an investment banking firm ("Mutually Acceptable Investment Banker") to make a value determination of the Venture Interest. If joint action fails, each Party shall separately designate an investment banking firm, and within [*number*] days after those appointment, the several firms shall select a single investment banking firm to make a final determination of value ("Neutral Investment Banker"). Within [*number*] days after the appointment of the Mutually Acceptable or Neutral Investment Banker, such Banker shall render its appraisal of the fair market value of the Venture Interest to be purchased, which appraisal shall be binding and conclusive on the Parties. The Parties shall share equally the cost of the appraisal.

3. The payment date of the purchase price pursuant to this Section shall not be later than [*number*] days after [*date*]. Any purchase of a Venture Interest pursuant to this Section shall take place on the payment date, and the certificates representing such Venture Interest so purchased shall be duly endorsed and delivered to the purchasing Party on the payment date.

4. If, on the occurrence of one of the events specified in #1. above, a Party that has the right to purchase the Venture Interest of the other Party does not exercise such right within the [*number*] day period specified in #1. above, then this Venture shall be liquidated and dissolved in the manner specified in this Agreement.

CHAPTER 17

Terminating the JV

COMMENTATORS HAVE SUGGESTED that more than 50 percent of international JVs survive no longer than five years. Although venturers sometimes contemplate such a short term initially, the more likely scenario is that a breakup of the JV will be unplanned, in the sense that it occurs before the end of the JV term specified in the formation documents. Most JV agreements include restrictions on the transfer of ownership and the ability of a venturer to withdraw unilaterally from the JV. These restrictions are designed to promote continuity in the relationship.

Nevertheless, when the JV is formed, it is important for the parties to consider carefully the procedures that might facilitate an orderly termination of the JV in the event that the relationship sours. Absent such an agreement, the parties may find themselves involved in a protracted and expensive dissolution battle, which could impair their ability to make new strategies for exploitation in the geographic and technical markets where the JV was active.

The termination provisions included in the definitive documents for the JV will depend to an extent on whether the JV will have a fixed term (e.g., completion of a specified project) or whether the parties originally contemplated a perpetual or indeterminate term for the business. When the JV is to run for a fixed term, it is important to have a post-termination plan as part of the initial arrangements, and that the plan set the rules for one or both of the parties to continue to operate in the JV's field of activity following termination of the business. When the JV does not have a fixed term, it is more difficult to draft definitive provisions relating to termination at the beginning of the JV; however, at a minimum, the parties should include some of the procedures described in Chapter 16 for regularly reviewing the continuing viability of the JV relationship before it implodes with disputes.

Restrictions on Transfers of Ownership

A transfer of a partner's ownership interest in the JV to a new party would effectively terminate the original business relationship between the parties, even if the JV entity continues. Accordingly, as a general rule, the parties will agree to strictly prohibit the sale or transfer of their ownership interests for a specified time, usually corresponding to the initial JV term. Precluded transfers will include not only an outright sale of the interests, but also any pledge or other encumbrance of the interests, although in some cases a party will be permitted to transfer the interest to a successor corporation or a wholly owned subsidiary of the party. Waiver of the restriction on transfer would require the consent of the other party.

After the restriction period has ended, the parties usually have a right of first offer or first refusal. A right of first offer obligates the party that seeks a purchaser for its interest to first offer it to the other party on the same terms at which the potential seller would complete the transaction. If the other party is unwilling to purchase the interest on those terms, the seller then has a specified time within which to find a purchaser on terms no less favorable than those originally offered to the other party. A right of first refusal is similar, but the selling party must first have an offer to purchase the shares from a third party before offering the same to the other party.

Pre-Termination Withdrawals of a JV Partner

In a variety of situations, one of the JV partners may be allowed, or required, to withdraw from the JV prior to the date on which the parties originally contemplated that the relationship would terminate. Such events tend to be major, fundamental changes or disturbances that affect the anticipated risks or goals of the JV or of its partners separately. The withdrawal of a party and the continuation of the business by the other party is obviously an alternative to simply dissolving and liquidating the entity. In some cases, continuing the business without both of the original parties is simply not a viable alternative, particularly when the withdrawing party takes with it certain resources, technical or otherwise, that are of fundamental importance to the success of the JV. However, because dissolution and liquidation often diminishes the value of the interests of both parties, some effort will generally be made to establish equitable procedures for liquidating the interests of one party without terminating the business itself.

WITHDRAWAL EVENTS

At the time a JV is formed, the parties should anticipate events that might raise one party's fears over the continued viability of the JV, whether on account of changes in the separate entities of the JV partners or within operation of the JV itself. In particular, the parties should consider the possibility of the following events that could trigger provisions for withdrawal of one JV partner:

- OPERATIONAL PROBLEMS OF A PARTNER An obligation to withdraw may be activated by events that reflect a downturn in the financial and business operations of the party, including the appointment of a trustee or receiver for all or any part of the assets or property of a party; the insolvency or bankruptcy of a party; any general assignment for the benefit of creditors by a party; or attachment of all or substantially all of the assets of a party.
- PARTNER'S CHANGE OF OWNERSHIP Another concern for one party would be a change in the ownership and management structure of the other party, including any transfer of all or substantially all of the assets of the party, or any merger, consolidation, or other transaction resulting in a change of ownership of a controlling block of ownership interests. In effect, the relationship is no longer between the same parties.
- MATERIAL CHANGE IN PARTNER'S BUSINESS A material change, adverse or otherwise, in the overall business activities of a party may be construed as disruptive to the JV. Obviously, the liquidation of a party qualifies as such a change. However, termination may also be appropriate when continued involvement with the JV is no longer compatible with the party's functional or product line objectives, even if the party stays financially solvent.
- OPERATIONAL PROBLEMS OF THE JV A right or obligation to withdraw from the JV may arise from acts and events relating to the JV itself. For example, some material breach of the JV agreement, if left uncured, should create a right

in the hands of the non-breaching party to assume ownership, as well as management control of the enterprise. In some cases the poor financial performance of the JV, or failure to meet a milestone of performance, will trigger an option in favor of one or both of the parties to buy out the other party and assume control of the JV. The loss of services of key personnel might also be such an event.

PROCEDURES FOR FACILITATING WITHDRAWAL OF A PARTY

A number of procedures may be used to facilitate the withdrawal of one party from the JV, either by the sale of the ownership interest of the withdrawing party to the remaining party, or by permitting the withdrawing party to secure some liquidity for its investment through transactions involving third parties. Among the provisions that might be considered by the parties are the following:

- OPTION TO LIQUIDATE Granting the right to either party, at its option, to liquidate and dissolve the JV. If such a right is provided, the parties should also include a valuation mechanism, and an option in favor of the other party to purchase the interest of the party that wishes to withdraw, thereby allowing the business activities of the JV to continue.
- PERMITTED SALE TO THIRD PARTY Permitting either party to sell its shares to a third party, perhaps in a public offering, subject to a right of first refusal in favor of the other party. An interesting variation on this alternative would permit either party to obtain an offer for the sale of the entire JV, with the other party having the right of first refusal to buy the interest of the withdrawing party on the same terms and conditions presented by the third party.
- BUY-SELL OPTIONS Use of a buy-sell option that permits one party to set a price on its shares and then allows the other party to choose between buying the shares or selling its own shares at the stated price. Alternatively, one party may be given the right to sell its interest in the venture to the other party after a fixed period of time at a price to be fixed by an independent appraisal. The other party must either purchase the shares or dissolve the JV. This method may be utilized when a certain milestone has not been achieved by a date specified by the parties.
- UNILATERAL PURCHASE RIGHTS In certain situations, one party may be provided with the unilateral right to purchase the shares of the other party after a fixed period of time, with the price to be determined at the time the option is exercised.

VALUING THE INTEREST OF THE WITHDRAWING PARTY

Assuming that the parties can reach agreement regarding the various events that might create a purchase right in one or both of them, the next item to consider is the price at which the JV interests may be purchased. Obviously, in those cases where the procedures contemplate an offer by a third party, then the price can be dictated by the terms and conditions of any such outstanding offer. However, in other cases, because no public market will exist for the JV interests, it will be necessary for the parties to use various appraisal procedures to determine the value of each interest to be purchased and sold.

COMMON VALUATION METHODS

Valuation provisions included in JV agreements generally are intended to provide the parties with some degree of certainty regarding the value to be assigned to their interest on their withdrawal from the JV. For the valuation provisions to achieve this basic objective, they must be drafted in a manner that conforms with certain guiding principles. First, the agreement must be clear and unambiguous with respect to the material terms, especially the transfer price, because, although the agreement is generally drafted when the parties are of one mind regarding the business and its prospects, disputes are quite likely to occur when the valuation provisions become applicable. Second, the agreement must provide a means for determining the transfer price and value of a departing partner's interest, whether the value is defined as a stated amount, a formula, or by reference to the determination of a third party. Third, the transfer price should be reasonable, which typically means that the agreement price represents the fair market value of the business interest on the date the agreement is signed.

Computing the value of an ownership interest in a JV that is privately held is difficult. No single valuation method is equally appropriate for all businesses, and a wide variety of valuation procedures have been used or proposed. In some cases, the parties merely agree on a person who will be entrusted with the task of establishing the value, such as when the agreement calls for the value to be set by mutual agreement of the parties, independent appraisers, arbitrators, or bona fide prospective purchasers. Alternatively, the parties may agree on the use of a specific valuation formula, generally keyed either to the value of the assets of the business or its value as a going concern. Among the common choices with respect to formula are: (1) the book value of the interest, (2) the cost of the interest to the partner plus an annual increment (e.g., 10% per annum since formation), (3) capitalization of earnings, or (4) some combination of two or more formula measures. In appropriate cases, minority and marketability discounts and control premiums are used to adjust valuations that are based on other factors.

When the value of an interest in a JV is to be determined, the acquisition price or a means of determining the price should always be determined in advance and set forth in detail and with great care as part of the agreement. It is important to avoid leaving anything to be settled at the time that a transfer is set to occur, because it is always easier for the parties to reach agreement while the buyer and seller are still unknown. However, given the fact that a number of years may pass before the valuation provisions will actually come into play, consideration should always be given to periodically reexamining the valuation formula over the period of the agreement, to take into account the changing financial and business conditions of the JV and the needs and roles of the parties to the agreement.

FACTORS IN DETERMINING VALUATION PROCEDURES

As difficult as it might be to identify the appropriate valuation method, there are still other factors that need to be considered, such as the following:

- TIMING A purchase price may be reasonably related to the timing of the event giving rise to the purchase right. For example, if one party goes bankrupt within a few months after the JV commences, a logical purchase price would be the amount originally paid for the shares less a pro-rata portion of any expenses incurred during the brief period that the JV was operating. The assumption is that the JV has not yet developed the capacity to generate a steady flow of income.

- ALTERNATIVE FORMULAS Assuming that the JV has been operating for some time when the purchase right event occurs, reference might be made to such customary measures of value as net book value, revenues, net income, or cash flow. If the parties anticipate that the JV will move through a number of stages of development, it may be best to choose alternative formulas as the business matures. If the parties are uncomfortable with this type of procedure, it may be possible to substitute a purchase price formula based on actual performance following the purchase of the interest. However, these earn-out provisions can become quite complex, and generally should be avoided if at all possible.
- USE OF INDEPENDENT PARTIES Because the dissolution of the JV and the JV relationship tends to be difficult, it may be easier to allow for the valuation by independent investment bankers mutually selected by the parties.

A FEW PRACTICAL CONSIDERATIONS

Whatever procedures are utilized to value the interest of one party in the JV, it will be almost impossible to capture the sense of anticipation and expected financial benefit that served as the original inducement for the relationship. Often, when the JV depends on the unique skills and contacts of a local partner, the right of the other partner to purchase the interest of the local partner on default is almost worthless, because it is unlikely that the other partner will be able to continue the operations of the business without access to the labor, facilities, and distribution channels offered by the local partner. In those cases, the parties may opt to simply liquidate and dissolve the enterprise and, in fact, it is not uncommon to provide for liquidation in the event that an exercisable purchase right is not utilized.

On the other hand, if the JV has reached the stage where its business activities can be sustained without the direct participation of one of the original parties, an effort may be made to seek additional transactions that provide a market and suitable liquidity for the interest of the departing partner and, if necessary, additional financing for the expansion or continuation of the business activities of the JV. Among the possible financing vehicles would be a public or private offering to investors who would purchase part of the interest of the departing partner, as well as newly-issued ownership interests of the enterprise. The creation of a public market for the interests of the JV would also allow the remaining party to realize a return on its investment through periodic sales of a portion of its own interest.

Termination of the JV

Despite the best intentions of the parties, it is often necessary to consider the circumstances under which one or both of the parties may elect to terminate the enterprise. Termination of the JV leads to liquidation and dissolution of the business entity, a process that is largely dictated by applicable law and any agreements between the parties regarding the distribution of specified assets of the JV. The business of the JV will largely cease during the period required to liquidate and dissolve, although the management of the enterprise, or any other persons appointed to supervise the liquidation of the venture, will continue to collect any receivables and pay any liabilities. Appropriate provision will be made for the contingent claims of creditors, and a final accounting will be made that records each of the JV's assets and permits the preparation of final tax returns. If a dispute arises regarding the final accounting, it may be necessary for the parties to engage third party experts and mediators to assist in valuation and similar matters. The liquidation provisions can be tailored to suit the specific activities of the JV.

In drafting liquidation provisions, consideration must be given to the interests of the various parties who may be involved with the JV. One set of interests includes the desire of the partners to maintain and preserve the assets that they may have contributed or otherwise made available to the JV. These assets can include capital (i.e., cash contributions), goods, and inventory transferred to the JV, often without formal documentation; technology; goodwill; trademarks; and employees. Another important group of interests belong to some of the other stakeholders in the JV, including the desire of the government in the host country to protect the jobs of local employees of the JV, the need to assure payment to the JV's creditors, and the goal of avoiding material disruptions in the expectations of the JV's other business partners (e.g., customers, suppliers, etc.). These stakeholder interests may complicate the liquidation and dissolution process, particularly if host government approvals are required.

PARTNERS' INTERESTS

The preservation of the original assets of the partners can present some interesting issues. For example, the goal of returning capital will presumably be less important as the length of the JV's operations increases, because the partners will presumably have received a sufficient amount of profits to ensure the requisite level of profitability and return on investment. If this is not the case, however, it is important to consider how the effects of inflation might be taken into account in establishing a liquidation preference for the partners.

Assets that are tangible, such as inventory, machinery, and raw materials, may be reclaimed by the contributor, either by simply taking each asset directly or by arranging for local sale. Intangibles, such as know-how, trademarks, and goodwill, present more difficult problems, and the contributor's ability to gain the full measure of value for these items will depend on the use and enforceability of noncompetition covenants, and other restrictions on the use of the know-how.

Although deference must be paid to applicable laws and regulations, in many cases the parties may be able to tailor their agreement with respect to liquidating distributions to suit the specific activities of the JV and the preferences of the partners. For example, when one or more of the assets of the JV are best suited to use by one, but not both, of the parties, and sale of the asset and distribution of the cash proceeds makes little sense, then an effort should be made to ensure that such assets are distributed to the party to whom they have the most value.

STAKEHOLDERS' INTERESTS

The interests of stakeholders are really most important if one of the partners intends to continue the business conducted by the JV in some other form following the termination of the relationship. In such situations, the actual termination and dissolution of the JV is similar in effect to the withdrawal of a partner, as described above, and the party that is seeking to continue the business must consider the following potential problems:

- KNOW-HOW Know-how disclosed during the course of the relationship cannot easily be recaptured, and local law may make it difficult to enforce a noncompetition agreement, thereby making it more difficult for the continuing venturer to operate the business free from potential competition, or to recruit another local partner.
- GOODWILL OF JV Rights to goodwill, and trademarks in particular, may be disputed by the noncontinuing party, and it will be extremely important for the continuing party to be able to recapture the benefits of the trademark to prevent others from diluting the continuing party's control over the quality of its products.
- DISTRIBUTION CHANNELS The continuing viability of distribution channels in the local market must be considered if the continuing party is not local. It may be prohibitively expensive for the continuing party to develop its own distribution channels, and some local dealers may be unwilling to deal with anyone other than the departed local partner of the JV.

Post-Termination Considerations

Even though the formal JV relationship is terminated and the entity is liquidated and dissolved, certain agreements between the parties will survive. Most importantly, the parties will remain obligated under the terms of their agreement with respect to the confidentiality of proprietary information that was exchanged or otherwise received. In most cases, each party will be required to return all documentation (including copies) received from the other party that may constitute confidential information. Also, it is important for the parties to reach agreement as to how customers of the JV are to be handled in the future.

In addition, consideration must be given to satisfying the claims of creditors and other third parties that may arise following the dissolution of the venture. Although reference must be made to applicable law regarding the liability of the venturers for the return of liquidating distributions, it is appropriate to consider maintaining insurance to cover any liabilities associated with defective products, labor claims, or, if appropriate, environmental matters. If such a claim is successfully asserted, the parties are presumably free to allocate responsibilities between them in accordance with various indemnification and contribution agreements.

CHAPTER 18

Venturers' Agreement

THE FOLLOWING COMPREHENSIVE FORM of Venturers' Agreement contains provisions for an international JV dedicated to the research and development of technologies and, ultimately, to production and distribution of the resulting products. The agreement covers the major areas of negotiation and discussion with respect to a JV, including formation, capitalization, representations and closing matters, management and control, operations, and termination. It should be noted that this type of agreement is most often formulated to reflect the interests of JV parties, whether they form a partnership, corporate entity, or other organization. The term "Venturers' Agreement" is used for convenience, but would usually be replaced with "Shareholders' Agreement," "Partnership Agreement," or the like.

This agreement is provided for illustrative purposes only, with commentary about individual contract provisions and the alternatives available. It is essential that your agreement be drafted for your specific circumstances. Drafting an agreement should not be taken lightly, particularly when it is for a cross-border JV. This complex task is full of legal traps for the unwary. Both parties should obtain separate legal counsel.

Sample Contract: Venturers' Agreement

THIS VENTURERS' AGREEMENT ("Agreement") is made and entered into at [*address*] this [*date*] by and among [*name*], a [*description of entity*] having its principal office at [*address*] ("Technology Venturer"), [*name*], a [*description of entity*], having its principal office at [*address*] ("Cash Venturer"), and [*name*], a [*description of entity*], having its principal office at [*address*] ("Company").

COMMENT: One venturer is referred to as the "Technology Venturer," because its primary contribution will be the technology necessary for the pursuit of the JV's activities. The other venturer is referred to as the "Cash Venturer," because it will provide a large amount of cash for the JV. These terms can obviously be varied. The JV Company is made a party to this Agreement, as soon as it has been formed because some contract obligations and rights will fall on the JV itself.

RECITALS

A. Technology Venturer has conducted research and has developed and possesses certain existing proprietary technical information, technology, and know-how relating to [*description*], which has enabled it to develop [*description*].

B. Technology Venturer and Cash Venturer believe that the aforementioned [*description*] techniques will have important application to the development of Products (as defined in Section 1.6 below).

C. Technology Venturer and Cash Venturer desire to form the Company to develop, manufacture, produce, and distribute [*territory*] the Products.

COMMENT: The recitals set out the primary intent of the parties for entering into the agreement. They usually include a brief description of the objectives of the venturers. In many cases, the recital will also include a description of the assets they intend to contribute to the JV.

NOW, THEREFORE, in consideration of the mutual promises, covenants, and conditions set forth in this Agreement, the parties mutually agree as follows:

1. DEFINITIONS

1.1. CORE TECHNOLOGY

The term "Core Technology" shall mean Technology Venturer's proprietary technical information, technology, and know-how, including without limitation, [*definition*], other than Transferred Technology, which is required to conduct the Company's business in the Field of Activity. Pursuant to that certain Assignment and License Agreement ("Technology Venturer's Assignment") attached as Exhibit [*number or letter*], the Core Technology shall be licensed by Technology Venturer to the Company exclusively with respect to its direct application to the Field of Activity.

COMMENT: Although "Transferred Technology" includes the base technology that is necessary to develop the Products, the Technology Venturer also has other proprietary information that may be useful in the development efforts of the Products. The Technology Venturer may choose to license, rather than assign, this Core Technology to the JV company strictly for use in the designated Field of Activity. Disclosure of such data is a concern for the Technology Venturer, who will be understandably reluctant to expose such information to the risk that the Cash Venturer or others might use it for purposes outside of the JV.

1.2. DEVELOPMENT PROGRAM

The term "Development Program" shall have the meaning set forth in Section 6.2 of this Agreement.

COMMENT: The "Development Program" refers to the development work that is to be conducted by the JV with the Core Technology. The parties will be obligated to agree on a development plan and budget within a specified period of time after formation of the JV, and the plan and budget would become part of the agreement.

1.3. FIELD OF ACTIVITY

The term "Field of Activity" shall mean the areas of development, manufacture, production, and commercial distribution of the Products within the Territory, and shall include but not be limited to [*description of activity*] and all other actions necessary to obtain the approvals required to conduct these activities.

COMMENT: The "Field of Activity" actually refers to the technical applications of the Core Technology agreed on by the parties, as well as the full range of functional tasks (e.g., research and development, manufacture, production, and commercial distribution) necessary for commercialization of the JV's products.

1.4. MARKETS

The term "Markets" shall mean [*definition of proposed consumers*].

COMMENT: The term "Markets" refers to the projected end users of the products to be developed by the JV.

1.5. PARTY

The term "Party" shall mean the Technology Venturer, Cash Venturer, or Company, as the context shall indicate, or, when used in the plural, the Technology Venturer, Cash Venturer, and Company, as the context shall indicate.

Comment: The term "Party" is defined to ease the drafting process, and refers to the JV company and/or one or both of the venturers, as the context dictates.

1.6. PRODUCTS

The term "Products" shall mean [*definition*] that are distributed in the Markets.

COMMENT: The term "Products" refers to the products the venturers have identified in advance as the objectives for research and development. The definition is important because it delineates the technical scope of the relationship between the parties. Presumably, the parties are free to work separately on any project that does not fall within the scope of the products as defined here.

1.7. SUBSIDIARY

The term "Subsidiary" shall mean a corporate entity other than the Company, of which at least [*number*] percent of the voting stock is owned or controlled, directly or indirectly, by a Party.

COMMENT: The term "Subsidiary" refers to other corporations that may be controlled by the JV company or either of the venturers.

1.8. TECHNOLOGY

The term "Technology" shall mean the Transferred Technology and the Core Technology, plus all improvements and enhancements to it developed by the Parties under the Development Program or otherwise under this Agreement, that have been used in the development of Products whether in or out of the Development Program.

COMMENT: The term "Technology" is intended to be all-inclusive, and would cover all the technology that has been contributed by the parties to the JV, as well as the technology that they have developed during the course of their venture.

1.9. TERRITORY

The term "Territory" shall mean [*definition*]. The term "Company Territory" shall mean [*definition*], the term "Technology Venturer Territory" shall mean [*definition*], and the term "Cash Venturer Territory" shall mean [*definition*].

COMMENT: This definition allocates among the JV and each of the venturers the geographic territories where they will have the primary responsibility for commercializing the products to be developed by the JV.

1.10. TRANSFERRED TECHNOLOGY

The term "Transferred Technology" shall mean all proprietary technical information, technology, and know-how that has been previously developed by Technology Venturer relating specifically to the Products, that is owned by Technology Venturer or is otherwise covered or protected by letters patent, patent applications, trademarks, service marks, trade names, copyrights, or licenses held by Technology Venturer as of the Closing Date, and that are required in the development, manufacture, production, testing, use, or distribution of the Products (including, without limitation, items that would be deemed to be Confidential Information under Section 7.4 below). The Transferred Technology shall be assigned to Company effective on the Closing Date pursuant to the Technology Venturer Assignment.

COMMENT: "Transferred Technology" includes all the proprietary information and statutory intellectual property rights owned by the Technology Venturer relating to the Products to be developed by the JV company. The Technology Venturer agrees to assign all the technology to the JV company as part of its original contribution. In attempting to define what should be included in the proprietary information for purposes of this definition, reference is made to the concept of "Confidential Information" that appears later in the agreement. The parties have also agreed to attach an exhibit to the agreement that lists the items to be included as part of the assignment, which items will have already been identified in the due diligence prior to the formation of the JV.

1.11. VENTURER

The term "Venturer" shall mean Technology Venturer or Cash Venturer, as the context shall indicate, or, when used in the plural, Technology Venturer and Cash Venturer, as the context shall indicate.

COMMENT: This provision merely clarifies usage of the term Venturer in singular or plural forms, allowing this more convenient usage when the context is clear.

2. FORMATION AND ORGANIZATION OF COMPANY

COMMENT: Technically, this agreement begins as a "preformation agreement," and includes the agreement of the parties regarding formation and organization of the JV. Once the entity has been formed, it will become a party to the agreement, and the agreement will govern the JV's activities while it exists.

2.1. FORMATION

On or before the Closing Date, Technology Venturer and Cash Venturer shall establish or cause to be established, "[*name of Company*]" which shall be a [*description of entity*] organized under the laws of [*state and/or country*] for the principal business purpose set forth in Section 2.5 below. Immediately after its formation, the Company shall become a Party to this Agreement.

COMMENT: The parties agree to cause the formation of the JV company prior to the chosen closing date of this agreement. At this point, the parties will have agreed on the type of entity, its domicile of organization, its name, and its principal business purpose. See Chapter 8 for a discussion of selecting the entity.

2.2. NAME

The designation of Company shall be "[*name of Company*]" or such other name as may be mutually agreed to by the Venturers.

COMMENT: The parties have selected a name for the JV. Presumably, a check has been made to make sure the chosen name is available and, if necessary, the name has been reserved for use. This provision allows flexibility for last minute changes.

2.3. PRINCIPAL OFFICE

The principal office and place of business of the Company shall be located at [*address*], or at such other place as may be mutually agreed to by the Venturers.

COMMENT: At the time of formation, the principal office of the JV may be located within, or near, the offices of one of the venturers. This facilitates the provision of ancillary services to the JV, and can ease the burdens of starting and operating the business. Once the JV grows and matures, it may seek its own facilities.

2.4. FISCAL YEAR

The fiscal year of the Company shall be [*month/day/year*].

COMMENT: The fiscal year of the JV may be the calendar year or any other 12-month period that may be appropriate to the JV's activities. Tax and accounting specialists should be consulted with regard to the proper choice of a fiscal year.

2.5. BUSINESS PURPOSE

The business purpose of the Company shall be to engage in the Field of Activity, to otherwise exploit the Technology for commercial purposes within the Territory by whatever means including, but not limited to, the license or sale of such Technology with mutual agreement of the Venturers, and to do all things necessary, appropriate, or advisable in furtherance of such purposes.

COMMENT: No JV should be consummated without a clear understanding between the participants regarding the general business purpose of the relationship. Although the ability of the participants to develop a concise and clear statement of the proposed business purpose is no guarantee of the overall success of the JV, it does ensure that the basic parameters of the future business activities have been discussed. See Chapters 9 and 10 for a discussion of selecting the business purpose.

2.6. PRE-FORMATION EXPENSES

All expenses incurred by the Venturers in connection with the preparation of the documents relating to the formation of the Company including, without limitation, registration fees and legal fees, shall be borne by the Company, and the Venturers shall cause the Company to reimburse such expenses to the Venturer that incurred them. In addition, the Venturers agree to cause the Company to reimburse to any Venturer all expenses incurred by such Venturer prior to formation of the Company to the extent that the benefit of such expense runs primarily to the Company and not to the Venturer that incurred such expenses.

COMMENT: Each venturer is likely to incur substantial legal and accounting expenses prior to incorporation with respect to the negotiation of the agreement and the various other documents relating to the operation of the JV's business. The parties have agreed that expenses associated with the formation of the corporation (e.g., franchise taxes, filing fees, legal fees for drafting basic corporate documents, etc.) will be reimbursed out of the funds contributed to the JV as pre-incorporation expenses. However, the expenses associated with negotiating the terms of the transaction must be borne by the venturers themselves.

3. CAPITAL AND CAPITAL ACCOUNTS

COMMENT: The first step in establishing any JV is to determine the contributions each party will be making to the enterprise. In this area, consideration should be given not only to the amount of cash that each party will be expected to contribute to fund the various activities of the venture, but also the content and valuation of any in-kind contributions. The parties must also decide the relative rights that are to be associated with the ownership instruments to be issued in connection with the capital contributions, their obligations to contribute additional capital to the venture or to guarantee any borrowings by the venture from commercial lending institutions, and finally, the nature of other contributions to the venture by the parties that are made other than in the form of a capital contribution.

3.1. PERCENTAGE INTEREST

Except as otherwise expressly set forth in this Agreement, the interest of the respective Venturers in the assets, liabilities, profits, and losses of the Company shall be as follows:
Technology Venturer....................[*number*]%
Cash Venturer................................[*number*]%

A separate capital account shall be maintained for each Venturer. The initial capital account of Cash Venturer shall equal the dollar amount of the Initial Capital Contribution of Cash Venturer. The initial capital account of Technology Venturer shall equal the dollar amount of the Initial Capital Contribution of Technology Venturer as set forth in Section 3.2. Except as otherwise provided in this Agreement, all items of income, gain, loss, or deduction shall be allocated equally between the Venturers and shall increase (if income or gain) or decrease (if loss or deduction) each Venturer's capital account. Distributions shall reduce the respective capital accounts.

COMMENT: The percentage interest of the Venturers depends on the value of their initial respective contributions, as well as the services and assets to be contributed to the JV during operations. The interests may be split 50-50, but the parties are obviously free to choose a different allocation.

3.2. CONTRIBUTIONS

a. **On formation of the Company, Cash Venturer shall contribute to the Company, as its capital contribution, $[*amount*] (the "Cash Venturer Initial Contribution"), and shall receive the ownership interest in the Company described in Section 3.1.**

b. **On formation of the Company, Technology Venturer shall contribute to the Company, as its capital contribution, (i) $[*amount*] and (ii) all of the Transferred Technology (the "Technology Venturer Initial Contribution"). In return, the Technology Venturer shall receive the ownership interest in the Company described in Section 3.1. The Venturers have agreed that the Technology Venturer Initial Capital Contribution has a fair market value of $[*amount*].**

COMMENT: This paragraph sets out the procedures for the delivery of the consideration, and contains an acknowledgment of the parties as to the fair market value of assets to be contributed to the corporation. The parties will be required to value all the forms of consideration contributed to the venture in exchange for securities. Obviously, the most difficult questions arise over contributions of intangible property because of the difficult task of accurately assessing the value of technology that has not been fully developed and for which no proven commercial application exists. Nonetheless, it is important to estimate the value of any item of intangible property, because allocation of the venture's income is usually based on the values of the respective capital contributions.

3.3. ADDITIONAL CAPITAL CONTRIBUTIONS

a. **Subject to Section 3.3(b), no additional capital stock may be issued by the Company other than by the mutual written consent of the Venturers. The Venturers shall meet no less frequently than annually following the formation of the Company to determine its capital needs for the next succeeding year.**

b. **In the event that the initial capital contributions to the Company pursuant to Section 3.2 (together with interest earned by the Company on the cash so contributed) are insufficient to fund the activities of the Company and the Development Program until all approvals (governmental or otherwise) have been obtained for the manufacture and sale of the Products in the Territory, then the Venturers may, but shall not be obligated to, agree to make additional capital contributions to the Company. Any such agreed on capital contributions shall be made in the proportion to which each Venturer's total capital contribution bears to the aggregate capital contributions of the Venturers from time to time existing. On written notification by the Company's Board of Directors to the Venturers that the Company does not have sufficient capital to fund the activities of the Company, the Venturers shall promptly meet with management of the Company to ascertain the amount of funding reasonably required under the circumstances. The Venturers shall thereafter enter into a mutually acceptable agreement with respect to such additional capital contributions, if any.**

COMMENT: It is often necessary to provide additional capital to the venture following the development stage. As part of the periodic budgeting process, the parties must consider the need for additional financing and must reach agreement regarding the timing and amount of the new contributions. If additional capital is necessary, each of the parties will usually be obligated to make the contribution in proportion to their then-existing interest in the income and assets of the venture.

3.4. WITHDRAWALS OF CAPITAL

Except as otherwise provided in this Agreement, neither of the Venturers shall have the right to withdraw or to demand a return of all or any part of its capital contribution to the Company.

COMMENT: Neither venturer will be permitted to withdraw any capital from the JV company without the consent of the other venturer.

3.5. DEFAULT ON ADDITIONAL CAPITAL CONTRIBUTION OBLIGATION

To the extent that either of the Venturers fails to contribute its proportionate share of any additional capital called for under Section 3.3, then from and after the date such capital was to have been contributed to the Company, the shareholding percentages of the Venturers shall promptly be adjusted to reflect the increase in capital contributed by either of the Venturers such that the shareholding interest of the Venturers shall accurately reflect the percentage of

each Venturer's total capital contribution as it bears to the aggregate capital contributions of both Venturers.

COMMENT: Should one party be unable or unwilling to make another capital contribution, the interests of the parties will be modified to reflect the actual amounts of capital contributed. However, in some cases, the failure to make an additional contribution may have more dire consequences, perhaps providing the non-defaulting party with the right to terminate the venture or purchase the interest of the other party.

4. REPRESENTATIONS AND WARRANTIES; INDEMNIFICATION

COMMENT: Although the representations and warranties from each JV party are intended to facilitate the appropriate level of due diligence prior to formation of the JV, they do carry with them the potential for liability between the participants if any of the representations and warranties should prove to be false or misleading in light of events that occur following consummation of the transaction. In most jurisdictions, each participant would be liable to the other for any fraudulent act or statement made during the course of the formation and operation of the JV. Nevertheless, it is common practice to include specific provisions governing indemnification obligations between the participants with respect to deficiencies in the representations and warranties.

4.1. REPRESENTATIONS AND WARRANTIES OF TECHNOLOGY VENTURER

To induce Cash Venturer to enter into this Agreement, Technology Venturer represents and warrants to Cash Venturer as of the date of this Agreement and as of the Closing Date as follows:

a. **Technology Venturer is a [*type of entity*] duly organized, validly existing, and in good standing under the laws of [*state and/or country*]. Technology Venturer has all requisite authority and power to own and operate its properties and assets, and to carry on its business as presently conducted and as proposed to be conducted.**

b. **Technology Venturer has all requisite legal and corporate power to execute and deliver this Agreement and any other agreement referred to herein to which Technology Venturer is a party (collectively the "Technology Venturer Agreements") and to carry out and perform its obligations under the terms of any of the Technology Venturer Agreements.**

c. **All actions on the part of Technology Venturer, and its owners, representatives, and management, that are necessary for the performance of Technology Venturer's obligations under any of the Technology Venturer Agreements have been or will be taken prior to the Closing Date. The Technology Venturer Agreements are each valid and binding obligations of Technology Venturer, enforceable in accordance with their respective terms, subject to laws of general application relating to bankruptcy, insolvency, and the relief of debtors.**

d. **The Technology Venturer's execution, delivery, or performance of any of the Technology Venturer Agreements or any other instrument to be executed in connection with this Agreement shall not:**

   i. **Conflict with, violate, or result in a breach of any term, condition, or provision of any indenture, material contract, or other material agreement to which**

Technology Venturer is a party or by which Technology Venturer or its properties is subject or bound.

ii. Constitute a material default under any instrument specified in (i).

iii. Result in the acceleration of any material obligation under any instrument specified in (i) or permit the termination of such instrument.

iv. Result in the creation of any mortgage, pledge, lien, encumbrance, or charge on any of Technology Venturer's properties.

v. Conflict with or violate the provisions of any judgment, decree, or order to which Technology Venturer is subject, the provisions of Technology Venturer's Articles of Incorporation or Bylaws or, to the best of its knowledge, any law or regulation.

e. Technology Venturer is not a party to any pending or threatened suit, action, or legal, administrative, arbitration, or other proceeding that might materially and adversely affect the transactions contemplated by any of the Technology Venturer Agreements or the business of the Company, the Transferred Technology or the Core Technology existing as of the date of this Agreement or to be in existence as of the Closing Date, nor does Technology Venturer know of any existing facts that are likely with the passage of time to give rise to such a suit, action, or proceeding.

f. No consent, approval, or authorization of, nor any designation, declaration, or filing with, any governmental authority on the part of Technology Venturer is required in connection with the valid execution and delivery of any of the Technology Venturer Agreements or the consummation of any other transaction contemplated by any of the Technology Venturer Agreements.

COMMENT: The representations and warranties included in Section 4.1 are made by the Technology Venturer. The representations and warranties are an important part of any commercial transaction and are usually supplemented by a legal and commercial due diligence investigation, to provide independent verification of statements made by the participants regarding their existing business activities and their plans and intentions in connection with the proposed JV.

4.2. REPRESENTATIONS AND WARRANTIES OF CASH VENTURER

To induce Technology Venturer to enter into this Agreement, Cash Venturer represents and warrants to Technology Venturer as of the date of this Agreement and as of the Closing Date as follows:

a. Cash Venturer is a [*type of entity*] duly organized, validly existing, and in good standing under the laws of [*state and/or country*]. Cash Venturer has all requisite authority and power to own and operate its properties and assets and to carry on its business as presently conducted and as proposed to be conducted.

b. Cash Venturer has all requisite legal and corporate power to execute and deliver this Agreement and any other agreement referred to herein to which Cash Venturer is a party (collectively the "Cash Venturer Agreements") and to carry out and perform its obligations under the terms of any of the Cash Venturer Agreements.

c. All actions on the part of Cash Venturer and its owners, representatives, and management that are necessary for performance of Cash Venturer's obligations under any of the Cash Venturer Agreements have been or will be taken prior to the Closing Date. The Cash Venturer Agreements are each valid and binding obligations of Cash Venturer, enforceable in accordance with their respective terms, subject to laws of general application relating to bankruptcy, insolvency, and the relief of debtors.

d. The Cash Venturer's execution, delivery, or performance of any of the Cash Venturer Agreements or any other instrument to be executed in connection with this Agreement shall not:

   i. Conflict with, violate, or result in a breach of any term, condition, or provision of any indenture, material contract, or other material agreement to which Cash Venturer is a party or by which Cash Venturer or its properties is subject or bound.

   ii. Constitute a material default under any instrument specified in (i).

   iii. Result in the acceleration of any material obligation under any instrument specified in (i) or permit the termination of such instrument.

   iv. Result in the creation of any mortgage, pledge, lien, encumbrance, or charge on any of Cash Venturer's properties.

   v. Conflict with or violate the provisions of any judgment, decree, or order to which Cash Venturer is subject, the provisions of Cash Venturer's Articles of Incorporation or Bylaws or, to the best of its knowledge, any law or regulation.

e. Cash Venturer is not a party to any pending or threatened suit, action, or legal, administrative, arbitration, or other proceeding that might materially and adversely affect the business of the Company or the transactions contemplated by any of the Cash Venturer Agreements, nor does Cash Venturer know of any existing facts that are likely with the passage of time to give rise to such a suit, action, or proceeding.

f. No consent, approval, or authorization of, nor any designation, declaration, or filing with, any governmental authority on the part of Cash Venturer is required in connection with the valid execution and delivery of any of the Cash Venturer Agreements or the consummation of any other transaction contemplated by any of the Cash Venturer Agreements.

COMMENT: The representations and warranties included in Section 4.2 are provided by the Cash Venturer, although the venturer will probably be involved in various other functional activities for the JV once the development work has been completed.

4.3. SURVIVAL OF REPRESENTATIONS AND WARRANTIES

The respective representations and warranties of the Venturers shall survive the Closing and shall continue in full force and effect for [*number*] years after the Closing Date.

COMMENT: Although an action for fraud will generally survive any time limit imposed in the JV documentation, the parties will usually agree that the representations and warranties will survive for a specified period following the consummation of the transaction. The period may be established to conform with the statute of limitations under applicable national law or may be tied to a specific technical or financial milestone relating to the JV's activities. It is also possible to single out areas of particular concern with respect to which great uncertainties exist, and to establish specific procedures relating to future risks associated with matters covered by one or more representations or warranties.

4.4. INDEMNIFICATION

a. Each Venturer shall indemnify and hold the other Venturer, Company, and their respective owners, directors, officers, employees, and agents harmless from and against any and all claims, liabilities, losses, costs, damages, and expenses, including

costs of investigation, court costs, and reasonable attorneys' fees, to which any of them may become subject arising from or in any manner connected with, directly or indirectly, any material misstatement, error, or omission in any representation or warranty of the indemnifying Venturer (the "Indemnifying Venturer") contained in this Agreement (without effect on the Indemnifying Venturer's liability under the various instruments and documents to be executed in connection with this Agreement).

b. The Venturer seeking indemnification under (a) ("Indemnified Venturer") shall give written notice to the Indemnifying Venturer of its indemnification claims, specifying the amount and nature of the claim, and giving the Indemnifying Venturer the right to contest any such claim represented by counsel of its choice. If any such claim is made by the Indemnified Venturer, such claim arises from the claims of a third party against the Indemnified Venturer, and the Indemnifying Venturer does not elect to undertake the defense of the third party's claim, then by written notice within [*number*] days after receipt of the original notice from the Indemnified Venturer, the Indemnified Venturer shall be entitled to indemnity pursuant to the terms of this Agreement to the extent of its payment in respect of such claim. To the extent that the Indemnifying Venturer undertakes the defense of such claim in good faith by proceeding diligently at its expense, and without materially impairing the financial conditions or operations of the Indemnified Venturer, the Indemnified Venturer shall be entitled to indemnity only if, and to the extent that, such defense is unsuccessful as determined by a final judgment of a court of competent jurisdiction or is settled with the consent of the Indemnifying Venturer. The Venturer defending a third party claim shall have the right to choose its own counsel.

COMMENT: As a general matter, each of the participants will agree to indemnify the other participant with respect to damages, losses, and liabilities suffered by the indemnified party as a result of any material misstatement, error, or omission contained in any of the representations and warranties delivered by the indemnifying party. The documentation will set forth procedures with respect to the indemnification, including notice provisions and, in most cases, the indemnifying party will have the right to assume the defense of any action for which indemnification is available. If the indemnifying party assumes defense of the action and pursues such defense in good faith without materially impairing the financial condition of the other party, the liability of the indemnifying party will usually be limited to the amount of any final adverse judgment.

5. MANAGEMENT

COMMENT: Devising an appropriate structure for the management and control of the venture is one of the most important matters to be negotiated between the parties. See Chapter 14 for a discussion of the management and control of a JV.

5.1. BOARD OF DIRECTORS

a. The Board of Directors of the Company shall consist of [*number*] directors, of which [*number*] directors shall be nominated by Technology Venturer and [*number*] directors shall be nominated by Cash Venturer. After the Closing, the respective rights of the Venturers with respect to the election of directors shall be governed by the provisions of this Section 5.1.

b. If a vacancy in any directorship should occur, for whatever reason, the Venturer who had nominated the former director shall nominate the replacement. The Venturers agree to vote their respective shares for the election of such nominee. Vacancies shall

be filled by vote of the Venturers as provided in the Bylaws. A Venturer may remove any director nominated by such Venturer, with or without cause, and may replace such director with his or its nominee, and the other Venturer shall vote its shares to effect such removal and replacement.

c. **The Board of Directors shall manage the business of Company and may exercise all powers commonly exercised by a Board of Directors, except for such powers as are required to be exercised by Venturers, all in accordance with the Certificate and the Bylaws and applicable statutes. All actions by the Board of Directors shall require the affirmative vote of a majority of the total members of Board of Directors at a meeting at which a quorum is present, except for such actions as to which a higher than majority vote is required pursuant to the provisions of this Agreement, the Certificate, the Bylaws, or applicable law.**

COMMENT: The procedures for selection of the board of directors may be set forth in the charter documents of the corporation, or in the agreements between the parties that describe their rights with respect to the voting of their shares. Among the issues that should be considered are:

- The actual size and composition of the board;
- The procedures for allocating control of the board in those cases when the parties do not choose equal representation;
- Selection of the chairman of the board of directors;
- The role of the board of directors in relation to the officers on the one hand and the shareholders on the other hand; and
- The circumstances under which control of the board may shift to one party.

It is important to remember that all of these provisions should be fully integrated with the language regarding voting and election of directors in the charter documents (e.g., articles, certificate of incorporation, bylaws, and so forth) of the company.

5.2. OFFICERS

The Company shall have a Chairman of the Board, President, Vice President - [*title*], Vice President - [*title*], Secretary, Assistant Secretary, Chief Financial Officer, and such other officers with such titles and duties as the Board of Directors may determine. Any two or more offices may be held by the same person. Officers shall be elected from candidates nominated by the parties at the initial meeting of the Board of Directors and thereafter at each meeting of the Board immediately following the Annual Meeting of Venturers as prescribed in the Bylaws. Officers shall serve for [*number*] year(s) and until their successors are elected and qualified, provided that any officer may be re-elected for successive terms. The Chairman of the Board, the Vice President - [*title*], the Chief Financial Officer, and the Assistant Secretary shall be nominees of Cash Venturer. The President, the Vice President - [*title*], and the Secretary shall be nominees of Technology Venturer.

COMMENT: The board of directors has the legal authority to select each officers of the JV company. Officers generally assume responsibility for the management of day-to-day affairs of the JV, subject to any obligations that might be imposed on them to report to the board of directors. A variety of methods can be used for selecting the officers of a JV company. One procedure that is sometimes used in the case of international JVs is to alternate various positions between the parties, such that a representative of one party serves as the president and chief executive officer every other year. In those years when a party does not have the right to elect the president, it will usually be allowed to name the executive vice president or chief financial officer.

5.3. MANAGEMENT COMMITTEE

Subject to review by the Board of Directors, a Management Committee consisting of [*name*], [*name*] and [*name*] shall be constituted with authority to decide such matters as may be delegated to it from time to time by resolution of the Board of Directors, including the following:

a. **Compensation, including salaries, bonuses, and incentive compensation to be received by the employees of the Company, other than officers;**

b. **The appointment and removal of any employee of the Company;**

c. **The establishment or modification of the Company's proposed annual budget for consideration by the Board of Directors;**

d. **The recommendation to the Board of Directors of appropriate bookkeeping and accounting policies, including the selection of the Company's bookkeeper; and**

e. **Except for the Services Agreements, the License Agreements, or the Development Agreement, entry by the Company into any agreement with any Venturer or a Subsidiary of any Venturer other than with respect to [*exception*] in the ordinary course of the Company's business.**

Regular meetings of the Management Committee may be held at such time and place as shall from time to time be fixed by such Management Committee, and no notice of the meetings shall be required.

COMMENT: The parties may elect to delegate authority for day-to-day decisionmaking to a subgroup of directors who will serve on the management committee. A management committee structure may be appropriate when the board itself is quite large, and includes senior executives of the venturers who wish to reserve their time and efforts for major decisions regarding the venture (e.g., any of the matters in Section 5.4 below), or when the directors are not all located near the site of the JV's activities. If a management committee is used, its members will include the senior officers of the JV company, and the authority of the committee will be limited to compensation and employment matters, budget preparation, and ordinary contract matters.

5.4. ACTIONS REQUIRING UNANIMOUS CONSENT

Notwithstanding anything contained in this Agreement to the contrary, the Company shall not take any of the following actions without obtaining the unanimous consent of the Venturers:

a. **Enter into any business outside of the Field of Activity;**

b. **Engage in lending or borrowing of money in an amount in excess of $[*amount*];**

c. **Acquire, mortgage, pledge, sell, assign, transfer, or otherwise dispose of any property of the Company having a fair market value in excess of $[*amount*] (other than in connection with the sale of products and services in the ordinary course of business) or any interest of the Company (regardless of value) in the legal or beneficial ownership of any other corporation or enterprise;**

d. Adopt any business plan, annual capital, operating or development plan, or budget, including any material modifications thereto;

e. Make a capital expenditure in excess of $[*amount*];

f. Engage in any transaction regarding buildings and land, including the lease, purchase, sale, or mortgage thereof;

g. Issue, repurchase, or redeem any equity or debt securities or instruments issued by the Company;

h. Increase or reduce the capital of the Company;

i. Merge into or with, or acquire all or a portion of, the business of, any other person or entity;

j. Dissolve or enter into voluntary bankruptcy proceedings;

k. Transfer in any one transaction or series of transactions all or a substantial portion of the Company's business or assets;

l. Fix the compensation of the officers of the Company, including bonuses;

m. Declare dividends on any outstanding securities of the Company; or

n. Engage in any act that constitutes a material breach of this Agreement.

COMMENT: The parties need to strike an appropriate balance between permitting the officers and managers of the JV to make appropriate decisions regarding the operation of the enterprise and reserving the right, as the owners of the venture, to review and approve certain matters. The matters that are subject to the shared control of the owners, thereby requiring approval of both JV partners, should be limited to those items that are material to the performance of the venture, because making numerous actions subject to a unanimous vote will diminish, or even eliminate, the ability of the venture to respond quickly to appropriate business opportunities and changes in competitive and other environmental conditions.

6. BUSINESS AND OPERATIONAL ACTIVITIES

COMMENT: The parties need to reach agreement on how the JV business will actually be operated once the company has legally formed and organized. In most cases, this will be done through a series of ancillary agreements covering the functional activities of the JV (see Chapter 15); however, the basic agreements of the parties should be included in the main agreement along with cross-references to the ancillary agreement(s) covering particular matters (e.g., development, technical assistance, distribution, etc.).

6.1. PREPARATION AND REVIEW OF BUSINESS PLAN

Within [*number*] days following the execution of this Agreement, the Venturers shall mutually develop and agree on an initial annual business plan for the Company covering the period ending on the date that is [*date*]. Without limitation, the business plan shall set forth in reasonable detail the plans, goals, and objectives of the Company with respect to research and development, manufacturing, distribution and licensing, including any monthly capital and operating expense budgets, cash flow statements, projected balance sheets, and profit and loss statements for each month and for the end of each year itemized in such detail as the Venturers may reasonably determine, and such other

matters as may be determined by the Venturers. The Venturers shall meet no less frequently than annually to review the then-current business plan, and shall develop and agree on subsequent business plans for the Company during the term of this Agreement.

COMMENT: The development of a business plan for a JV is discussed in Chapter 10.

6.2. RESEARCH AND DEVELOPMENT ACTIVITIES

The Venturers agree to conduct on behalf of the Company, on an accelerated and coordinated basis, such research and development activities as may be necessary for the Venturers to engage in the Field of Activity and manufacture and sell Products in their respective Territories. The research and development activities to be conducted by the Venturers are referred to as the "Development Program". The scope and content of the Development Program shall be as set forth in that certain Development Agreement ("Development Agreement") attached to this Agreement as Exhibit [*number or letter*]. Within [*number*] days following the Closing Date, Technology Venturer and Cash Venturer shall agree on a Preliminary Development Plan and Budget with respect to the Development Program, which Development Plan and Budget shall be appended to the Development Agreement and be made a part of it. The Company will retain responsibility for, and with the consent of both the Venturers may enter into agreements similar to those contemplated in this Section for, the conduct of studies, trials, and product registration for the purpose of securing all approvals (governmental or otherwise) necessary for the Company to engage in the Field of Activity and to manufacture and sell Products in the Company Territory.

COMMENT: Development activities and planning are discussed in Chapter 15.

6.3. MANUFACTURING ACTIVITIES

The Company shall not, without the prior consent of both Venturers, enter into any agreement or appropriate any funds for the construction of a manufacturing facility for the purposes of engaging in the Field of Activity in the Company Territory. At such time as the Board of Directors believes that such a capacity would be beneficial to the Company's activities, it shall consult with each of the Venturers with respect to the proposed project, with the intent of determining whether existing manufacturing facilities operated by one or both of the Venturers can be used by the Company under a mutually acceptable arrangement to be approved by the Venturers.

COMMENT: In this situation, the venturers have agreed to defer any decision regarding the construction of manufacturing facilities until the development work has been completed. At that time, the venturers will either appropriate funds for the construction of internal manufacturing facilities, or may consider entering into a manufacturing agreement with one of the venturers. If such an agreement is completed, it will generally include most of the terms referred to above.

6.4. DISTRIBUTION ACTIVITIES

As more fully set forth in the License Agreements, the Venturers agree that:

a. **Technology Venturer will have an exclusive right to manufacture and sell the Products in the Field of Activity in the Technology Venturer Territory pursuant to the Technology Venturer Agreement, and in no other territory without the prior written consent of Cash Venturer and Company. The Technology Venturer License**

Agreement will contain specific terms with respect to the calculation and payment by Technology Venturer to the Company of a royalty equal to $[*amount*].

b. Cash Venturer will have an exclusive right to manufacture and sell the Products in the Field of Activity in the Cash Venturer Territory pursuant to the Cash Venturer License Agreement, and in no other territory without the prior written consent of Technology Venturer and Company. The Cash Venturer License Agreement will contain specific terms with respect to the calculation and payment by Cash Venturer to the Company of a royalty equal to $[*amount*].

c. The Venturers agree that the Company may license one other entity in addition to the Venturers for the manufacture of Products in the Field of Activity in the Company Territory and may license other entities in addition to the Venturers for the marketing of Products in the Field of Activity in the Company Territory; provided, however, that the Venturers may mutually agree to amend this Agreement and the appropriate License Agreement at any time to permit Technology Venturer and/or Cash Venturer to manufacture and sell the Products in the Field of Activity in parts of the Company Territory. The rights of the Company to grant further licenses as set forth above shall not be diminished thereafter with respect to the remainder of the Company Territory.

COMMENT: The provision regarding distribution rights reflects the breakdown of territorial responsibilities discussed above. See Chapter 15 for a discussion of distribution activities.

6.5. INTERNAL CONTROLS

a. The Venturers shall cause the management of Company to conduct the business of the Company at all times in accordance with high standards of business ethics and to maintain the Company's accounts in accordance with generally accepted accounting principles consistently applied and, specifically, to:

   i. Maintain full and accurate books, records, and accounts that shall, in reasonable detail, accurately and fairly reflect all transactions of Company and shall be kept according to generally accepted accounting principles, consistently applied, employing standards, procedures, and forms conforming to established practice in [*country*]; and

   ii. Devise and maintain a system of internal accounting controls sufficient to provide reasonable assurances that: (i) transactions are executed in accordance with general or specific authorizations, (ii) transactions are recorded as necessary to permit preparation of financial statements and tax returns in conformity with generally accepted accounting principles and to maintain accountability for assets, (iii) access to assets is permitted only in accordance with general or specific authorizations, and (iv) the recorded accountability for assets is compared with existing assets at reasonable intervals and appropriate action is taken with respect to any differences.

b. Access to the books, records, and accounts of the Company shall be made available to each of the Venturers at all times during standard business hours, and each Venturer shall have the right to have such books of account audited by its representatives.

c. The Company will employ independent certified public accountants selected by the unanimous vote of the Board of Directors of the Company. The independent certified public accounting firm of [*name*] shall act as the initial independent accountants to Company pursuant to that certain engagement letter attached to this Agreement as

Exhibit [*number or letter*]. Such firm shall be retained in such capacity by the Company until the Venturers shall have agreed on another firm as independent auditors. The Company will have annual audits made by such independent public accountants in the course of which such accountants shall make such examinations, in accordance with generally accepted auditing standards.

c. The Company will obtain and maintain in force such property damage, public liability, business interruption, worker's compensation, indemnity bonds, and other types of insurance as the Company's executive officers shall determine to be necessary or appropriate to protect the Company from the insurable hazards or risks associated with the conduct of the Company's business.

d. All funds of the Company shall be deposited in the name of the Company in such bank account or accounts as shall be determined by mutual agreement of the Venturers. All withdrawals therefrom shall be made on checks signed on behalf of the Company by any one officer, except for: (a) amounts in excess of $[*amount*], and (b) any payments to be made to Technology Venturer and/or Cash Venturer, in which case all such checks shall require the signature of one (1) officer of each of the Venturers.

e. The law firm of [*name*] shall act as general counsel for Company until otherwise mutually agreed between the Venturers.

COMMENT: The parties must reach agreement on the establishment of accounting and internal controls, including the selection of an independent public accountant to audit the books and records of the venture. The parties should agree that each of them will cause the JV company to maintain full and accurate books and records of account. In addition, the managers of the JV company will be required to devise and maintain a system of internal accounting controls.

6.6. FINANCIAL INFORMATION

a. The Company will deliver to each Venturer: (a) an unaudited balance sheet, statement of operations, and statement of cash flows for each month within 30 days following the end of such month; (b) an unaudited balance sheet, statement of operations, and statement of cash flows for each quarter within 45 days following the end of such quarter; and (c) an audited balance sheet, statement of operations, and statement of cash flows for each fiscal year within 90 days following the end of such year. Unaudited statements will be prepared in accordance with the books and records of the Company, and will fairly present the financial condition and results of operations of the Company for the respective period. Audited statements will be prepared in accordance with generally accepted accounting principles consistently applied.

b. Each Venturer has the right to visit and inspect any of the properties of the Company, and to discuss their affairs, finances, and accounts with their officers, all at such reasonable times and as often as may be reasonably requested.

c. Each Venturer agrees that any confidential, proprietary, or secret information that such Venturer may obtain from the Company, and that the Company has prominently marked "confidential", "proprietary," or "secret" or has otherwise identified as being such, pursuant to financial statements, reports, and other materials submitted by the Company as required under this Agreement, or pursuant to visitation or inspection rights granted under this Agreement, shall be deemed to be Confidential Information (as defined in Section 7.4 below).

COMMENT: Financial reporting is an essential part of monitoring the progress and management of the JV company. The parties need to agree on the scope and content of the financial information regarding the enterprise that is generated and distributed by management in cooperation with the venture's independent public accountants. A good deal of the information may be readily available to the parties involved with the activities of the venture on a day-to-day basis. However, if one party is removed, either geographically or otherwise, from the physical facilities of the JV company, financial information becomes a key part of the venturer's ability to assess the viability of its investment.

6.7. DISTRIBUTIONS OF INCOME AND APPLICATION OF FUNDS

a. Subject to the terms of the Certificate or any other contractual agreement between the Venturers, distributions of operating income shall be made to the Venturers in accordance with their respective aggregate capital contributions. Such distributions shall be made at times mutually determined by the Venturers.

b. Subject to Section 6.7(a), the Venturers shall mutually determine the application of funds internal to the Company (and related investment and financial policies).

COMMENT: The activities of the JV will presumably generate income to the enterprise. Moreover, any sale of assets that might be owned by the JV will also provide cash that would be available for distribution to the shareholders or for reinvestment in the activities of the business. Because external financing opportunities for the JV may be limited, it is important for the parties to carefully consider the policies that are to be followed with respect to distributions of operating income and the internal application of funds. As such, it is important to maintain an ongoing capital budgeting process that ensures that the enterprise will not distribute funds that are better utilized for expansion and related purposes.

6.8. SERVICES AGREEMENTS

To ensure that the Company will receive adequate staff, training, and professional services and other products and materials at the Company's request during the period of [*number*] years commencing on the Closing Date, the Company will enter into Services Agreements with each of the Venturers.

COMMENT: Although the venturers intend for the JV company to be self-supporting at some point in the future, they recognize that various services will need to be provided to the JV during the early stages of development. This provision contemplates services agreements covering the matters described in Chapter 15.

7. VENTURER DUTIES AND OBLIGATIONS

COMMENT: Depending on the circumstances, the parties may include a variety of additional covenants in the JV documents covering:

- General obligations to cooperate with one another and support the JV's activities;
- Covenants to adhere to their fiduciary duties in relation to the JV company and not to engage in competitive activities; and
- Provisions regarding the protection of confidential information if there is no separate agreement on the subject.

7.1. COOPERATION AND SUPPORT

Each of the Venturers agrees to cooperate fully with each other to realize the purposes of the Company and the objectives otherwise set forth in this Agreement. Without limiting the generality of the foregoing, the Venturers agree that they shall assist the Company in complying with all applicable federal, state, and local regulations with regard to the development, manufacture, and distribution of the Products and shall provide the Company with support and assistance as more fully provided for in the Services Agreements.

COMMENT: The parties will agree to cooperate in complying with applicable federal, state, and local regulations for the development, testing, manufacture, and distribution of the venture's products and services. This is particularly important when the products must be approved by government regulators prior to sale to the public. Other support obligations might include construction of plants and facilities, sale of equipment and machinery, and additional financing.

7.2. FIDUCIARY DUTIES AND OBLIGATIONS

The Venturers, the officers, and the directors of the Company shall all have fiduciary responsibility for safekeeping and use of all of the funds and assets (including records) of the Company, regardless of whether the funds or assets are in their immediate possession or control, for exclusive benefit of the Company and the Venturers.

COMMENT: The documents may contain specific provisions relating to the obligations of the parties to adhere to certain fiduciary duties in dealing with each other during the course of the JV and in managing the JV's assets and resources.

7.3. NON-COMPETITION AND OTHER BUSINESS ACTIVITIES

Except as specifically authorized by the respective License Agreements, the Venturers agree that they shall not, directly or indirectly, engage in any business of a substantially similar nature to the business of the Company in the Field of Activity for a period of [*number*] years from and after the Closing Date, anywhere throughout [*area*], nor shall they permit any of their respective subsidiaries or affiliates, as applicable, to engage in such activities. The Venturers acknowledge that the business of the Company shall be [*business*]. Notwithstanding the foregoing, the Venturers may engage in or possess an interest in other business ventures of any nature or description, independently or with others, whether presently existing or later created, other than for the purpose of the development, manufacture, production, and sale of the Products.

COMMENT: The parties may include various agreements relating to their other business activities, including a covenant not to engage in any activities that might compete with those of the venture for a specified period of time, including some period following the expiration of the contemplated term of the enterprise. In most jurisdictions, such a convenant must be reasonable to be enforceable, because restraints of trade are usually permitted with reluctance.

7.4. PROHIBITION AGAINST DISCLOSURE OF CONFIDENTIAL INFORMATION

a. "Confidential Information" shall mean trade secrets, know-how, data, formulas, processes, computer software and related documentation, tools and techniques,

software algorithms and routines, intellectual property or other information, tangible or intangible, of one Party that becomes known by another Party.

b. Except as expressly authorized by any other Party, each Party agrees not to disclose, use, or permit the disclosure or use by others of any Confidential Information unless and to the extent such Confidential Information:

   i. Is not marked or designated in writing as confidential, and is provided for a purpose that reasonably contemplates disclosure to or use by others, provided, however, that information disclosed orally that is designated in writing within three days of such oral disclosure as confidential shall be treated as Confidential Information,

   ii. Becomes a matter of public knowledge through no action of the Party receiving the Confidential Information,

   iii. Was in the receiving Party's possession before receipt of such Confidential Information,

   iv. Is rightfully received by the receiving Party from a third party without any duty of confidentiality,

   v. Is disclosed with the prior written approval of the party providing such Confidential Information, or

   vi. Is independently developed by the receiving Party without any use of the Confidential Information.

COMMENT: Confidentiality agreements are discussed in Chapter 7.

7.5. RESTRICTIONS ON TRANSFERS OF SHARES

a. Without the prior written consent of the other Venturer, no Venturer shall sell, transfer, pledge or otherwise encumber any Shares during the period of [*number*] years beginning on the date of this Agreement. Unless such prior written consent is given, the proposed sale or transfer may not take place, and any attempted sale or transfer in derogation hereof shall be deemed null and void. If for any reason any clause or provision of this Section 7.5(a) should be held unenforceable, invalid, or in violation of law by any court or tribunal, then the nontransferring Venturer shall have the right, exercisable in writing within [*number*] days of the date of final determination of invalidity or unenforceability, to purchase all of the Shares of the transferring Venturer pursuant to the terms of Section 7.5(b) below that such transferring Venturer purported to sell or transfer.

b. If after [*number*] years from the date hereof, either Venturer shall desire to sell all or a part of its Shares, such Venturer shall first provide the other Venturer with written notice of its desire to sell, including a description of the number of Shares to be offered, their proposed price and the financial terms on which they will be offered. The other Venturer shall have [*number*] days after receipt of such notice to exercise, by mailing to such selling Venturer a written notice thereof, a right of first refusal or option to purchase such Shares at the price and on financial terms offered by the selling Venturer. If the other Venturer exercises such right of first refusal or option to purchase, it shall have an additional period of [*number*] days after such exercise within which to make payment for, and take title to, such Shares. If the other Venturer does not exercise such right of first refusal or option to purchase, the selling Venturer shall have a [*number*] day period in which to sell the Shares at a price and on financial terms no less favorable to the selling Venturer than those specified in the selling

Venturer's notice to the other Venturer, provided that the purchaser agrees in writing to be bound by the terms and conditions of this Agreement.

c. The provisions of Sections 7.5(a) and (b) notwithstanding, a Venturer may transfer all (but not part of) the Shares held by it to any corporation that succeeds to all or substantially all of such Venturer's business and properties, or that wholly owns or is wholly owned by, such Venturer; provided, however, that the transferee shall have agreed to be bound jointly with the transferring Venturer by all of the terms and conditions of this Agreement.

d. The Company shall not record the transfer of Shares by a Venturer in violation of this Section 7.5, and shall affix the following legend on any stock certificate representing Shares subject to this Section 7.5:

> "Any sale, assignment, transfer, pledge, bequest, or other disposition of the shares of stock represented by this Certificate is restricted by and subject to the terms and provisions of a Venturers Agreement dated [*date*] by and among this Company, Technology Venturer, and Cash Venturer, a copy of which Agreement is on file in the principal office of this Company, and which Agreement may from time to time hereafter be amended. The shares of stock evidenced by this Certificate have not been registered with the Securities and Exchange Commission, but have been issued pursuant to the private offering exemption under the Securities Act of 1933, as amended."

COMMENT: Provisions relating to transfers of shares typically cover restrictions on transfers, which preclude a venturer from being able to withdraw its ownership interest in the JV company without complying with specified procedures. Also, the venturers will often agree that certain events will create an option in favor of one of them to purchase the shares held by the other on terms and conditions agreed to in advance and made part of the agreement. For convenience, this provision assumes that the company is a corporate entity that has issued shares of stock subject to United States laws. This language will, of course, have to be modified to reflect the type of entity and the requirements of the national laws where the JV is formed. See Chapter 17 for a discussion of restrictions on transfer.

8. TERM AND TERMINATION

COMMENT: The parties must consider the term, or duration, of the JV, as well as events that may lead to termination before expiration of the original fixed term.

8.1. TERM

This Agreement shall take effect as of the date stated at the beginning and, unless otherwise provided herein, shall remain in full force and effect until the earlier of:

a. The mutual written consent of the Venturers to terminate this Agreement;

b. The unilateral election of [*name*] to terminate this Agreement in the event that the Conversion Event does not occur on or before [*date*];

c. The election of one of the Venturers to terminate this Agreement on the occurrence of one of the events specified in Section 8.2.

COMMENT: The JV documents must include provisions that specify the duration of the enterprise. A number of issues need to be considered with respect to establishing the duration of the JV. In concept, a successful JV may enjoy perpetual existence and the parties will seek ways in which the basic relationship can be expanded to include new opportunities in function, technology, product line, and market. However, at the outset the venturers may well be satisfied with establishing an initial term for the enterprise that fits within the realistic business horizon for each of the particular activities to be undertaken and provides the parties with a reasonable opportunity to achieve a proper return on their investment of time, capital, and other resources.

8.2. TERMINATION EVENTS

Either of the Venturers shall have the right to terminate this Agreement on the occurrence of any one of the following events:

a. The appointment of a trustee or receiver for all or any part of the assets or property of the other Venturer;

b. The insolvency or bankruptcy of the other Venturer;

c. Any general assignment for the benefit of creditors by the other Venturer;

d. Any transfer or attachment of all or substantially all of the assets of the other Venturer;

e. Any liquidation, dissolution, merger, consolidation, reorganization, or transfer of more than [*amount*] percent of the issued and outstanding stock of the other Venturer;

f. Any material breach of this Agreement by the other Venturer that is not cured within [*number*] days following written notification to such breaching Venturer from the other Venturer, which notice shall specify the nature of the breach and reference the rights of the non-breaching Venturer as provided herein; or

g. The accumulated losses of the Company during the [*number*] year period ending on [*date*] exceeds the sum of the paid-in capital of the Company as of such date.

Any termination of this Agreement effected by either of the Venturers shall be effective: (i) in the case of one of the events specified in (a) - (e) above, immediately on the delivery of written notice to the other Venturer; (ii) in the case of the event specified in (f) above, at the end of the [*number*] day period specified for the cure of the material breach of this Agreement; and (iii) in the case of the event specified in (g) above, at the end of the [*number*] day period following delivery of written notice to the other Venturer. Each Venturer agrees to notify the other Venturer promptly in writing of the occurrence of any of the events specified above.

COMMENT: In spite of the best intentions of the parties, it is often necessary to consider the circumstances on which one or both of the parties may elect to terminate the enterprise. It is likely that the parties will contemplate the termination of the venture on the occurrence of a fundamental change relating to one party, a material breach by one party of its obligations to the relationship, or the failure of the venture to attain specified technical or financial milestones.

8.3. EFFECT OF TERMINATION OF AGREEMENT

The termination of this Agreement shall not in any way operate to impair or destroy any of the rights or remedies of either Venturer, or to relieve any Venturer of its obligations to comply with any of the provisions of this Agreement that shall have accrued prior to the effective date of termination.

On termination of this Agreement, the Venturers shall vote their respective Shares and cause the Board of Directors to take such actions as are necessary to liquidate and dissolve the Company in accordance with all applicable laws.

COMMENT: Even though the formal JV relationship is terminated and the entity is liquidated and dissolved, certain agreements between the parties will survive the completion of the formal business relationship. Most importantly, the parties will remain obligated under the terms of any agreement with respect to the confidentiality of proprietary information that was exchanged or otherwise received in the course of the JV. In most cases, each party will be required to return all documentation (including copies) received from the other party that may constitute confidential information. Also, it is important for the parties to reach agreement as to how customers of the JV are to be handled in the future.

In addition, consideration must be given to satisfying the claims of creditors and other third parties that may arise following the dissolution of the venture. Although reference must be made to applicable law regarding the liability of shareholders for the return of liquidating distributions, it is appropriate to consider maintaining insurance to cover any liabilities associated with defective products, labor claims, or environmental matters, if appropriate.

If claims are successfully asserted, the parties are presumably free to allocate responsibilities by means of indemnification and contribution agreements.

9. DISSOLUTION AND LIQUIDATION OF COMPANY

On the dissolution of the Company, the Venturers will follow and abide by the following procedures:

a. **The Company's independent certified public accountants shall make a complete and accurate accounting from the date of the last accounting to the date of dissolution, and all required tax returns shall be timely filed.**

b. **The Venturers shall each appoint three (3) individuals who shall jointly act as liquidators to wind up Company (collectively "Liquidator"). The Liquidator shall have the power and authority to take full account of Company's assets and liabilities and to wind up and liquidate the affairs of Company in an orderly and business-like manner as consistent with obtaining the fair value thereof on dissolution. The Company shall engage in no further business thereafter other than as necessary to operate on an interim basis, collect its receivables, pay its liabilities, and liquidate its assets. All proceeds from liquidation shall be distributed in this order of priority: (i) first, to payment of all creditors of Company and the expenses of Liquidator; (ii) second, to a reserve account that the Liquidator deems reasonably necessary for any contingent, known, or unforeseen liabilities or obligations of Company; and (iii) third, the balance: [*amount*], to be distributed as follows: [*distribution plan or methodology*].**

c. **On completion of the distributions in liquidation of the Company as provided in this Section 9, the Liquidator shall cause the cancellation of all share certificates and shall take all other actions appropriate to dissolve and liquidate the Company.**

COMMENT: Termination of the JV leads to liquidation and dissolution of the business entity, a process that is largely dictated by applicable law and any agreements between the parties regarding the distribution of specified assets of the JV. The liquidation provisions can be tailored to suit the specific activities of the JV. For example, when one or more of the assets of the JV are best suited for use by one, but not both, of the parties, and sale of the asset and distribution of the cash proceeds makes little sense, then an effort will be made to ensure that such assets are distributed to the party to whom it has the most value.

10. MISCELLANEOUS PROVISIONS

COMMENT: The agreement will generally contain additional standard clauses and provisions. Among the more important are those that set out the procedures for notices and communications between the parties, as well as the procedures for amending the agreement. In addition, the parties may include language relating to dispute resolution procedures (e.g., arbitration), governing law, force majeure, remedies, and fees and expenses associated with the negotiation of the agreement.

10.1. NOTICES

All notices, requests, demands and other communications required or permitted to be given under this Agreement shall be in writing and shall be mailed to the Party to whom notice is to be given, by telex or facsimile, and confirmed by first class mail, registered or certified, return receipt requested, postage prepaid, and properly addressed as follows (in which case such notice shall be deemed to have been duly given on the [*number*] day following the date of such sending):

[*Set forth contact person and address for each party*, e.g.,
Attn: Corporate Secretary of (*name of Venturer or Company*)
At: (*address for acceptance of notice*)
With a copy to: (*name*)]

Any Party by giving notice to the others in the manner provided above may change such Party's address for purposes of this Section 10.1.

COMMENT: The agreement should specify the procedures for notices and other communications between the parties, including the address where communications should be sent, the manner in which notices may be sent, and any other requirements, such as delivery of communications to a specified representative.

10.2. PUBLICITY AND DISCLOSURE

Subject to limitations placed on [*party*] by the securities laws of the United States of America (including regulations of the Securities and Exchange Commission), the timing and content of any announcements, press releases, and public statements concerning the transactions contemplated under this Agreement will be by mutual agreement of the Venturers and the Venturers agree, to the extent reasonable, to keep the terms of this Agreement and the other Agreements contemplated by this Agreement confidential.

COMMENT: The parties often agree not to publicly announce the formation of a JV or the details of its operations and performance without the consent of both parties. In some cases the parties may be required to make certain disclosures to various regulatory agencies (e.g., Securities and Exchange Commission), and these disclosures are typically excluded from this provision.

10.3. ENTIRE AGREEMENT

This Agreement, together with all Exhibits attached to it and all documents and instruments delivered in connection with it, constitutes the full and complete agreement and understanding between the Venturers and shall supersede any

and all prior written and oral agreements concerning the subject matter contained in it, including the Memorandum of Agreement; provided, however, that any obligations of the Venturers contained in any confidentiality or non-disclosure agreement shall, to the extent they are not inconsistent with this Agreement or any other agreement contemplated by it, remain in full force and effect.

COMMENT: This is a standard provision which expressly states that the terms of the agreement constitute the entire agreement and understanding between the parties concerning the relationship. In particular, the parties will want to include an acknowledgment that the definitive agreement supersedes any earlier letter of intent or memorandum of understanding. In this case, the parties have provided that the terms of any confidentiality agreement will continue to apply to the extent they are not inconsistent with the agreement.

10.4. AMENDMENT OR MODIFICATION

This Agreement may not be modified or amended except in writing duly signed by the authorized representatives of each of the Venturers. Any condition or provision in any document or communication whatsoever, other than a writing amending or modifying this Agreement in accordance with the first sentence of this Section 14.4, shall be deemed inapplicable to the obligations between the Venturers.

COMMENT: This provision makes clear that no modification or amendment to the agreement will bind either of the parties unless made in writing and duly signed by an authorized representative of each party.

10.5. SEVERABILITY

If any one or more of the non-material provisions contained in this Agreement shall be invalid, illegal, or unenforceable in any respect, the validity, legality, and/or enforceability of the remaining provisions contained in this Agreement shall not in any way be affected or impaired by such action. All non-material provision or provisions deemed invalid shall be validly reformed so as to approximate as nearly as possible the intent of the Venturers and, if they cannot be reformed, shall be severed and deleted from this Agreement. In the event any one or more of the material provisions contained in this Agreement shall be invalid, illegal, or unenforceable in any material respect, the Venturers shall promptly meet to renegotiate the material provisions of this Agreement.

COMMENT: Provisions may be included that make it clear that if a provision of the agreement is found to be invalid and unenforceable, the remainder of the agreement will remain valid and in force in accordance with its terms.

10.6. WAIVER

No failure or delay by a Venturer to insist on strict performance of any term, condition, covenant, or provision of this Agreement, or to exercise any right, power, or remedy under it or arising from any breach of it, shall constitute a waiver of any such term, condition, covenant, agreement, right, power, breach, or remedy, nor shall it preclude the Venturer from exercising that right, power, or remedy at any later time or times.

COMMENT: The agreement should make clear that waivers of performance will not affect a party's right to assert nonperformance at a future date.

10.7. ENFORCEMENT

The Shares are unique and cannot be readily purchased or sold in the open market. For this reason, among others, the Venturers will be irreparably damaged if this Agreement is not deemed to be enforceable by specific performance, and the Venturers agree accordingly that this Agreement shall be specifically enforceable. Such remedy shall be cumulative, not exclusive, and in addition to any other remedy that the Venturers may have.

COMMENT: The agreement includes a "specific enforcement" provision which applies to each obligation of the venturers included in the agreement. The rationale is that the ownership interests in the JV are unique and not readily transferable if a venturer wishes to withdraw its investment in the enterprise. Valuation difficulties also make it imperative that the venturers have a reasonable expectation that their rights will be enforced, particularly when a purchase and sale of the shares between the venturers is called for under the agreement.

10.8. REMEDIES

No right, power, or remedy conferred on or reserved to any Venturer in this Agreement is intended to be exclusive of any other right, power, or remedy, and each and every right, power, and remedy of any Venturer pursuant to this Agreement now or later existing at law, in equity, by statute, or otherwise shall to the extent permitted by law be cumulative and concurrent, and shall be in addition to every other right, power, or remedy pursuant to this Agreement, or now or later existing at law, in equity, by statute, or otherwise. The exercise or beginning of the exercise by any Venturer of any one or more of such rights, powers, or remedies shall not preclude the simultaneous or later exercise by any Venturer of any or all such other rights, powers, or remedies.

COMMENT: The agreement should make clear that any remedy included in the agreement is not intended to be exclusive, and that each party retains the right to pursue all remedies available to it at law and equity.

10.9. HEADINGS

Headings in this Agreement are included in it for the convenience of reference only and shall not constitute a part of this Agreement for any purpose.

COMMENT: A provision should be included to make clear that the headings used are intended only for convenience and not as an integral part of the agreement.

10.10. ATTORNEYS' FEES AND COSTS

In the event of any action at law or in equity between the Venturers to enforce any of the provisions of this Agreement, the unsuccessful party or parties to such litigation shall pay to the successful party or parties all costs and expenses, including actual attorneys' fees, incurred therein by such successful party or parties. If the successful party or parties shall recover judgment in any such action or proceeding, such costs, expenses, and attorneys' fees may be included in and as part of the judgment. The successful party shall be the party who is entitled to recover costs of suit, regardless of whether the suit proceeds to final judgment. A party not entitled to recover costs shall not recover attorneys' fees.

COMMENT: The successful party in any action for the interpretation or enforcement of the agreement is entitled to an award of reasonable attorneys' fees and costs.

10.11. GOVERNING LAW

This Agreement shall be construed in accordance with the internal laws, and not the law of conflicts, of [*state and/or country*] applicable to agreements made and to be performed in such jurisdiction.

COMMENT: The JV documents are intended to express the will of the participants regarding the rules that will govern the conduct of the operations of the enterprise, and the relationship between the venturers. However, if disagreement arises over the interpretation of a provision, or if a participant fails to perform an obligation, reference must be made to the governing law to construe the agreement. The "governing law" consists of the statutory laws and court decisions to be applied to analyze and determine the respective rights and duties of the participants.

As a general matter, the participants may freely choose the law that governs their JV relationship, allowing them to predict by reference to precedents in the specified jurisdiction how disputes might be resolved. The participants should try to choose a governing law that has detailed and favorable provision for the type of transaction, as well as for general commercial matters. For example, in the United States, the laws of California or New York are often preferred.

Whether the choice of governing law will be followed by a court depends on the laws and policies of the jurisdiction. In the United States, a choice of law will be honored unless the chosen jurisdiction has no substantial relationship to the participant or the transaction and there is no other reasonable basis for the parties' choice, although due respect will be given to the fundamental policies of a state that has a materially greater interest in the determination of a particular issue. Practices differ in other countries and it is important to anticipate the court's view of a governing law clause. If the participants do not choose a governing law, the courts will infer one from the conduct of the participants and will often simply apply the law of the forum where the dispute is being litigated, or the law of the jurisdiction with the most significant relationship to the issues or concerns.

10.12. ARBITRATION

a. **In the event of any dispute arising out of or relating to this Agreement, or the breach of it, either Venturer, by notice (hereinafter referred to a an "Arbitration Notice") given no later than [*time*], may demand that the dispute be submitted to final and binding arbitration before a single arbitrator selected by the parties in accordance with the then-existing rules of the [*specify*, e.g., International Chamber of Commerce]. All arbitration proceedings and records shall be in English and shall be held in [*location*] in accordance with the laws of [*state and/or country*]. Issuance of an Arbitration Notice shall suspend the effect of any default under this Agreement, including but not limited to any judicial or administrative proceedings instituted in connection with the default, for the duration of the arbitration proceedings. If the Venturers cannot agree on the identity of a single arbitrator within [*number*] days of receipt of the Arbitration Notice, each of them shall appoint one (1) arbitrator and the Venturer-appointed arbitrators shall appoint within [*number*] days of their appointment a third arbitrator.**

b. **The arbitrator or arbitrators shall forthwith determine whether a default has occurred, and shall deliver its or their decision within [*number*] days of the date of receipt of the Arbitration Notice. The decision shall specify such remedy (including individually, in combination money damages, or specific performance) as shall fully**

implement the intent and purposes of this Agreement and as shall indemnify non-breaching parties for and hold them harmless from all losses, cost, and expenses (including costs of arbitration and reasonable attorneys' fees) resulting from any breach or from defending against any allegations of a breach determined to be unfounded. Termination of any rights and licenses shall not be awarded except if a substantial breach cannot be remedied by money damages or if there has been a pattern of breaches (even if timely cured or remediable by money damages) that have materially undermined the intent of the parties. The right to demand arbitration and to receive damages or specific performance shall be the exclusive remedy in the event of the giving of an Arbitration Notice, and all other rights or remedies, in law or in equity, are now forever waived.

COMMENTS: Whether the JV is a 50-50 company or one party owns more than 50 percent of the venture but has agreed to supermajority voting provisions, the possibility of deadlock must be taken into account in structuring the enterprise. Although it may be somewhat awkward to spend inordinate amounts of time before the JV is formed debating the consequences of any failure of the parties to agree, some procedures for resolving a dispute between the parties without having to resort to the costs and aggravations of litigation are usually desirable. See Chapter 16 for a discussion of dispute resolution mechanisms.

10.13. EXHIBITS

All exhibits attached to this Agreement and referred to in it are incorporated within it as though fully set forth at length.

COMMENT: This language makes it clear that the various exhibits attached to the agreement and referred to therein are to be construed as if part of the agreement.

10.14. COUNTERPARTS

This Agreement may be executed in one or more counterparts by the Parties. All counterparts shall be construed together and shall constitute one agreement.

COMMENT: If appropriate, provision should be made for execution of the agreement in counterparts when the parties cannot sign it at one time in one place. This is a typical provision in international contracts when the cost, time, and expense of travel may preclude the parties from meeting for the final execution.

10.15. FORCE MAJEURE

Any Venturer shall be excused for failures and delays in performance of its respective obligations under this Agreement caused by war, riots, insurrections, laws and regulations (including, without limitation, imposition of export restrictions or controls), strikes, floods, fires, explosions or other catastrophes beyond the control and without the fault of such Venturer. This provision shall not, however, release such Venturer from using its best efforts to avoid or remove such cause and such Venturer shall continue performance under this Agreement with the utmost dispatch whenever such causes are removed. On claiming any such excuse or delay for non-performance, such Venturer shall give prompt written notice to the other Venturer. Notwithstanding the foregoing, if an event of force majeure remains in effect for a period of [*number*] months, then the Venturer agrees to renegotiate promptly the terms of this Agreement, and if no such agreement can be reached within [*number*] days of

such [*number*] month period, then this Agreement shall automatically terminate and be of no further force or effect.

COMMENT: A venturer's performance under the agreement will be excused on the occurrence of certain specified catastrophic or uncontrollable events, including natural disasters, strikes or labor disputes, war or other violence, or government actions. However, the agreement may permit the venturer so affected to take all reasonable steps to avoid or remove the causes of nonperformance, and the affected party may be obligated to resume performance with dispatch once the event or cause for suspension of performance has been removed. The agreement provides that if the force majeure condition continues for a certain number of months, the parties will have a specific time to try to renegotiate the terms so as to account for the performance problems. If they are unsuccessful, the agreement will terminate.

10.16. ASSIGNMENT ON WRITTEN CONSENT

This Agreement, and any documents that are exhibits to it or are contemplated by it, are confidential between the Venturers. Except as provided in Section 7.5, this Agreement and the ownership interests of the Venturers issued under it may not be wholly or partly assigned by either Venturer except with the other Venturer's prior written consent. Subject to this restriction, this Agreement shall be binding on and shall inure to the benefit of the Venturers and their respective successors and assigns.

COMMENT: In general, rights and obligations under the agreement may not be assigned by a party without the consent of the other parties or following compliance with the provisions relating to transfer of shares. The agreement is intended to be binding on the respective legal successors and assignees to the parties.

IN WITNESS WHEREOF, the undersigned have caused this Agreement to be executed by their duly authorized representatives in the manner legally binding on them.

TECHNOLOGY VENTURER, INC., a [*state and/or country*] corporation

By [*name of representative*]
[*typed name and title*]

CASH VENTURER, INC., a [*state and/or country*] corporation

By [*name of representative*]
[*typed name and title*]

COMPANY, INC., a [*state and/or country*] corporation

By [*name of representative*]
[*typed name and title*]

CHAPTER 19

Glossary

ACT OF GOD CLAUSE See FORCE MAJEURE CLAUSE.

AFFILIATED COMPANY A business enterprise that is directly or indirectly owned or controlled by another entity.

AGENDA The list of topics to be covered during a meeting, such as a negotiation session. An agenda is usually arranged in either ascending or descending order of importance. Control of the agenda is important to negotiation strategy.

AMENDMENT An addition, deletion, or other change in a legal document.

ANTITRUST AND COMPETITION LAWS National and regional laws that regulate business collaborations, including JVs, that might have a material adverse impact on the level of competition in the country or region. Many countries have published guidelines that regulate provisions typically included as part of the documentation for a JV.

ARBITRATION The resolution of a dispute between two parties through a voluntary or contractually required hearing and determination by an impartial third party. The impartial third party is called the arbiter or arbitrator and is chosen by a higher or disinterested body, or by the two disputing parties. In the United States, the major national arbitration body is the American Arbitration Association; 140 West 51st Street; New York, NY 10020 USA; Tel: [1] (212) 484-4000. Internationally, the main arbitration body is the International Chamber of Commerce (ICC); 38 Course Albert 1er; 75008 Paris, France; Tel: (1) 49-53-28-28; Fax: (1) 49-53-29-42. For the U.S. representative of the ICC, contact: U.S. Council for International Business; 1212 Avenue of the Americas; New York, NY 10036 USA; Tel: [1] (212) 354-4480. See ARBITRATION CLAUSE.

ARBITRATION CLAUSE A contract clause included in many international contracts stating for example: "Any controversy or claim arising out of or relating to this contract, or the breach thereof, shall be settled by arbitration in accordance with the Commercial Arbitration Rules of the [name of organization], and judgment on the award rendered by the arbitrator(s) may be entered in any court having jurisdiction thereof." See ARBITRATION.

BOILERPLATE Standard contract terms usually printed in small type on the reverse of a pre-printed contract form. Also called fine print, this term refers to the minute details of a contract.

BREACH A violation of law or agreement.

CHARTER (law) (a) An instrument issued by a government to the governed people, a specific part of the people, a corporation, a colony, or a dependency confirming or conferring described rights, liberties, or powers. (b) A legislative act that creates a business corporation or that creates and defines a corporate franchise.

CISG See CONVENTION ON CONTRACTS FOR THE INTERNATIONAL SALE OF GOODS.

CLOSING CERTIFICATES Documents that are executed and delivered by the parties in connection with the legal formation of a JV company and the delivery of initial capital contributions. Certificates include statements from the officers of each party as to compliance with specified closing conditions, and may include an opinion from each party's legal counsel.

COMMERCIAL LAWS The set of laws, rules and regulations that govern market-based transactions among independent contracting parties. Notable examples include the laws of contracts, sale of goods transactions, debtor-creditor laws, and laws governing the form and use of promissory notes, security agreements, and commercial paper.

COMPANY LAWS See ENTERPRISE LAWS.

CONFIDENTIALITY AGREEMENT An obligation to protect the confidentiality of proprietary information exchanged between parties exploring a commercial relationship. Also referred to as a nondisclosure agreement (NDA). Use of a confidentiality agreement is generally a condition to the availability of trade secret protection in most countries. See DUE DILIGENCE INVESTIGATION.

CONFLICT OF INTEREST A financial or ethical conflict between an official's private interests and official duties.

CONSIDERATION The price or other motivation that induces a party to make a contract. For example, a buyer may agree to pay a sum of money or to furnish certain products as consideration for receiving the seller's goods.

CONVENTION ON CONTRACTS FOR THE INTERNATIONAL SALE OF GOODS (CISG) A United Nations convention that establishes uniform legal rules to govern international contracts for the sale of goods between nationals of member countries. If cross-border traders are nationals of countries that have ratified the CISG, their contracts for the sale of goods will be subject to the CISG unless the contracts specify otherwise.

CORPORATE CULTURE The social and traditional bonds that hold an organization together. It incorporates an organization's values, norms of behavior, policies, and procedures, and is heavily influenced by national cultural values, ownership structure, and the nature of the industry in which the corporation operates.

CORPORATION An association or entity created by persons under the authority of the laws of a particular jurisdiction. A corporation is treated as distinct from the persons (referred to as shareholders) who created it, therefore the shareholders enjoy limited liability and the corporation has certain legal rights, such as the right to own property, enter contracts, and bring suit, similar to rights held by individuals. *See* PERSON. See Business Entities Worldwide in *Dictionary of International Trade* (World Trade Press) for a detailed listing of corporate-type entities in various countries around the world.

COUNTRY MARKETING PLAN (U.S.) An analysis of a country's business and economic climate, giving emphasis to marketing and trade issues. Usually prepared by the U.S. embassy in the subject country and published by the U.S. Department of Commerce, International Trade Administration. Also available on CD-ROM in the National Trade Data Bank, and available from the U.S. Department of Commerce; 14th Street and Constitution Ave.; Washington, DC 20230 USA; Tel: [1] (202) 482-2000.

COUNTRY RISK (economics) The financial risks of a transaction that relate to the political, economic, or social instability of a country.

CROSS-CULTURAL A comparison of beliefs and attitudes of different cultures or nationalities with another set of beliefs and attitudes. In management, it is a concept that deals with the challenge of managing a team of workers from different cultures.

CULTURE A set of learned core values, beliefs, standards, knowledge, morals, laws, and behaviors shared by individuals and societies that determines how an individual acts, feels, and views himself/herself and others.

DAMAGES A monetary amount claimed and awarded to a person for loss or injury to the person or the person's property. Types of damages include *actual* (compensation for amounts in fact incurred), *expectation* (compensation for amounts that a person could have reasonably anticipated receiving from a transaction had it not failed), *incidental* (expenses reasonably incurred in mitigating, or otherwise in association with, losses), and *liquidated* (an amount fixed by contract as reasonable compensation in the event a party defaults).

DEVELOPING COUNTRIES (economics) Countries that generally lack a high degree of industrialization, infrastructure, capital investment, sophisticated technology, widespread literacy, and advanced living standards among their populations as a whole. These countries are sometimes collectively designated as the "South," because a large number of them are in the Southern Hemisphere. In general, most of the countries of Africa (except South Africa), Asia and Oceania (except Australia, Japan, Korea and New Zealand), Latin America, and the Middle East are considered "developing," as are a few European countries (Cyprus, Malta, Turkey, and countries of the former Yugoslavia and Soviet Union for example).

DISPUTE SETTLEMENT Resolution of a conflict, usually through a compromise between opposing claims, sometimes facilitated by an intermediary such as an arbiter or mediator.

DISTRIBUTION AGREEMENT In the context of a JV, an agreement by which one party or a third party agrees to distribute goods produced and/or sold by the JV. See DISTRIBUTOR.

DISTRIBUTOR An agent who sells directly for one or more suppliers and maintains an inventory of the suppliers' products.

DOCUMENTATION The financial, commercial, and legal documents relating to a transaction.

DUE DILIGENCE INVESTIGATION Preliminary research and exchange of data between parties contemplating a commercial transaction such as a potential JV. The data covers each party's business and affairs and specific matters relating to the proposed business plan for the JV. See CONFIDENTIALITY AGREEMENT.

ENTERPRISE LAWS The laws governing the formation and operation of legal entities, such as corporations, limited liability companies, and partnerships. Each country has its own set of enterprise laws that apply to legal entities formed within its borders.

EXHIBIT A document attached to a contract or agreement. For example, a document entitled "Exhibit A" might list product specifications attached to a purchase order.

FORCE MAJEURE CLAUSE A contract clause that excuses a party who breaches the contract when performance is prevented by the occurrence of an event—such as a natural disaster, war, or labor strike—that is beyond the party's reasonable control.

FOREIGN CORRUPT PRACTICES ACT (FCPA) (U.S. law) The FCPA makes it unlawful for any United States citizen or firm (or any person acting for a U.S. citizen or firm) to offer, pay, transfer, promise to pay or transfer, or authorize a payment, transfer, or promise of money or anything of value to any foreign appointed or elected government official, foreign political party, or candidate for a foreign political office for a corrupt purpose (that is, to influence the official's discretionary act or decision) and for obtaining or retaining business.

A U.S. business owner is also prohibited from making such an offer, promise, payment, or transfer to any person if the U.S. business owner knows, or has reason to know, that the person will offer, give, or promise directly or indirectly all or any part of the payment to a foreign government official, political party, or candidate. The term knowledge means both *actual knowledge* (the business owner in fact knew that such a payment was included) and *implied knowledge* (the business owner should have known from the facts and circumstances of a transaction that a bribe was paid, but failed to investigate reasonably).

The FCPA does not prohibit payments made to facilitate a routine government action. A facilitating payment is made in connection with an action that a foreign official must perform as part of the job. In comparison, a corrupt payment is made to influence an official's discretionary decision. For example, payments are not usually corrupt if made to cover an official's overtime for expediting the processing of export documentation for a legal shipment of merchandise or to cover the expense of additional crew to handle a shipment.

FOREIGN INVESTMENTS The flow of foreign capital into local business enterprises in which local residents have significant control. Many countries have adopted extensive laws and regulations governing the amount and type of foreign investment allowed in the country.

FOREIGN PERSON Any person resident outside a country or subject to the jurisdiction of another country. See PERSON.

GOVERNING LAW CLAUSE A contract provision that specifies the law that the parties have selected for the interpretation of their contract. Whether a court respects the choice of the parties is discretionary, because parties are not permitted to deprive a court of jurisdiction.

INDEMNIFY (insurance/law) To compensate for actual loss sustained. Many insurance policies and all bonds promise to "indemnify" the insureds. Under such a contract, the insured cannot recover until actual loss is suffered, at which time he or she is entitled to compensation for the damage (i.e. to be restored to the same financial position enjoyed before the loss).

INTELLECTUAL PROPERTY Intangible rights that can be protected because of their novelty, uniqueness, and value to the creator. These rights include copyrights, trademarks, service marks, designs, and patents.

JOINT VENTURE (law) (a) A combination of two or more individuals or legal entities who together undertake a transaction for mutual gain or engage in a commercial enterprise with mutual sharing of profits and losses. (b) A form of business partnership involving joint management and the sharing of risks and profits as between enterprises based in different countries. If joint ownership of capital is involved, the partnership is known as an equity JV.

LEGAL ENTITY (law) Any individual, proprietorship, partnership, corporation, association, or other organization that has, in the eyes of the law, the capacity to make a contract or an agreement, and the abilities to assume an obligation and to discharge an indebtedness. A legal entity is a responsible being in the eyes of the law and can be sued for damages if the performance of a contract or agreement is not met. *See also* PERSON.

LETTER OF INTENT (LOI) See MEMORANDUM OF UNDERSTANDING (MOU).

LICENSING AGREEMENT (law) A contract by which the holder of a trademark, patent, or copyright transfers a limited right to use a process, sell or manufacture an article, or furnish specialized services covered by the trademark, patent, or copyright to another firm.

LIMITED LIABILITY (law) Restricted liability for business obligations. Liability may be limited, for example, to the amount of a shareholder's capital in a corporation.

LIMITED PARTNERSHIP (law) A partnership in which at least one partner has general liability and at least one of the other partners has limited liability.

LIQUIDATED DAMAGES See DAMAGES.

MANAGING BOARD A business organization's executive body that exercises overall management and control. In the case of a corporation, the managing board would be the board of directors.

MEMORANDUM OF UNDERSTANDING (MOU) Sometimes referred to as a Letter of Intent (LOI), an informal document that states the basic intentions and points of agreement between two or more parties and that serves as the basis of a future, more detailed contract.

NEW YORK CONVENTION The New York Convention on the Recognition and Enforcement of Foreign Arbitral Awards of 1958, which set out the conditions under which foreign arbitral awards rendered in any jurisdiction that is a party to the Convention will be honored in any other jurisdiction that is also a party to the Convention.

NONDISCLOSURE AGREEMENT See CONFIDENTIALITY AGREEMENT.

OFFICERS The persons assigned with responsibility for the day-to-day operations of a business organization. Officers may include the President, Vice Presidents, Secretary, and Treasurer (Chief Financing Officer). Officers are elected by the managing board, and in a JV the agreement of the parties with respect to election of officers may be set out in the venturers' agreement.

PARTY (TO A TRANSACTION) An individual, group, or entity that represents one side of a question, contract, or dispute.

PERSON (law) An individual or legal entity recognized under law as having legal rights and obligations. In the United States, for example, corporations and partnerships are legal entities recognized as persons under the law. In countries that allow the formation of limited and unlimited liability companies, those companies are recognized as persons under the law.

POLITICAL RISK (economics) Extraordinary measures of foreign countries and political events abroad that make it impossible for a debtor to comply with a contract or that lead to the loss, confiscation of, or damage to goods belonging to the exporter (e.g., war, revolution, annexation, and civil war) and that can have detrimental effect on the exporter. An exporter may be able to cover this risk by utilizing a confirmed letter of credit, or by applying for cover from export credit agencies.

SERVICES AGREEMENT A contract between a JV and one or more of the parties to the JV, pursuant to which the party(ies) provide various administrative services to the JV. Services may include financial, legal, personnel, public relations, and general management support.

STRATEGY The art or science of creating a plan using all the social, economic, political, legal, cultural, and other forces available to achieve a goal.

TECHNOLOGY TRANSFER The transfer of knowledge generated and developed in one place to another, where is it is used to achieve some practical end. Technology may be transferred in many ways: by giving it away (technical journals, conferences, emigration of technical experts, technical assistance programs); by industrial espionage; or by sale (patents, blueprints, industrial processes, and the activities of multinational corporations).

VENTURERS' AGREEMENT The agreement between the parties to a JV that sets out their understanding regarding capital contributions to the JV, management and control, and business operations. The name and format of the venturers' agreement will vary depending on whether the JV is a corporation (shareholders' agreement), partnership (partnership agreement) or limited liability company (operating agreement).

WAIVER (a) The abandoning of a claim or right. (b) The document acknowledging the abandoning of a claim or right.

WARRANTY A contract provision by which one party represents to the other that certain facts are true. In an international JV, the parties will make various warranties to each other regarding their capacity to enter into the arrangement, the title to assets contributed to the JV, and the absence of third-party claims that might materially impact the JV's operation.

CHAPTER 20

Resources

Aaker, David A. *Managing Brand Equity*
Free Press, New York, New York. 1991.

Bendaniel, David J. and Arthur H. Rosenbloom. *International Mergers and Acquisitions, Joint Ventures, and Beyond: Doing the Deal*
John Wiley & Sons, Inc. 1997.

Bergquist, William, Julie Betwee, and David Meuel. *Building Strategic Relationships: How to Extend Your Organization's Reach Through Partnership, Alliances, and Joint Ventures*
Jossey-Bass Inc. 1995.

Breen, George & A.B. Blankenship, *Do-It-Yourself Marketing Research*
McGraw-Hill, New York, New York. 1989.

Charles, Ronald and Charles Wolf. *Effective International Joint Venture Management: Practical Legal Insights for Successful Organization and Implementation*
M.E. Sharpe, Inc. 2000.

Child, John and David Faulkner. *Strategies of Cooperation: Managing Alliances, Networks, and Joint Ventures*
Oxford University Press, Inc. 1999.

Cyr, Dianne J. and Cascio Wayne. *The Human Resource Challenge of International Joint Ventures*
Greenwood Publishing Group 1995.

Das, Dilip K. *Migration of Financial Resources to Developing Countries*
St. Martin's Press, New York, New York. 1986.

Editor, *Accounting for East-West Joint Ventures*
United Nations. 1992.

Editor, *Public Joint Ventures in Developing Countries: Organization, Management, and Critical Issues*
United Nations. 1989.

Hinkelman, Edward G. *Dictionary of International Trade, 4th Edition*
World Trade Press, Novato, California. 2000.

Lewis, Jordan D. *Partnerships for Profit: Structuring and Managing Strategic Alliances*
Simon & Schuster. 1990.

Lynch, Robert Porter. *Business Alliances Guide: The Hidden Competitive Weapon*
John Wiley & Sons, Inc. 1993.

Matthews, Clifford. *Managing International Joint Ventures*
Kogan Page Ltd. 2000.

Shippey, Karla C. *A Short Course in International Contracts*
World Trade Press, Novato, California. 1999.

Triantis, John E. *Creating Successful Acquisition and Joint Venture Projects*
Greenwood Publishing Group. 1999.